PRACTISE TO DECEIVE

PRACTISE TO DECEIVE:
Learning Curves of Military Deception Planners

BARTON WHALEY

Introduction by A. Denis Clift

Edited by Susan Stratton Aykroyd

Naval Institute Press
Annapolis, Maryland

Naval Institute Press
291 Wood Road
Annapolis, MD 21402

© 2016 by U.S. Naval Institute
All rights reserved. No part of this book may be reproduced or utilized in any form or by any means, electronic or mechanical, including photocopying and recording, or by any information storage and retrieval system, without permission in writing from the publisher.

First Naval Institute Press paperback edition published in 2020.
ISBN: 978-1-68247-642-0 (paperback)

The Library of Congress has cataloged the hardcover edition as follows:
Whaley, Barton.
  Practise to deceive : learning curves of military deception planners / Barton Whaley; introduction by A. Denis Clift ; edited by Susan Stratton Aykroyd.
    pages cm
  Includes bibliographical references.
    ISBN 978-1-61251-982-1 (hardcover : alk. paper) — ISBN 978-1-61251-983-8 (ebook) 1. Deception (Military science) 2. Deception (Military science)—History. 3. Deception (Military science)—Case studies. 4. Military planning. I. Aykroyd, Susan Stratton. II. Title.
    U167.5.D37.W53 2016
    355.4'1—dc23

2015035352

♾ Print editions meet the requirements of ANSI/NISO z39.48-1992 (Permanence of Paper).

9 8 7 6 5 4 3 2 1

The views herein are the author's and not necessarily those of the Foreign Denial & Deception Committee.

O, what a tangled web we weave,
When first we practise to deceive!
— Sir Walter Scott, *Marmion* (1808),
  Canto 6, Stanza 17

But, if we practise for a while,
We'll get a wizard knack for guile.
— BW, 11 Jan 2010, with apologies to
  J. R. Pope

To

J. Bowyer Bell
(1931-2003)

who immersed me in his real world of terrorists
while I introduced him to war gaming and the theory of deception.

Contents

Executive Summary: Findings & Recommendations xi
    0.1. Discontinuities xi
    0.2. Planners as Individuals xiv
    0.3. Overall Competence xv
    0.4. Recomended Research xvii
    0.5. The Planning Process in a Nutshell xviii

Introduction by A. Denis Clift xxi

PART ONE: Introduction 1

Chapter 1: Intent 2

Chapter 2: Scope 3

Chapter 3: Sources 5

PART TWO: The Case Studies 7

Chapter 4: Learning to Deceive 8
    Cases 1-22

Chapter 5: Planners in Specific Operations 58
    Cases 23-64

Chapter 6: Selling the Commander 127
    Cases 65-76

Chapter 7: Institutional Deception Planning 148
    Cases 77-88

PART THREE: Analysis & Conclusions 179

Chapter 8: The Planning Process 180
    8.1. The Basic Process 180
    8.2. The Things Manipulated 182

Chapter 9: Social/Institutional Factors: Networks, Institutions, & Traditions 184
    9.1. Policy Constraints and the Supreme Command 184

9.2.	Commanders and Their Staffs	185
9.3.	Intelligence or Operations?	186
9.4.	Level of Operations: The Tactical-Strategic Continuum	188
9.5.	Enemy Capabilities & SOP	189

Chapter 10: Cultural Factors 190
    10.1. Ethical Constraints 190
    10.2. Deception and National Character 191
    10.3. National Military Doctrines 191
    10.4. The "Not Invented Here" Syndrome & Its Alternatives 193

Chapter 11: Personality Factors 194
    11.1. The Maria Theresa Syndrome: Break the Rules to Make Your Own 195
    11.2. The Pleasures of Deceiving: An Odd Sense of Humor 197
    11.3. The Empathic Mind: Know Your Enemy 200
    11.4. The Prepared Mind: Know Your Subject 205

Chapter 12: Selection of Deception Personnel 206
    12.1. Prior Experience 206
    12.2. Selection 207
    12.3. Teaching & Training 209

Appendices 210

Appendix A: "Guidelines for Deception of the Enemy," 15 February 1941, *Basic German Strategic Deception Plan for Operation BARBAROSSA (invasion of Russia)* 211

Appendix B: Chronology of 67 Further German BARBAROSSA Deception Plans, 1941 215

Appendix C: Plan CLOAK, 25 January 1945, *British Tactical Deception Plan against Japanese in Burma, February 1945* .. 216

Appendix D: Checklist of Other Deception Plans 222

Bibliography 224

List of Cases 241
    Cases 1-88 in order presented

Executive Summary: Findings & Recommendations

The royal road to learning how to deceive in war has been paved with speed bumps. It is widely assumed that this learning process has been incremental, a gradual accumulation of experience in combat, lessons learned in staff studies, scholarly analysis of historical cases, the passing of knowledge from master to apprentice, and practical experience in combat. In other words, the art of military deception is generally seen as improving slowly but steadily through a long chain of theory and practice. However, the reality is very different.

0.1. Discontinuities

In fact, discontinuity is the universal pattern of deception found in every cultural and national tradition studied. The most usual specific pattern is one of more-or-less short periods of fairly rapid growth in experience and theory followed by sudden loss of this skill at guile through either demobilization or being superceded by a theory of naked force. In this way, the pendulum always swings between the polar opposites of "force and fraud", to use the terms of Machiavelli and Hobbes. Thus, whenever deception gets reintroduced in war, it typically requires rebuilding from scratch—reinventing the proverbial wheel. And these reinvented wheels are, more often than not, more clunkingly square than smoothly round.[1]

This pattern of discontinuity between high and low levels of guileful warfare has been studied in detail in 15 major cultures or cultural types from antiquity to the present.[2] These are:

- Tribal Warfare
- The Classical West
- Decline in the Medieval West
- The Byzantine Style
- The Scythian Style
- The Renaissance of Deception in Europe
- Discontinuity: "Progress" and Romanticism in the 19th Century

---

1 See Whaley, "Deception—Its Decline and Revival in International Conflict," in Lasswell, Lerner, Speier (*editor*), *Propaganda and Communication in World History*, Vol.2 (Honolulu: University Press of Hawaii, 1980), 339-367.
2 Whaley, *The Prevalence of Guile* (FDDC: 2007), Part One, pp.11-57.

- The Chinese Way
- The Japanese Style
- India plus Pakistan
- Arabian to Islamic Cultures
- Twentieth Century Limited
- Soviet Doctrine
- American Roller-coaster and the Missing Generation
- Twenty-first Century Unlimited: Asymmetric Warfare Revisited

All of these cultures, types of culture, and sub-cultures employed deception. But each showed wide swings in levels of deception practiced across time—none of these levels remaining either consistently high or low. Consequently, such unqualified stereotypes that "the Chinese are crafty" or that the Byzantines were, well, "byzantine", are flat-out wrong. We must qualify such broad claims. The anecdotal evidence of this present paper, being consistent with the findings of the earlier systematic paper, *The Prevalence of Guile* FDDC, 2007), reinforces its findings.

Here are the 6 main findings, all somewhat surprising and all important for improving deception doctrine, particularly the currently weak deception & surprise doctrine in the American services:

- **Some cultures are clearly more deceptive than others *but only during any given slice of time*. No single culture has excelled in deceptiveness throughout its history.** (Chapter 10.3)

    For example, while the Chinese did rise to the highest level of military deviousness during the time of Sun Tzu (c.350 BC), they had low levels before Master Sun, and afterwards largely lost it during three long periods, only to regain it each time. (Case 20)

    The most recent Chinese loss was when they fell to the lowest level from the late 1700s until being conquered in 1948 by the stratagemic Chinese Communists (PLA). Thence the PLA has displayed high if not the highest levels of deceptiveness, although there are indications that, beginning in 2002, they are again on the upswing. (Cases 20 & 21)

- **The levels of guilefulness at any given time can be quite different *across the major disciplines* of military, domestic politics, foreign diplomacy, and commercial business.** (Chapter 10)

Perceived practical considerations of greed and survival do sometimes override religious, moral, or ethical factors to produce deceptive behavior. (Case 1)

- **The levels of guilefulness at any given point in time *between any two contemporary armed entities* (nations, insurgents, or terrorists) are apt to be asymmetric.** (Chapters 10.4 and 11.1)

One example: In 1945 the Soviet Army conducted a vastly more deceptive campaign in Manchuria than did the Japanese defenders (Case 87). Another example: In the period 1928 to 1948 the battle doctrine & practice of the Chinese Communist Army (PLA) was far more deceptive than its main enemy, the Chinese National Army (Case 21).

- **Deception sophistication is independent of technological change. *Within each culture* deception varies widely in its levels of sophistication.**

High, medium, and low levels were found in every culture at different times and regardless of its level of technology. The reason? Because deception is a mind game, it is played only between or among humans. And this condition will remain as long as machines such as computers lack artificial intelligence (AI). (Case 20)

- **Because deception is a mind game, the variations in guilefulness between opposing individuals or groups can be crucial in deciding the victor in combat.** (Chapter 11)

    RULE: In combat, deception can strengthen the weaker side—the David-vs-Goliath Effect. Moreover, *when all other factors are equal, the more deceptive player or team will always win.* (Part Two)

- **Deceptiveness, the ability to deceive, can be learned by individuals or teams.** (Chapter 4)

    - Historically (prior to the mid-1900s) this learning came mainly from trial-anderror experience in combat, as with Washington (Case 25), Monro (Case 4), Zhukov (Case 9), or Dayan (Cases 60 & 61).

    - Or from observing others, as with Wavell (Case 10).

    - Or by being inspired by reading military history or biography, as with MacArthur (Case 71), Yadin (Case 57), and Schwartzkopf's planners (Case 87).

    - Or by transferring & applying deception theory from some non-military discipline to the military domain, as with R.V. Jones (Case

19) in applying practical jokes) or Dudley Clarke (Case 88) in applying conjuring theory, or Barkas (Case 12) and Fairbanks (Case 51) in applying cinematic special effects.

- Beginning around WW1 these methods for learning deception have been slowly supplemented by formal teaching & training (Chapter 4), specifically as with camouflage and other deception units (Cases 12, 14, & 80).

0.2. Planners as Individuals

This study also supports 10 general conclusions about *those individual military deception planners who have been consistently successful*:

- **Deception planners are first & foremost single individuals.**

  Those studied in this paper range from novices to experienced experts. (Cases 1 to 21).

- **Excellence at deception is independent of either rank or branch of service—military or otherwise.**

  All three military services have contributed (including their naval equivalent ranks)—from 3 lowly lieutenants, through 2 captains, 8 majors, 6 lieutenant colonels, 10 colonels, 4 brigadiers, 5 major generals, 8 lieutenant generals, 11 generals, up to 2 field marshals. Civilians contributed 4 intelligence officers, 1 bureaucrat, 3 defense ministers, and 6 heads of government (presidents, prime ministers, or dictators). (Chapter 2)

- **The chief deception planner will often direct a small team of deception planners (seldom more than 5 or 6) whose members are drawn from varied backgrounds and specialties.** (Chapter 2.4)

- **They usually—perhaps always—bring to this art a talent for deception based on a prior understanding of deception, however vague. This understanding comes from either the study of military deceptions or from personal experience with deception in non-military fields.** (Case 19)

- **They have an acute awareness of the incongruities amidst congruity, both in their own camp as well as that of the enemy.** (Case 19 and Chapter 11.1)

- **Some will learn deception from personal experience in war. However, as few have the opportunity to plan much less command in many battles, this can be a very slow trial-and-error process.**

- Consequently, most learn fastest from studying the experiences of others, their failures as well as their successes.

  This second-hand knowledge is best found in case studies of deception, biographies of the consistently successful individual deceivers (and those of their dupes), and *theories or analyses* of the subject by such individual teachers as Sun Tzu, Byzantine Emperor Maurice, Machiavelli, or R. V. Jones. Many students will also benefit from cross-disciplinary reading of the actual deception *operations* of consistently successful practitioners—particularly magicians, mentalists, con artists, and practical jokers. (Chapter 12)

- **All modern military deception planners work within a bureaucratic structure that requires that they "know" their friends and colleagues as well as they do their enemies.** (Chapters 9 and 11.3)

- **The deception planners must not only know their Commander's goal for each operation but they must be prepared to "sell" their plan to that Commander or joint staff.** (Chapter 6)

- **Finally, the single most important conclusion of this study is that Commanders should play an active role in deception planning.**

  If they don't do this on their own initiative, the planners must at least get them to state their goals and priorities or work this through the Chiefs of Staff. (Case 11)

0.3. Overall Competence

> The perfection of this man who could use infantry and cavalry, artillery and Air Force, Navy and armoured cars, deceptions and irregulars, each in its best fashion!
>
> — T. E. Lawrence, *Seven Pillars of Wisdom* (1936), 615

In the above quote, Lawrence of Arabia fulsomely but accurately assayed the overall competence of his commander, General Allenby. But, by implication, he is defining the ideal commander as any officer who blends a talent for "deceptions" with the other more conventional military skills. As important as deception is to a successful military outcome—whether outright victory or simple survival—it is only one among several components of that success.

That was the loud and clear finding of the RAND Corporation study by Feer & Whelan.[3]

That study in the mid-1980s systematically examined the highly realistic war games then currently being conducted by the U.S. Army National Training Center (NTC) at Fort Irwin in California's remote Mojave Desert. Fred Feer and Bill Whelan closely observed over 90 of these "Blue" brigade (BLUFOR) versus "Red" regiment (OPFOR) battles. They were surprised, as was I, by two overarching conclusions:

First, although the Red regiment (a permanent cadre at the NTC) was always the smaller and less well equipped force, it "won" in all but one of the first 50 battles. That's an astonishing 98%. Feer attributed Red's dominance to two main factors: much more intensive training as a unit (including familiarization with the local terrain) and much more sophisticated use of deception. Moreover, Red performed almost as well in the next 40 battles.

Second, while all the top performing "Blue" teams (including the one or two that "won") used deception, all their commanders also showed considerably higher levels of overall ability

—what Feer and Whelan themselves summed up in the term "competence". They defined this overall competence operationally as superior marks in at least four specific skills: communications (particularly through exercising control through briefings and delegation of authority), rehearsal (of units), intelligence (mainly through pressing for aggressive reconnaissance to establish ground truth including penetrating enemy camouflage), and planning (with particular attention to deception).

How do these two main conclusions of the Feer-Wheland study match up with our present set of case-studies in deception planning? First, intensive and sophisticated application of deception can compensate for smaller numbers and inferior technology. Second, this intensity and sophistication is probably best learned through frequent practice. Third, practice can be supplemented, perhaps even replaced, by studying historical cases of successful deception operations.

---

3 Fredric S. Feer, *Tactical Deception at the National Training Center* (Santa Monica: RAND Corporation, Mar 1989). I have not seen that study. However, the insights from the NTC's war games are summarized in several RAND and non-RAND publications. See particularly, Fredric S. Feer, *Thinking-Red-in-Wargaming Workshop: Opportunities for Deception and Counterdeception in the Red Planning Process* (Santa Monica, CA: The RAND Corporation, May 1989, iii+12pp; James S. Hodges, "Analytical Use of Data From Army Training Exercises: A Case Study of Tactical Reconnaissance," *Journal of the American Statistical Association*, Vol.89, No.426 (Jun 1994), 444-451; Martin Goldsmith, Jerry M. Sollinger, Jon Grossman, *Quantifying the Battlefield: RAND Research at the National Training Center* (Santa Monica: RAND, 1993, xi+26pp. AR-105-A); John D. Rosenberger, *An Assessment of Reconnaissance and Counterreconnaissance Operations at the National Training Center* (Ft. Knox: Army Armor School, Feb 1987, 44pp); and Richard Randazzo, "OPFOR Counterreconnaissance At the National Training Center," *Armor*, Vol.107, No.2 (Mar-Apr 1998), 12-13.

Frequent practice in real situations against real opponents clearly provides the most effective learning experience. However, even the most battle-experienced military commanders seldom get the opportunity to design and direct more than a dozen deception operations in an entire career. The most experienced senior commander of WW2, Soviet Marshal Zhukov, designed only about 40 battles. German Field-Marshal Rommel commanded in only eight, two of which were in World War I. British Field-Marshal Alexander and U.S. General MacArthur directed a few more, one of MacArthur's having been in the Korean War; General Patton less. With such limited opportunities to learn by trial-and-error, it is not surprising that so few generals and admirals manage to become expert at the deception game.

Much has been learned about deception by studying deceptive military operations, but only because they are so well documented. More can be learned by studying better experienced deceivers, particularly magicians because they have, by far the most experience (in both frequency & depth of sophistication). For example, professional conjurors such as David Copperfield or Ben Robinson typically give two performances a night, each show containing around a dozen separate tricks, that is, miniature deception operations. Consequently, the average magician performs more deception operations in one week than any single military commander or counter-intelligence officer ever has in a lifetime career.

Moreover, the typical professional magician generally performs deceptions much more frequently than any other type of professional deceiver. The conjuror's closest competitors are card sharps and con artists. But, they plan, carry out, and get feedback on deceptions at a much lower rate than magicians. Even so, their rate of practice exceeds that of any military deceptionist.

0.4. Recommended Research

The main findings of this study illuminate several major weaknesses in our theory and data. To strengthen these, research on the following four questions is recommended for future research:

- **How can we break the Law of Small Numbers?**

    This is the simplest research question. It also has the simplest answer—increase the number of case studies, that is, enlarge the data base. But, dollar-wise, it is expensive. The 88 case studies presented here may seem large, but it is only an "opportunity sample", therefore carrying no statistical weight. At best, it pretty well covers the range of most typical types of deception planning situations. But that is a very strong start in tackling any research problem.

- **What types of individuals make the best deception *planners*? Or the best deception *operators*?**

    Who make the better ones? Professional soldiers and intelligencers (like those in Clarke's "A" Force) or civilian amateurs (like Masterman's Double-Cross Committee)? What differences, if any, are there between the best planners and the best operators? How can we identify these persons? By what interview or test questions?

- **Which organizational structure produces the best deception plans? Or the best operations?**

    In other words, having selected our deception planners, how do we best organize them? The case studies strongly support the conclusion that small teams—of, say, 5 to 10 members—are most productive, even for the most elaborate operational and strategic level operations. However, we have seen single individuals design effective deceptions when they are either the commander or have close access to the commander.

- **Where in the organization chart do these units best fit?**

    This last is the most difficult research question. And also the most costly—both in money and potentially in effectiveness. Brigadier Dudley Clarke, in recommending the British WW2 strategic & operational deception system to the Americans, rightly pointed out (Case 88) that while certain basic principles drive all attempts to deceive an enemy, the organizations to plan and carry out deception are not a "one size fits all" matter. Those specialized units are best tailored to fit each specific national military system.

0.5. The Planning Process in a Nutshell

As condensed from Chapter 8.1, all deception planning can be described by a single set of ten steps. Note that, unlike many planning processes which are circular, deception planning is usually linear, although with feedback for fine tuning.

1. **Understanding the GOAL of the operation, military or otherwise.**

    This is usually (and ideally) defined by the Commander.

2. **Deciding how we want the target to REACT.**

3. **Deciding what we want the target to PERCEIVE.**

    Not merely what we want the target to THINK. (See Case 11)

4. **Deciding specifically which facts or objects are to be HIDDEN and which SHOWN.**

5. **Analyzing the PATTERN of the REAL thing to be hidden to discover the specific characteristics ("signatures") that must be deleted or added to create another pattern that will suitably dissimulate it.**
6. **Doing the same for the FALSE thing to be shown to create a pattern that will suitably simulate it.**
7. **At this point the planner has designed a desired EFFECT together with its concealed METHOD.**

   He must now explore the means available for presenting this effect to the target. If the deception assets available for the job are inadequate, the planner must either get them or abort the plan and go back to step 4 or 5. If no plan seems feasible, it is desirable to so inform the Commander and recommend that he select an alternative goal.

8. **Having designed the effect and the method, the planning phase has ended and the OPERATIONAL PHASE begins.**

   However, the planner should informed of developments in steps 8-to-10 in order to be able to effect modifications or take advantage of unexpected developments.

9. **Selecting the CHANNELS through which the various false characteristics are to be communicated.**
10. **For the deception to succeed, the target must accept ("buy") the EFFECT, perceiving the projected illusion.**

    Deception will fail at this point only if the target takes no notice of the presented effect, notices but judges it irrelevant, misconstrues its intended meaning, or detects its METHOD. Conversely, the target will:

    - take notice, if the effect is designed to attract his ATTENTION;
    - find it relevant, if the effect can hold his INTEREST;
    - form the intended hypothesis about its meaning, if the projected pattern of characteristics is CONGRUENT with patterns already part of his experience and memory; and
    - fail to detect the deception, if none of the ever-present characteristics that are INCONGRUENT are accessible to his sensors.

Introduction

> We must significantly reduce our vulnerability to intelligence surprises, mistakes, and omissions caused by the effects of denial and deception on collection and analysis.
>
> — Weapons of Mass Destruction Commission, 2005

In 1883, writing in the Naval Institute *Proceedings*, Commodore Stephen B. Luce called for the creation of a more extended course of study on the art of war for naval officers. A year later, the Naval War College was created with Luce as its first President.

Following World War II, Fleet Admiral Chester W. Nimitz, as Chief of Naval Operations, and General of the Army Dwight D. Eisenhower, as Chief of the Army Staff, separately created the Naval Intelligence School and the Army Strategic Intelligence School. Both leaders were concerned that no good, extended intelligence training had been available to the intelligence officers under their commands.

In 1962, the two schools would be joined as the Defense Intelligence School, which in the years to follow would become the regionally accredited, degree-granting Defense Intelligence College, the Joint Military Intelligence College, the National Defense Intelligence College, and—today—the National Intelligence University offering baccalaureate and master's degree programs on the art of intelligence.

It was my privilege to serve as President and to lead this intelligence institution of higher learning from 1994 to 2009. A research center, a university press, an international center, and a science and technology in intelligence center were created. Curricula changes and introduction of more highly credentialed faculty were all part of the college's steady advancement to university status.

In 2002, R. Kent Tiernan, Vice Chairman of the Director of Central Intelligence's Foreign Denial and Deception Committee called on me to propose that the college add a Denial and Deception Advanced Studies Program to the curriculum. My response on the spot was positive. What could be more important to the study of the art of intelligence?

National denial and deception embarrassments were fresh in my mind. In May 1998, for example, the Government of India had caught the U.S. intelligence community by surprise when it tested nuclear weapons at its desert test site.

"It's not a failure of the CIA," the Associated Press had quoted Indian nuclear researcher G. Balachandran. "It's a matter of their intelligence being good, our deception being better."

We added four denial-and-deception teachers to the faculty and made the courses in the advanced studies program available either as a subset of the master's degree or as a separate certificate program. All participants were required to complete an eight-day off-site capstone exercise. The most important readings in the advanced studies program were, and are, the writings of Barton Whaley.

During his lifetime, Barton Whaley became the undisputed dean of U.S. denial and deception experts. He knew the history of denial and deception across time, disciplines, and culture. He was a foremost authority on the intricacies of denial and deception strategy, tactics, and operations—the crafting of successful operations. At the same time he was an authority on crafting the denial and deception double cross, and on designing and managing a skillful and effective exit when an operation failed.

He was gifted with both wisdom and wit. He would remind of Goldfinger's caution to James Bond: "Mr. Bond they have a saying Chicago. Once is happenstance. Twice is coincidence. The third time it's enemy action."

Whaley's writing was as sharp as his thinking and analysis. His acclaimed published works included *Barbarossa, Covert German Rearmament, 1919–1939* and *Stratagem: Deception and Surprise in War*. His papers, published and unpublished, became the lifeblood of classroom discussion, thesis inspiration, and exercise preparation in the advanced studies program.

In *Practise to Deceive: Learning Curves of Military Deception Planners*, Whaley presents 88 case studies under the headings: learning to deceive, planners in specific operations, selling the commander, and institutional deception planning. His goal is two-fold: to make his readers aware of the kinds of threats posed by any opponent's military deception operations, and to suggest ways we can initiate and improve our own deception practices.

Deception in his analysis is a mind game, and the variations in guilefulness between opposing individuals or groups can be crucial in deciding the victory in combat. First, he writes, intensive and sophisticated application of deception can compensate for smaller numbers and inferior technology. Second, this intensity and sophistication is probably best learned through frequent practice. Third, practice can be supplemented, even replaced, by studying historical cases of successful deception operations.

His case studies are rich in history with vivid descriptions of deception planning and actions. They range from Gideon's Trumpet, Israel c. 1249 BC, and Sun Tzu and the Chinese tradition of deception, to General Schwarzkopf's deception planners, Iraq, 1991. They include Winston's Churchill's 1914 creation of a dummy war fleet to deter the German High Seas Fleet and lure its submarines into traps, and British World War II deception genius R. V. Jones who persuaded the Germans that their U-boat losses were being caused by a fictitious airborne infrared detector. The U-boats were repainted with hastily-developed anti-infrared paint; improved British radar continued to track them.

Whaley recounts Commander Douglas Fairbanks Jr.'s World War II role in the Mediterranean in the naval part of the Genoa deception plan. "With only two gunboats, four PTs and a command ship, Fairbanks steered toward Genoa, noisily simulating a large task force and landing 67 commandos near Cannes at 0410 hours. Although the commandos were captured, Radio Berlin credited Fairbanks with the command of 'four or five large battleships.'" In a citation to Fairbanks, Secretary of the Navy James Forrestal would underscore his role in the original development of tactical deception and diversionary warfare.

The book's pages range across Washington at Yorktown, Arabia and T. E. Lawrence, Gallipoli, the Spanish Civil War, North Africa, Midway, Inchon, the Bay of Pigs, and the Six-Day War. Throughout, Whaley's talent for capturing different personalities stands out.

"If the reader detects a tone of lightheartedness, even occasional frivolity, in the case studies, this faithfully reflects the attitude of the majority of deception planners themselves," Whaley writes. "... [H]umor requires precisely the same manipulation of congruities and incongruities that defines deception. Consequently, it is not surprising that the more clever military deception planners tend to have highly developed senses of humor."

Practise to Deceive is both fascinating reading and instruction at the highest level. Each of Whaley's dips into history is riveting. His lessons, if read and heeded, will contribute to the future strength, security, and well-being of the Nation.

A. Denis Clift
President Emeritus
National Intelligence University

PRACTISE TO DECEIVE

PART ONE:
Introduction

> Lurgan Sahib has a shop among the European shops. All Simla knows it. Ask there—and, Friend of all the World, he is one to be obeyed to the last wink of his eyelashes. Men say he does magic, but that should not touch you. Go up the hill and ask. Here begins the Great Game.
>
> — Rudyard Kipling, *Kim* (1901), Ch.8

War is an uncertain business. Its proverbial "fog" permeates the entire enterprise, creating uncertainly. This pervading uncertainty is the *objective* overall cause of the each victim's *subjective* perception of surprise. Superb intelligence that gives more-or-less complete knowledge of the battleground is the only tool that can dispel this fog, this uncertainty. And deception is the only weapon that a warrior can wield that, to the extent it succeeds, will impose uncertainty and the element of surprise on the opponent. In other words, surprise is the intended result of deception. But that has been the overarching subject—the lesson—of all the previous papers in this author's series for the Foreign Denial and Deception Committee (FDDC). The subject of *this* specific paper is designed to give a different point of view, that of the planners themselves.

CHAPTER 1:
Intent

The subject of this study is military deception planners—their planning process and their plans. The subsequent deception operations are sketched only enough to indicate the degree and type of success or failure achieved.[4] This research is focused on how these people think about the dilemmas posed and why they propose one deception plan rather than another and how they get it implemented. Our theme is devious minds picking their way among limited options.[5]

The purpose or intended goal of this paper is twofold. First, to make us aware—acutely aware—of the kinds of threats posed by any opponent's military deception operations. Second, to suggest several major ways we can initiate or improve our own military deception efforts—as individuals or as teams.

---

4   Significant failures and partial failures have been analyzed in depth in Whaley, *When Deception Fails: The Theory of Outs* (FDDC, August 2010). Successes were first systematically and statistically analyzed in Whaley (1969/2007 reprint).

5   I conceived and began preliminary research on this study on a freelance basis in 1987. At that time my original (or, at least, an early) draft proposal to Fredric Feer and William Whelan at The RAND Corporation in Santa Monica tentatively identified 57 case studies of successful deception planning and outlined a rough framework for categorizing and analyzing these cases. Feer & Whelan had intended that piece (together with a second study of deception failure) as historical backgrounders to their larger study of the then ongoing OPFOR Red-Blue type battalion-sized combat exercises at Fort Irwin. Unfortunately, their overall project experienced difficulties and my research was cancelled before I could submit any draft material. Consequently, copyright remained with me.

CHAPTER 2:
Scope

This report covers the entire range of military deception planning in support of large-scale strategic operations to small-scale tactical ones. Moreover, it also covers the range across land, sea, aerial, and space environments. The assumption is that the planning process, the thinking behind deception plans, is relatively independent of both their scale and their military environment. This assumption—strongly supported by previous studies—is one of several hypotheses to be re-explored in this study.[6]

A central question is what is the role of the Commander? And at whatever level of command he or she may sit. How does that person effect the "bodyguard of lies" that can protect the overall military goal? Encourage or discourage deception? Actively participate in the deception process? Or favor types of operations that make deception planning harder or easier?

The report surveys and analyzes the published accounts of military deception planners (plus occasional reference to interviews by the author). Its main purpose is to identify the planners by their background, relevant training and experience, place in the organization they served, what constraints the Commander gave them, who initiated the plan, how they planned, what they planned, how they got approval, and their effectiveness in translating these plans into operations. Only secondarily and briefly does it evaluate the success or failures of the actual operation. Thus, this study tightly focuses on the thinking and procedures of individual planners rather than on the battles that flowed from their plans. To do that would require an order-of-magnitude greater effort with, I believe, little additional payoff.

The cases examine only explicit statements about the planning process. They exclude inferences that could be drawn by working backward from known results. They also exclude any inferences obtainable by working forward from knowledge of the institutionalized organizational structures of specific deception planning teams. To include either type of inference would require greatly expanding the number of case studies. But that would be at the cost of what I judge to be unacceptability vague and uncertain speculation. By way of partial compensation, Chapter 7 gives 12 cases of deception planning at the institutional level, in an attempt to capture that broader context where deception planning goes far beyond the original individual planner.

---

6 See particularly Whaley, *Stratagem* (1969/2007), Chapter 5, which did comparative studies of deception & surprise in a) strategic versus operational levels, b) land, sea, air, & amphibious environments; and c) whether in offensive or defensive modes.

This paper summarizes 88 cases: the 57 identified in my original Proposal of 6 July 1987 plus 31 others that came to light during the research. To encourage and simplify further research, it reports all relevant bibliographic references used. Because of the great variation in the volume of relevant source materials among separate cases, these summaries range from a few paragraphs to 7 pages. And because of the wide variation in types of problems faced by individual cases, the format for each has been kept flexible. However, all are reported in a manner consistent with three existing computerized data bases: my DECEPTR data-base of 230 "strategic" and "operational" cases, Fredric Feer's large system. and Feer's smaller "universe" of 140 NTC "tactical" cases. This has been done to anticipate the likelihood of future coding and incorporation in a larger and expandible computerized data-base.

The report draws several general conclusions that emerged from the data and establishes a model or framework for analyzing and incorporating any additional cases in the future.

If the reader detects a tone of lightheartedness, even occasional frivolity, in the case studies, this faithfully reflects the attitude of the majority of deception planners themselves. The subject is literally deadly serious; but most planners who mention their personal reaction describe it almost as play—a curious attitude whose important implications for selection and training of deception planners will be examined in Chapter 3 on "Analyses & Conclusions".

CHAPTER 3:
Sources

Several thousand books and articles have been written that include material on military deception. However, only a small proportion of these give evidence directly relevant to our narrow theme of its planning phase. The first stage of the winnowing or filtering process needed to identify these essential sources produced the Whaley Collection at the CIA Library's Barton Whaley Deception Research Center and its accompanying reference work, *Detecting Deception: A Bibliography of Counterdeception across Time, Cultures, and Disciplines* (Third Edition, FDDC: 2009 with Supplement). The final stage was to draw on this more manageable body of sources for those most relevant to this paper's specific topic of deception planning.

Because this paper focuses more on individuals than organizations, most—indeed the best—data is found in memoirs and biographies. Histories, particularly official histories, have an unhappy tendency to depersonalize or even suppress the contribution of staff planners and give an often exaggerated impression of the planning abilities of the commanders who get highlighted. For example, a reading of the official accounts of U.S. generals Eisenhower or Mark Clark or of British Field-Marshal Montgomery leads the unwary into the false assumption that these senior commanders must have had a major impact on the deception planning process. Their own autobiographies along with the many memoirs of their subordinates dispels this myth. Montgomery prided himself on his cumbersome strategic "master plans" and left the details—including all deception planning—to the experts he had inherited. Gen. Clark reveals himself as too preoccupied with outwitting British and fellow-American generals to give more than passing notice of the Germans, Greek Communists, or North Koreans and Chinese that his troops happened to be fighting. Even General Eisenhower took little interest in deception, but at least left it to his capable chief of staff. In fact, these three commanders neither encouraged nor discouraged their deception experts; they ignored them at the time and forgot them afterwards. Their only impact on the lowly deception planners was to set strategic or tactical parameters. But the best of their planners took such constraints in stride—a challenge to ply their devious art.

It is also instructive to see how professional military historians treat the contribution of misinformation, rumors, and deception to the outcome of battle. While most memoirs of participants recognize the very real effect that misinformation in general and deception in particular had on the enemy's decisions, most historians overlook this factor in their zeal to strip out the relevant contemporary perceptions of the decision makers and substitute their own ex post facto reconstructions of "fact". Nor can these writers universally plead the censor's red pencil. Many, particularly those who published in the 1920s, 1930s, and from 1970 until today, have worked relatively uncensored and with sufficient access to the relevant sources.

Unfortunately the record is incomplete, the blank squares in my mental "questionnaire" greatly outnumbering the filled-in ones. Until the 1960s most military and intelligence historians were simply unaware of deception as a significant factor in winning or losing battles. And since the early 1970s only a few have become more than amateurishly aware of this factor. Even the military commanders and staff officers who contributed the deceptions are usually unable to fully articulate much less consciously understand exactly how they thought about and planned them. Consequently, with few exceptions (such as the realistic RED-BLUE war games at Fort Irwin), most case studies leave far more questions unanswered than answered. And other studies pose new and perhaps unexpected questions.

There is, of course, the ever-present problems of exaggerated, mistaken, and downright deceitful sources. This is particularly true of memoirs where the usual legitimate memory tricks too often get magnified by deliberate lies, as with Col. Richard Meinertzhagen who lied whenever he thought he could succeed. The only reliable test of truth is by independent corroborative evidence. Because I prefer to exclude cases that did not meet this criterion of verifiability, all but two or three of the cases presented here have at least one independent source of confirmation.

Finally, I deplore invented dialogue as fit only for historical fiction and even approach "remembered" verbatim conversations with the same caution I would undocumented memoirs. In this case I have included several cases of "remembered" dialogue when it is the deception planners themselves speaking, because these passages probably come as close to their thinking as we can get.[7]

---

[7] A footnote on style: Editors and close readers will note many inconsistencies in titles and spellings. Titles and ranks of individuals are those held at the time under discussion, so that Rommel appears under his progressive ranks from lieutenant to field-marshal and Wavell moves up from plain mister through a knighthood to the peerage. Similarly, rank and unit designations, conform to local and temporal usage, such as American lieutenant generals and the British hyphenated lieutenant-generals. Abbreviations also conform to contemporary national usages.

PART TWO:
The Case Studies

> Gentlemen, I notice that there are always three courses open to the enemy, and that he usually takes the fourth.
>
> — General Count Helmuth von Moltke, c.1869

The 88 case studies are clustered under four headings: Learning to Deceive, Planners in Specific Operations, Selling the Commander, and Institutional Deception Planning. Each of these categories is an important topic in its own right; but, because they obviously overlap one another, the specific examples to illustrate each have been chosen mainly by the amount of available detail.

While the format varies case-to-case due to gaps in both data and the particular type of problem posed, I give for each case separate paragraphs to the following categories of information, if readily available:

1) career and personality background on the principal planners;

2) the specific problem and planning constraints faced by each;

3) detailed account of their consequent deception plan;

4) summary of the actual deception operation; and

5) the results (briefly stated).

CHAPTER 4:
Learning to Deceive

> In the first Deception Plan I ever tackled I learned a lesson of inestimable value.
>
> — Brig. Dudley Clarke, 1972

Here we meet 17 men at the outset of their careers as effective military deception planners. We see something of their personality and biases and how they were initiated into the rules of the Great Game and how these early experiences taught them to become "deception minded", leading to their subsequent contributions to the practice and/or theory of deception. And in most cases in their own words. Because of this extra detail, these special cases tend to be longer than the others.

CASE 1:
Maj.-Gen. Sir Garnet Wolseley, Night Advance on Tel el-Kebir, Egypt 1882

> As a nation we are bred up to feel it a disgrace even to succeed by falsehood; the word spy conveys something as repulsive as slave; we will keep hammering along with the conviction that 'honesty is the best policy,' and that truth always wins in the long run. These pretty little sentences do well for a child's copy-book, but the man who acts on them in war had better sheathe his sword for ever.
>
> — Col. Wolseley, *The Soldier's Pocket-Book for Field Service* (London: 1869), 169

The above words were by one of Britain's few deception-minded military commanders of the 1800s. It was Colonel Garnet Wolseley's clear diagnosis of every deceiver's ethical dilemma and its cause. I assume it reflected his distinguished combat experiences in Burma, the Crimea, India, and China plus his observations of the American Civil War in 1862 from the Confederate side. The twice-wounded, one-eyed lieut.-colonel had been properly impressed by the somewhat imaginative accomplishments and tactics of Generals Lee and Longstreet and, particularly, of Generals Stonewall Jackson and Nathan Bedford Forrest. His chapter, "Intelligence Department", from the 1874 3rd Edition, proved sufficiently timeless to be reprinted 89 years later by the CIA in its in-house classified journal.[8]

Further distinguished imperial service brought Lieut.-General Sir Garnet Wolseley to Egypt to suppress the Urabi Revolt led by Ahmed Urabi.[9] Mustering his joint British army at the Mediterranean port of Alexandria he first tried a straight 110-mile thrust south along the Nile valley and river—toward the rebel-held capital, Cairo. After five weeks of unsuccessful attempts to force his passage by that direct route, one stoutly defended by the well-entrenched enemy under Ahmed Urabi, Wolseley switched to an indirect strategy—to capture the recently opened Suez Canal to the east of Cairo and then move upon Cairo from behind. Advised by Ferdinand de Lesseps on this point, Urabi had completely discounted this as a realistic option for their enemy. Consequently, Urabi left the Canal undefended and Wolseley easily captured it by September 6th.

On the 12th, having quickly staged his main force at the southern Canal port of Ismailia, he set out from there. His attacking force comprised two divisions of British infantry, a brigade of British cavalry, with an Indian brigade acting as a flanking force—a total of some 18,500 troops and 70 cannon. They advanced west along the railway and feeder Sweetwater canal toward Cairo, which was about 70 miles distant but over almost flat and easily traversed flat and hard desert.

Urabi hastily set up a poorly dug-in blocking army of about 15,000 Egyptians with 60 cannon at Tel el-Kebir, between Cairo and the advancing British-Indian force. Although the British force was better trained, as the attackers against even a lightly dug-in force of comparable strength, they would seem to be at a marked disadvantage.

Wolseley now planned to reinforce the strategic surprise of his indirect approach on Cairo from the Canal side by gaining tactical surprise as well. The tactic would be the conventional and therefore expected full-frontal attack on the rebel line. However Wolseley intended to make it an entirely unconventional *night attack*. This was an almost unheard of tactic among large forces comprised of several separate units whose coordinated movement required the kind of close communication that was then possible mainly through visual means—namely in daylight.

---

8   *Studies in Intelligence*, Vol.7, No.4 (Fall 1963), A19-A24.
9   The ensuing battle is best described covered in Joseph H. Lehmann, *All Sir Garnet: A Life of Field-Marshal Lord Wolseley* (London: Jonathan Cape, 1964). See also *Wikipedia*, "Battle of Tel el-Kebir" and "Garnet Wolseley" (both accessed 5 Oct 2010).

Wolseley made several personal reconnaissances. From these he saw that the rebels did not man their outposts at night. He knew that with good acoustical discipline he could get his assault force quite close to the sleepy Egyptian line. He launched his final approach in the predawn darkness on the 13th. Indeed, his three-brigade assault force got to 300 yards of the enemy force when at 5:45 am, just when dawn was breaking, Egyptian sentries noticed them and opened fire.

The ensuing battle was decided in little more than a half hour. At a cost of 57 British KIA to about 1,400 Egyptians, the battle ended in the rebels' complete rout. The brigade of British cavalry swept forward to Cairo, accepting the surrender of the fleeing Urabi along the way. Wolseley and his staff arrived in Cairo the next day by train. The revolt was over.

CASE 2:
Lieut.-Col. G.F.R. Henderson, the Relief of Kimberley, South Africa 1900
The Commander's chief of Intelligence emulates Stonewall Jackson.

In the late 19th Century, Lieutenant-Colonel G.F.R. Henderson was Britain's most unorthodox military scholar. His classic study of the American Civil War, published in 1898, identified a whole range of strategic and tactical ruses used by the rebel Confederate generals, particularly the highly unorthodox "Stonewall" Jackson. Henderson's research had led him to explicitly attribute the Rebels frequent attainment of surprise to their use of tactical deceptions.[10]

Two years later Henderson got the rare opportunity to apply his academic theories to real war when he accompanied General Lord Roberts into the hitherto—for the British—disastrous quagmire of the Boer War. As head of Robert's Intelligence Service, Colonel Henderson devised the carefully coordinated plan of feint and deception that relieved Kimberley and permitted the move against Bloemfontein.[11] As Gen. Wavell later described it.[12]

> In its essentials Roberts' plan was, like most successful plans in war, simple almost to the point of crudity—a feint at Cronje's right and then a quick-step around his left. The rest depended on the marching powers of man and horse. But elaborate arrangements were made to deceive the enemy and to make the outflanking force mobile; in the careful execution of these details lay the difficulties and success of the plan. ... [And]

---

10   Whaley (1969), 26.
11   A. P. Wavell, *Allenby*, Vol.1 (London: Harrap,1940), 80.
12   Wavell (1941), 80.

> other steps were taken by ... Henderson to prevent the real plan being guessed.

This combination of simulative and dissimulative deception measures achieved Robert's purpose when his campaign began on 11 February 1900.

After that war, Henderson returned to military scholarship to do battle with the majority of soldiers—those tiresome skeptics who forever insist that new technology invalidates lessons of history. In 1902 he wrote prophetically:[13]

> It is repeated ad nauseam that in consequence of the vastly improved means of transmitting information, surprise on a large scale is no longer to be feared. It should be remembered, however, that the means of concentrating troops and ships are far speedier than of old; that false information can be far more readily distributed; and also, that if there is one thing more certain than another, it is that the great strategist, surprise still being the most deadly of all weapons, will devote the whole force of his intellect to the problem of bringing it about.

In later cases we shall see that Henderson's writings and personal example as a deception planner influenced two other future deception planners: Allenby and Wavell, thereby starting a chain-reaction of person-to-person teaching that would peak in WW2.

CASE 3:
Major Ernest Swinton, The Boer War, South Africa 1900
A Royal Engineer sets two ambushes.

> The enemy ... expected to surprise us, and was himself surprised.
>
> — Swinton

Ernest Dunlop Swinton was born in 1868 in Bangalore, India, the fourth son of a British judge in the Indian Civil Service, but from a family with a strong tradition of military service. Educated at various public schools including Rugby, he entered the Royal Military Academy at Woolwich from which he graduated to a commission in the Royal Engineers in 1888, specializing thereafter in railway engineering and bridging.

---

13 [Colonel] G.F.R.H[enderson], "War", *Encyclopaedia Britannica*, 10th Edition, Vol.33 (1902), 747. This brilliant article was written for the 10th Edition and was reprinted in the 11th (1911). Then it was replaced by a dull piece by a conventionally-minded author.

Swinton was an intelligent, genial man with a keen sense of humor (selling cartoons to *Punch* and other magazines) and a minor flair for practical joking. This latter talent had emerged by age 14, when early in his one term at Cheltenham College he devised an ingenious ruse to induce Intelligence feedback:[14]

> I soon discovered a specimen of the unpleasant type of youth who is very friendly with lonely new boys so long as their pocket-money lasts, and in confidence worms intimate family secrets out of them, which he retails to other boys, to the confusion of the innocent newcomer. I suspected him, and bought him ices so long as I could afford to do so. I also supplied him with some confidential and scandalous and entirely bogus "facts" about my family. When this fictitious information came round to me—there was no doubt as to its source and I had a very satisfactory settlement with my false friend, which repaid me for all the pocket-money I had expended on him.

In 1899, 31-year old Captain Swinton went off to his first war—the Boer War, which was then raging in South Africa between the Dutch settlers and the British invaders. As an acting major he commanded a 400-man battalion of the newly and locally raised 1st Railway Pioneer Regiment, whose task was to rebuild bridges blown by Boer commandos. Now, in May and early June 1900, Swinton devised his first military ruse.[15]

> As, at that period, many supply trains travelling north at night, with a "guard" of a few half-frozen men on top of slippery tarpaulins just arrived in the country, had been held up and captured with all they contained, ... I resolved that we should have a fighting chance, if attacked. From the naval dockyard at Simonstown we got up some loopholed bullet-proof plates to fit behind the green sides of the usual goods trucks [freight cars]. On board the train we should have ammunition, food and water and 300 to 400 men all practised in taking action without awaiting orders. Some were to tumble out on one side of the train, some on the other, and lie down well away from the rails. A third party was to shoot from the truck and so draw the enemy fire, whilst trenches were being dug from which to carry on the fight after daylight. We were very proud of our innocent looking supply train, and hoped it might give a nasty surprise to "Brother Boer".

---

14 Swinton (1951), 31.
15 Swinton (1951), 116.

To Swinton's disappointment, the Boers never attacked his battalion while moving cross-country during June 7th through 12th in its camouflaged armored "Q-boat"-on-rails. However, on June 13th, he set an ambush at his battalion's new post. They had just joined another battalion of railway engineers and a battalion of militia to repair a knocked-out bridge over a thinly populated stretch of the Zand River. One of Major Swinton's captains reconnoitered the area and with "Scottish canniness" voiced his unease about the position. Swinton rode out with the officer to view the several camps and work sites and immediately realized that:[16]

> For our constructional work the whole post was conveniently arranged—*if the Boers did not attack*. But if they did, our position was absolutely hopeless. They could approach at night under cover, up and down the river bed, and at dawn shoot us up in our tents, capture the whole garrison, burn the [temporary bridge] ..., and so cut the communications at the Zand River for the second time.

First, Swinton had to convince the senior construction engineer who, though anxious to get on with the bridging, wisely left the military countermeasures to the professional. Then:[17]

> We put our views to the Commandant, and suggested that we should leave the camps standing and spend the day in entrenching in the cover of the thorn bush along the river, and the night standing to arms in the trenches, where we would, for a change, have the enemy at a disadvantage in the open, probably wasting ammunition, shooting into our empty tents. The nights are extremely cold on the High Velt of the Orange Free State, and my proposal of sleeping in the open was not at all welcome. The colonel was inclined to leave things as they were, and loath to make any change. In fact, it was not until I pointed out, firmly but tactfully, that as the senior Regular officer present and a sapper at that, I should in the event of a "regrettable incident", be blamed for any failure in the defensive measures, and asked for his refusal in writing, as Commandant, to adopt my suggestions, that he gave way.

Swinton entrenched the garrison and the first freezing night passed without incident. The second night, June 13th-14th, the Boers slipped past the British cavalry patrols and attacked the camp in force at first light. It was a 700-man Commando led by General "Fighting Parson" Roux with a field gun and a pom-

---

16 Swinton (1951), 118.
17 Swinton (1951), 119.

pom. The fire-fight ended at noon when the Boers withdrew. Their casualties were 21 killed and 31 wounded. The British had two killed and 12 wounded. As Swinton concluded:[18]

> Zand River was a case of the biter being bit. The enemy, judging from other experiences, had expected to surprise us, and was himself surprised. As Boer women had been allowed to come in from the neighboring farms with eggs and butter, it was not to be wondered that the raiders knew the position of the camps sufficiently accurately to plan a deadly attack at a time when the troops would be asleep in their tents. The tents were where expected, but, unluckily for the Boers, the occupants were not in them, but as snugly situated as the attackers themselves.

In 1909 Swinton published a most unusual collection of 11 short stories about war and soldiers. As a serving officer it was mandatory to publish under a pseudonym; and he chose "Ole Luk-Oie" from Hans Christian Andersen's fairytale character Ole Lukie meaning "Shut-Eye". The collection appeared as *The Green Curve And Other Stories* and was twice reprinted during WW2 when the then retired author's real name was revealed on the titlepage. While all these tales show either psychological depth or technological foresight (rapid-fire guns, aerial observation, vertical envelopment, etc.), two are unique. The title story is the first account—fictional or otherwise—of what would later be invented and called Operational Research, now better known, particularly in the USA, as Operations Research or simply OR. The other story, 'The Second Degree", is relevant here. It is the first fictional tale of military counterdeception, as apt today as when written nearly 80 years ago.

This story is set on a battlefield in an anonymous land at an unspecified but clearly modern time between two unnamed armies. The protagonist is a young Chief of Staff to his old Field-Marshal. They are on the defensive, awaiting the attack of their stronger enemy. They have just learned that the newly appointed enemy commander is a man that the Chief of Staff had known when they were both boys at the same school. At this point the Chief of Staff recalls his miserable schooldays with "the Ferret" whose "chief peculiarity was that though he sometimes lied, he often told the truth. It was also his success, for no one knew which way to take him, and he always attained his object when he wished to deceive." The Chief of Staff recalled the vicious deceptions of the Ferret and also his parting advice:[19]

---

18 Swinton (1951), 122-123. See also Major-General Sir Ernest D. Swinton, *Eyewitness* (Garden City, NY: Doubleday, 1933), 5-6.

19 "Ole Luk-Oie" [ErnestSwinton], *The Green Curve And Other Stories* (Edinburgh and London: William Blackwood & Sons, 1909), 59.

To *get on* it was necessary to be ahead of every one else, to anticipate what they would think or would do, to know their natures, and he added a good deal more stuff which then appeared to be sheer nonsense. He concluded by saying that lying—good lying—was useful in moderation, and his last words were: "To a stranger I never lie until I am forced—then I lie well; the other man thinks I am telling the truth—and is misled. That's the First Degree of Cunning. Next time I wish to deceive that man, I tell the truth. He, of course, thinks that I am lying, and so again is misled—the Second Degree."

Armed only with these memories, the Chief of Staff begins a deadly game of deceptioncounterdeception with the Ferret. Although fiction, Swinton's "The Second Degree" belongs in any textbook of deception to remind us that it is at heart a psychological game whose specific "assets" (such as camouflage netting, dummy tanks, decoy missiles, bogus radio traffic, ECM/ECCM, or double agents) are only the means to communicate deception material. The misperception itself always takes place in the victim's mind.

On his first visit to the one-month old Western Front in 1914, Swinton observed the chaos and slaughter created among British troops by German machine guns. He determined to find a countermeasure. Combining his earlier trial with an armored train with his knowledge of a new American agricultural machine, the Holt Caterpillar Tractor, Swinton conceived a revolutionary weapon. At first he met only lack of either imagination or cooperation from senior officials. It took a visionary First Lord of the Admiralty, Winston Churchill, to get R&D underway by diverting £270,000 of Admiralty money to this strictly Army project. At this point Swinton decided his machines should have a cover name to keep them secret until they could be built and deployed in large enough numbers for a devastating surprise attack. Accordingly in 1915 he chose the then quite innocuous word "tank", thereby coining the term by which it soon became universally known.[20]

Swinton was also one of the first (and few) soldiers to understand that, if you have a new technological weapon, you should unleash it as a total surprise weapon in a crucial battle in numbers sufficient to be decisive. You don't disclose it to the enemy in a series of minor "trials by combat". He urged this point on his superiors, but they didn't understand. Consequently, the tank premiered on 15 September 1916 with too few (36) to achieve any more than "technological surprise" and local panic.

---

20 Major-General Sir Ernest D. Swinton, *Eyewitness: Being Personal Reminiscences of Certain Phases of the Great War, Including the Genesis of the Tank* (Garden City, NY: Doubleday, Doran & Company, 1933), throughout.

Swinton was knighted in 1923; and from 1925 through 1939 he taught his mildly deceptive views as the Chichele Professor of Military History at Oxford University.

CASE 4:
Lieut.-Gen. Charles Monro, Suvla Bay and Anzac Beach, Gallipoli 1915
Wherein the Commander throws away the rule books and succeeds.

> A feint which did not fully fulfill its purpose would have been worse than useless ....
> —Monro, despatch, 6 Mar 1916

On 7 December 1915 the British Cabinet agreed to begin liquidating the Allied fiasco on the Gallipoli Peninsula. After seven months and 250,000 casualties, the three beachheads had failed to even link up much less achieve the intended breakout. The Cabinet decided to abandon two of these beaches, holding on with face-saving pride only at the tip position at Cape Helles—a bad compromise.

This embarrassing political-military decision had been made with the concurrence of the War Committee, the Minister for War (Lord Kitchener), Lieut.-Gen. Sir Charles Monro (Ian Hamilton's recent successor as commander in the Aegean), all of Hamilton's former staff (now under Monro), and two of the three corps commanders on Gallipoli itself.

Monro was being set up as the fall-guy. His unenvied task was to get some 100,000 Allied troops off the shores of Suvla Bay and nearby Anzac Beach in the face of roughly equal numbers of, but better positioned, Turkish soldiers who tightly ringed these two small beachheads. Moreover, the Turks dominated the hills overlooking the beechs

The decision to evacuate had been made in full agreement with the harrowing predictions of appalling casualties expected during withdrawal. The former commander, Gen. Ian Hamilton, had informed London just before being relieved that evacuation would entail 50% casualties and loss of all guns and stores. Although this was a lie told to forestall a decision to cancel his pet operation, even Hamilton privately expected fully 35% to 45% casualties in such an event. Monro's inherited staff, though generally biased for withdrawal, presented their new commander with a careful estimate that reckoned on 50% loss in troops and 66% in guns. Monro gave London his own estimate: 30% to 40% of both material and men (i.e., up to 40,000 casualties). War Minister Kitchener, who had come out to see for himself, was more optimistic, telling

London he expected only 25,000 casualties, that is, 25% of the total force. At that point, this was also the reduced estimate of Monro's staff. However the British Army General Staff in London held to an estimate of 50,000 casualties (i.e., 50%).

These predictions of huge losses assumed the evacuation would be contested. Accordingly, Lord Curzon, the Lord Privy Seal, pictured to the Cabinet the operation in these gloomy terms:[21]

> [The] evacuation and the final scene will be enacted at night. Our guns will continue firing until the last moment ... but the trenches will have been taken one by one, and a moment must come when a final *sauve qui peut* [each man save himself] takes place, and when a disorganized crowd will press in despairing tumult on to the shore and into the boats. Shells will be falling and bullets ploughing their way into this mass of retreating humanity .... Conceive the crowding into the boats of thousands of half crazy men, the swamping of craft, the nocturnal panic, the agony of the wounded, the hetacombs of slain ....

The differences among these various casualty predictions were directly proportional to the predictor's bias for or against evacuation. The few advocates for escalation pressed forward the more pessimistic figures, and the pro-evacuation crowd promoted the optimistic estimates. Moreover, those individuals who changed their policy position on evacuation, simultaneously adopted the psychologically appropriate statistics. The most striking instance was Lord Kitchener who backed down from 50% casualties to 25% and then, when leaving the scene where he had reluctantly concluded that evacuation was inevitable, blurted out to stay-behind Colonel Aspinall that, "I don't believe a word about those 25,000 casualties ... you'll just step off without losing a man, and without the Turks knowing anything about it."[22] Perhaps he was only consoling an officer he thought doomed. Or perhaps he had some glimmer of Monro's plan.

Once London ordered the evacuation, most staff officers in the Aegean suddenly revised their *private* estimates downward to a comforting 15%.[23] All these casualty estimates—far from being rational military calculations, much less seen in human terms—were used by the military and political professionals alike as political tools and psychological crutches. The only exception to this

---

21 As quoted in The Earl of Ronaldshay, *The Life of Lord Curzon*, Vol.3 (London: Benn, 1928), 130-131.
22 Quoted in Alan Moorehead, *Gallipoli* (New York: Harper, 1956), 333.
23 Henry W. Nevinson, *The Dardanelles Campaign* (New York: Holt, 1919), 387.

sorry morass of emotional self-seeking irresponsibility was the man who had to "carry the can"—General Monro.

Monro rejected the conventional feints or demonstrations as a supplement to the various ruses at the beachheads themselves. Knowing he was setting precedent, Monro reasoned that:[24]

> The attitude which we should adopt from a naval and military point of view in case of withdrawal ... had given me much anxious thought. According to text-book principles and lessons from history it seemed essential that ... evacuation should be immediately preceded by a combined naval and military feint in the neighborhood of the peninsula, with a view to distracting the attention of the Turks from our intention. When endeavoring to work out the concrete fact how such principles could be applied to the situation of our forces, I came to the conclusion that our chances of success were infinitely more probable if we made no departure of any kind from the normal life which we were following both on sea and on land. A feint which did not fully fulfill its purpose would have been worse than useless, and there was obvious danger that the suspicion of the Turks would be aroused by our adoption of a course, the real purport of which could not have been long disguised.

Indeed, as Monro had come to expect, evidence of the decision to evacuate Gallipoli had been gradually accumulating before both public and enemy eyes. Thus, the original commander of the expeditionary force, Hamilton, was relieved by Monro on October 14th. That same day, withdrawal was first openly advocated in the House of Lords by Milner. On November 2nd Prime Minister Asquith bluntly admitted to the House of Commons that the latest offensive had failed. On the 11th the announcement of a reconstituted War Committee (to replace the Dardanelles Committee) revealed that the two leading public proponents of the adventure, Churchill and Curzon, had been dumped. Finally, on the 18th. Lord Ribblesdale, an outspoken advocate of withdrawal, revealed in the House of Lords that General Monro had "reported in favor of withdrawal from the Dardanelles, and adversely to the continuance of winter operations there."[25] What was the Turkish reaction to all these authentic public indicators of both a possible forthcoming change in British policy but its timing as well? We know only their estimate of Lord Milner's public advocacy of withdrawal; they discredited it as a deliberate effort at deception. The Turks expected the

---

24 Monro despatch of 6 March 1916, as quoted in Major-General Sir C. E. Callwell, *The Dardanelles* (London: Constable, 1919). 276-277.
25 Nevinson (1919), 378n.

Allies to stay. So, the Allied withdrawals would at least enjoy the advantage of *strategic* surprise.

The carefully planned evacuation took place over a 10-day period, from December 10th through the 20th. Some troops were embarked in daylight under cover of tarpaulin. Most slipped off at night. As units drifted away and positions were abandoned, neighboring units took over the job of simulating a visually unchanged state. According to the planned schedule, they used such daytime ruses as maintaining the empty tents and increasingly moving about in the open. At nighttime all the usual campfires were lit. Normal levels of patrol activity and counter-battery fire were maintained. Aviation patrols kept the few German spotter planes from getting too close a look at the denuded positions, particularly on the final day when five Allied aircraft flew almost continuous air cover.

As the last day began at 0100 hours, only about 3,500 troops remained on the two beachheads; at 1715 the last 200 were safely away. The casualties? No dead and 5 wounded. Of the 200 guns, only 10 were left behind. Of some 5,000 draft animals, only 56 mules remained. Even most of the 2,000 carts had been removed.

The cost-effectiveness of Monro's deceptive surprise withdrawal was so little understood that many credited the rumor that the Turks had been bribed to withhold their attack.[26] A more generous and more accurate appraisal was given by a German military correspondent who was there: "So long as wars exist, the British evacuation ... will stand before the eyes of all strategists of retreat as a hitherto unattained masterpiece."[27]

CASE 5:
Lieut.-Gen. Monro, Helles Point, Gallipoli 1916
If the trick worked once, play it again.

> The Italians have a Proverb, He that deceives me Once, it's his Fault, but Twice, it is my fault.
>
> — Sir Anthony Weldon, *The Court and Character of King James* (1650)[28]

---

26 Nevinson (1919), 387.
27 Anonymous, *Vossische Zeitung*, 21 January 1916, as quoted in Nevinson (1919), 400n.
28 Weldon's is the only citation for this famous quotation that I deem credible. Google's "deceive" or "fool" or "hurt" and "shame" versions of this stock quotation have more than a thousand hits. But they give, at best, outlandish origins—Chinese, Dutch, Scots, Native American, Texan (according to George W. Bush), Southern, B. B. King/Jennings/Sample (1992), "a child's saying", "old maxim", or "current saying". I located only one other specific citation. That was to Nathan Bailey, *An Universal Etymological English Dictionary* (1721). But I couldn't find it there under "deceive", "fool", or "shame". Perhaps it is in the 1736 edition, as cited by G. L. Apperson, *English Proverbs and Proverbial Phrases* (1929).

Gen. Charles Monro's successful evacuations of Suvla Bay and Anzac Beach on 20 December 1915 hurried the inevitable decisions to liquidate the one remaining beachhead—Helles Point at the very tip of the peninsula. Three days later the War Committee recommended this action, the Cabinet debated four days before agreeing, and Monro was notified the next day, December 28th. He began evacuation the following day.

The situation again seemed desperate. The four Allied divisions (35,000 troops) comprising VIII Corps were crowded into the 12-square mile beachhead. Facing them was a vastly larger force of Turks directed by German General (and Turkish Field-Marshal) Liman von Sanders who had now concentrated his entire force of 21 divisions (120,000 troops) against this last remaining Allied position. It was certain that a contested evacuation would be costly, perhaps even disastrous.

Could Monro pull off a second surprise withdrawal? And only a fortnight after the last? He thought he could and adopted the same basic deception plan, choosing to simulate normalcy and avoid any feints.[29]

One new technique was added: this evacuation was to be carried out under the pretense of reinforcement and relief. As some relief and reinforcement had already been in effect since early December, "normalcy" at Helles meant busy comings-and-goings between ships and shore. Now, however, beginning on the 29th, the pattern of relief shifted slightly to bring in only small units of IX Corps, which just having extricated itself from Suvla was experienced in the special camouflage techniques needed. Phony orders were given out that IX Corps was relieving VIII Corps. This ruse succeeded so well that even the troops on the beachhead did not fully realize what was underway until sometime later.

And once again the enemy was completely fooled. During the 12 days of evacuation they failed to launch a single major attack. The final day, January 9th, the last contingent of 3,877 troops slipped away with only 5 casualties. Left behind were only 17 of 150 cannon, 508 of the 4,197 horses and mules, 1,590 carts, and some quantities of stores, mostly destroyed.[30]

---

29 Despatch of 16 March 1916, as quoted in Callwell (1919), 310.
30 On the deception see Callwell (1919), 310, 311, 314, 322-323; Moorehead (1959), 349-355; Sanders (1927), 101, 103; and James (1965), 344.

CASE 6:
Lt. Erwin Rommel, Italy 1917
The future "Desert Fox" learns the value of surprise and practices his first deceptions.

> ROMMEL: Tell me, general, what's the best way to command a panzer division?
> SCHMIDT: You'll find there are always two possible decisions open to you. Take the bolder one—it's always best.

This exchange, spoken in a stage whisper in a February 1940 receiving line of senior German officers, was a jest between Gen. Rudolf Schmidt and Lieut.-Gen. Erwin Rommel on the occasion of Rommel's transfer of command from infantry to armor. The joke's point was that Rommel had already always followed the bolder course and Schmidt knew it.[31]

Erwin Rommel was born in 1891, the middle son of a Swabian schoolteacher in a family without military tradition. A weakling until his teens, he slowly overcame this by a rigorous program of physical exercise; and, on his father's urging, reluctantly joined the Army at age 20 as a private in the Infantry. Seventeen months later, in 1912, he was commissioned second lieutenant. Nothing in his background or behavior suggested he would become other than a very ordinary soldier.[32] The Great War was about to change this.

In the first month of the war he had his first skirmish. On patrol with his platoon for 24 hours—exhausted, dirty, and ill from food poisoning—he came upon a small Belgian village with what at first looked like only 20 French defenders. Scouting ahead with an NCO and two privates he immediately attacked the equally surprised but hesitant enemy. When his full platoon arrived, they captured some 50 French soldiers.

Next month, when a German attack stalled, Rommel seized a rifle and charged forward alone through the bushes. Stumbling upon five French soldiers he shot two and then, with an emptied magazine, pressed his attack by bayonet until dropped by a bullet. For this bold action he won the Iron Cross, 2nd Class.

On 29 January 1915 he led his 200-man company through the 100-yard deep barbed wire in a surprise attack that captured four tactically important French blockhouses. For this he won the Iron Cross, 1st Class, the first for a lieutenant in his regiment. Transferred to the Rumanian front in August 1917, 1st Lieutenant Rommel infiltrated his company at night several miles behind

---
31 Irving (1977), 40.
32 See particularly Irving (1977).

enemy lines, waited for the defenders to go to sleep, and then, by a surprise attack, got their quick surrender, bringing back 400 prisoner.[33]

Next month the 26-year old 1st lieutenant was again transferred, now to the Italian front where he would gain his greatest successes in WW1. His orders were to secure the mountainous Alpine flank of the Austro-Hungarian and German army when they began their great offensive in late October. Exceeding these orders, he led his 600-man Abteilung secretly through the Italian front lines. Moving quickly, his unit forced surrender-after-surrender—more than 1,000 Italians that morning; 50 officers and 2,000 troops of the crack 4th Bersaglieri Brigade taken by ambush that afternoon; 43 officers and 1,500 men taken the next dawn. After 50 hours his prisoners totaled 150 officers and 9,000 men; and—more important—Rommel had assaulted up the 5,400-foot slope of strategically sited Monte Matajur, taking the summit with its 120 defenders at the cost of only one of his own men killed.

Two weeks later, after several other successes, Rommel's unit captured an entire 8,000-man Italian division at Langarone at a cost of less than 14 dead. For these prodigious and successful efforts by aggressive bluff, bravado, surprise attacks from both front and rear, and rapid pursuit, Rommel was promoted captain and received the Pour le Mérite, the coveted "Blue Max", which he wore throughout his career.[34]

These brilliant successes won Rommel his reputation for *Fingerspitzengefühl*—literally intuition in the fingertips, a sixth sense. But this type of "intuition" is a rational, if largely unconscious, process. It only seems mystical or mysterious because its practitioners are usually too unaware to fully understand it themselves much less find the words to explain it to others.[35] We'll see this quality emerge in Rommel on three occasions—once in WW2 (Case 6) and twice in his North African campaign (Cases 42 & 43) where he earned his nickname, the Desert Fox.

By the end of the Great War Rommel's personality was firmly set. He drove himself as hard as he did his officers and troops, demanding competence. War was his only passion; he had no hobbies and his reading was limited to military works and war news. He was a strictly monogamous family man with little time even for his family. He did not smoke and had only an occasional glass of wine with a hasty meal. He was not convivial and what carefully controlled humor he had was only for his few closest comrades and, casually, with his troops.

---

33 Samuel W. Mitcham Jr, *Triumphant Fox* (New York: Stein and Day, 1984), 31-33; Irving (1977). 14-15.

34 Irving (1977), 15-20; Mitcham (1984), 34-35.

35 This scientific theory of intuition, first comprehensively formulated in 1905 by French mathematician Henri Poincaré has only gradually become the dominant theory among cognitive psychologists. See Whaley, *Textbook of Political-Military Counterdeception* (FDDC: 2007), 84-89.

He believed he deserved high rewards; and pushed his cause at any superiors who tended to overlook him as, having a short stature, was both literally and psychologically easy for most of them to do. He, like Montgomery, made enemies more easily than friends.

In 1937 Rommel published *Infantrie Grieft an* [The Infantry Attacks]. His book reported shamelessly on the author's personal experiences in the Great War. However, in doing so, it proved that his experiences directly inspired much of his thinking about tactics. Specifically simple ruses but, more importantly Rommel's firm belief that the commander must *always* seize the initiative at the *earliest feasible moment* in order to surprise the enemy. The book became a best-seller in Germany.

In fall 1939 Major-General Rommel headed Hitler's battlefield headquarters during the Polish campaign. There he was impressed most by the mobility of the tank units. Next February, the General Staff wished to assign him command of a mountain infantry division, but Rommel went directly to the Führer, requesting and getting command of a panzer division. Rommel gave ten copies of his book to his unit commanders to make sure they would understand the unorthodox style that he intended to apply to armored warfare. And in May and June he followed his own precepts throughout his dashing drive—up to 150 miles a day—across France at the head of 7th Panzer Division that earned its nickname, "Spook Division", from the baffled enemy. During the six-week campaign Rommel's division had taken 97,500 prisoners (including 20 generals and 5 admirals), captured or destroyed 458 tanks and armored cars, and 79 aircraft—the most successful bag by any Wehrmacht division. However, the absolute cost was also the highest for any single German division: 20% of his tanks and men (42 of his original 218 tanks and 2,594 casualties out of his original 13,000 troops). Even so, this was a war-winning cost-beneficial strategy between two closely matched opponents—an investment of 1 armored vehicle to win 2 and 1 casualty to win 37.

CASE 7:
Lt. Col. George C. Marshall, St.-Mihiel, France 1918
The future US Army Chief-of-Staff learns to practice deception and creates a cadre of deceptive American commanders.

> "Rather think we outfoxed 'em."
> — Pershing

George Catlett Marshall got his first exposure to deception in 1918 when, as a lieutenant colonel on General John J. Pershing's G-3 (Operations) staff, he did the detailed planning for the Battle of St.-Mihiel, the American Expeditionary Force's first all-American offensive on the Western Front. Pershing stressed the need for surprise and his staff helped him get it. Although Marshall's role was mainly limited to the intricate pre-attack deployments of the "Doughboys", he was witness to the rather sophisticated deceptions pieced together by others on the staff that assured a major surprise.[36]

In 1927 Lieutenant Colonel Marshall was appointed Assistant Commandant of the Infantry School at Fort Benning, Georgia. This appointment carried with it the headship of the Academic Department. Appalled by the unrealistic pedantry of the curriculum and training techniques, this highly imaginative and unorthodox officer set in motion a "quiet and gradual revolution".[37] Until then, deception—while practiced with considerable verve by individual American commanders—had been ignored by U.S. Army doctrine. Now, under the man who had designed the first and most elaborate American strategic deception operation of WW1, it gained a tenuous foothold. A small but significant portion of America's WW2 and post-war military leaders thereby benefitted from continuity of the knowledge of surprise and deception so painfully learned in the Great War.

Marshall began a private and secret project of his own at Fort Benning that would have great pay-off in the coming war. He bought what he called "my little black book" in which he recorded the names of every young officer whose talents impressed him—"for future reference", as he put it. Those who made his list at Benning included Lt. Col. Joseph Stilwell, Maj. Omar Bradley, Capt. J. Lawton Collins, Lt. Charles T. Lanham from the staff. And, from the students, he listed Capt. Matthew B. Ridgeway, John H. Hilldring, and John R. Deane. Marshall had picked well—not only would all those named become generals in WW2 but all served with distinction. Once asked if he also used his little black book to jot down the names of officers who lacked talent, Marshall replied, "There wouldn't have been room."[38]

Although Marshall left the Infantry School in 1931, his curriculum and lecture work culminated in 1934 in publication of a book, *Infantry in Battle*, that incorporated his doctrine and drew heavily on historical examples and experience from the Great War. This still useful book had an immediate small success both at home and abroad.[39] The chapter on surprise is excellent and modern but, surprisingly, only vaguely implies its connection, with deception.

---

36 George C. Marshall, *Memoirs of My Services in the World War, 1917-1918* (Boston: Houghton Mifflin, 1976), 126-1 47.
37 Forrest C. Pogue, *George C. Marshall*, Vol.1 (New York: Viking Press, 1963), 248-260.
38 Leonard Mosley, *Marshall: Hero for Our Times* (New York: Hearst Books, 1982), 96.
39 [Major Edwin F. Harding (*editor*)], *Infantry in Battle* (1st ed., 1934; [Capt. C. T. Lanham (*editor*) (2nd ed., Washington, DC: The Infantry Journal, Inc., 1939), Chapter 8 ("Surprise", pp.107-121). The "Introduction" was by Marshall. See also Pogue, Vol.1 (1963), 255, 259.

It characterized surprise as "the master key to victory" and proceeded to demonstrate this otherwise sterile homily. It shows that surprise can be gained by the defender as well as an attacker. And, perhaps most original, it stresses that surprise "should be striven for by all units, regardless of size, and in all engagements, regardless of importance."[40] The book illustrates these points by citing in passing three major surprise offensives and then analyzing in detail four small-unit operations, as was appropriate for a school intended primarily for company grade infantry officers.

Throughout WW2 General Marshall served in Washington as Army Chief of Staff. In that high post he did not directly involve himself in deception planning. However he did use it to encourage and support the development of an institutionalized deception capability. Specifically he brought out his "little black book" and began surrounding himself with his chosen best-and-brightest officers. When he found that the rigidity of the War Department bureaucracy prevented him from arbitrarily promoting and reassigning these men, he simply plugged them into the War Plans Division, particularly General Wedemeyer. And we can assume that Marshall was highly predisposed to accept British recommendations for centralized U.S. and joint U.S.-British deception planning. In August 1942 the British Chiefs of Staff urged that the U.S. Joint Chiefs of Staff (JCS) create an organization equivalent to the LCS. The outcome of this partial meeting of minds was a compromise, the JCS giving oversight of all deception in early September to the Joint Security Control (JSC), which like the British Inter-Services Security Board (ISSB) exercised general supervision of security questions.[41] In late September the JCS was briefed jointly by Col. Bevan of the LSC and Col. Clarke of "A" Force who were visiting Washington for this purpose.

CASE 8:
Maj. Heinz Guderian, The Swedish Connection 1929
The future Panzer general learns the ways of deception.

In 1929 the then 40-year old Major Heinz Guderian drove his first tank, a Swedish M21, while a guest of the Swedish Army's lone tank company. It was a covert operation. This so-called M-21 was actually one of 10 German light Lk.II tanks that Joseph Vollmer had smuggled out of Germany in defiance of the Treaty of Versailles and sold to Sweden as the M-21.[42]

Unfortunately, we don't have Guderian's first-hand views on deception, and the moreor-less detailed second-hand accounts of his planning and operations

---

40 Harding (1934), 107, 118.
41 Cruickshank (1979), 214.
42 Whaley, *Covert German Rearmament, 1919-1939: Deception and Misperception*. Frederick, Maryland: University Publications of America, Inc., 1984).

make little reference to it. However, given the general deception-blindness of these distant writers, we should not conclude that deception wasn't at least at the back of his mind. Liddell Hart and Wavell saw him as a master of the "indirect approach". And, like most Great Captains, his operations have that air of overall "competence" that Fredric Feer and William Whelan identified in the mid1980s as among then current American brigade commanders, which always includes a stratagemic sense. Consequently, a reevaluation of Guderian from this perspective would have value as a school research paper.

CASE 9:
Corps Commander Georgi K. Zhukov, Khalkhin-Gol, Mongolia 1939
A future Marshal of the Soviet Union acts as his own deception planner.[43]

Since July 1938 the USSR had fought off Japanese incursions in a series of minor and inconclusive engagements along the Siberian frontier with Communist Outer Mongolia and Japanese-occupied Manchuria. Then, in the summer of 1939, Stalin decided to end this festering situation by a quick surprise attack. For this test he chose the troublesome Japanese position centered at the Manchurian town of Nomonkhan on the eastern bank of the Khalkhin-Gol river, which marked the border with Outer Mongolia. The Japanese Kwantung Army in Manchuria had assigned the Khalkhin-Gol front to its Sixth Army, which mustered 25 infantry battalions, 17 cavalry squadrons, 120 tanks, 450 planes, and 135 guns. Kwantung Army HQ had ordered this substantial force to launch its own offensive on August 24th.

In early August, the local Soviet forces were heavily reinforced and incorporated into the 1st Army Group headed by a promising but unblooded 43-year old Corps Commander named Georgi K. Zhukov. He commanded a crack force of 35 rifle battalions (4 divisions), 20 Mongolian cavalry squadrons (2 divisions), 498 tanks, 346 armored cars, 581 aircraft, and 266 guns. It is plain that Zhukov would not be permitted to fail.

The key to his strategy was to obtain a sufficiently secret build-up that the Japanese would be unable to match his strength. He did this through a combination of tight security, speedy deployment, and tactical deception. Zhukov's somewhat imaginative deception plan was designed to mask his offensive intent. Thus on D-minus-10 trucks stripped of their mufflers were paraded along the front to cover the characteristic noise of the tanks moving into their final pre-attack positions. A handbook titled *What the Soviet Soldier Must Know in Defense* was widely circulated to dissimulate his offensive intent.

---

43 See Whaley (1969/2007), Case A15, for details and sources.

On Aug 20th—preempting the Japanese by 4 days—Zhukov's offensive began. Following a short (3½ hour) artillery barrage to soften the well-fortified Japanese positions, the tank-and-aircraft supported infantry assault went in. The Japanese were surprised by Zhukov's intent and strength. The Soviet-Mongolian forces slogged ahead slowly but surely and without regard to casualties. On D+7 the Japanese conceded their local defeat and began a general break-out from their virtually encircled position. Although the Kwantung Army prepared an autumn counter-offensive, the Japanese Government had been sufficiently impressed by the unexpected show of Soviet strength, proficiency, and resolve to end the border war on September 16th with an armistice-in-place. Zhukov had achieved a decisive victory at a cost (8,000 KIA, 15,000 WIA) generally thought to be less than the Japanese casualties (officially only 8,500 KIA and 8,800 WIA). And he had won Stalin's confidence.

Throughout WW2 Marshal Zhukov served as Chief-of-Staff of the Soviet armed forces. Although he seldom again engaged directly in deception planning, he encouraged it in his staff. Indeed it is doubtful whether the General Staff could have adopted and developed systematic deception as rapidly as it did under any other senior Soviet officer.

CASE 10:
Gen. Wavell creates the world's first deception team, Cairo 1940
The origin of "A" Force.

> I have always had a liking for unorthodox soldiers and a leaning toward the unorthodox in war.
> — Wavell, *The Good Soldier* (1948), 56

> Perhaps the most elementary principle of all deception is to attract the enemy's attention to what you wish him to see and distract his attention from what you do not wish him to see. It is by these methods that the skillful conjurer obtains his results.
> — Wavell, "Ruses and Stratagems of War" (1942)

Although the British had become the acknowledged masters of deception during the Great War, they had virtually lost this technique by the beginning of WW2.[44] The sole repository of such wisdom in a position of command was General Sir Archibald "Archie" Wavell, then the G.O.C.-in-C. Middle East. How had he obtained this rare knowledge?

Wavell was born in 1883, the son of an English Army officer in an Army family. Educated at Winchester College and the Royal Military College at Sandhurst, he was that rare hybrid (even for an Englishman), a scholar-soldier. He had a keen memory. He was a poet, fluent in writing but nearly inarticulate in conversation, highly introspective, private and secretive to the point of off-putting. He was intuitive and somewhat empathic. He was supportive of his subordinates and dangerously outspoken with his superiors. He had a dry sense of irony and the ridiculous.

At age 18, Second Lieutenant Wavell got his first opportunity to observe military deception when he joined Gen. Lord Roberts and his intelligence-cum-deception chief, Col. Henderson (Case 2) in the last, successful stages of the Boer War. Wavell was sufficiently impressed to later write most favorably about Henderson's role.

At the outbreak of the Great War in 1914 Wavell was put in charge of M.O.5, the key staff section of the Military Operations Directorate charged with security, the secret service, ciphers, and general military intelligence. (At that time, the British Army still combined Intelligence and Operations.) One of his many odd jobs was the "last-minute improvisation" of a field intelligence service, the Intelligence Corps. From September to November he was in France at British Expeditionary Force GHQ, personally setting up the Intelligence Corps, whose 30 or 40 officers were distributed singly or in pairs among the corps and divisions of the BEF.[45]

After Wavell was reassigned to other staff duties, this brand new Intelligence Corps soon came to virtually monopolize the few keen British advocates of deception on the Western Front. However, for two very long years its superiors rejected deception as fit only for "comic opera", as one put it during the mindless butchery at the Somme in 1916.[46]

Wavell's journeyman lessons in military deception were the result of firsthand observation of the plans and operations of others in the Great War. His mentors were Allenby, Alleby's staff, and Lieut. Col. T. E. Lawrence. Wavell closely watched Allenby's unorthodox victories-through-deception in the Palestine campaigns with admiring approval as he did those more distant guerrilla

---

44 Whaley (1969), 29.
45 John Connell, *Wavell* (London: Collins, 1964), 92-94.
46 Captain Ferdinand Tuohy, *The Secret Corps* (London: Murray, 1920), 213-215.

operations of T.E. Lawrence. Their innovative approach astonished Wavell after the "dull, unimaginative, heavy-footed business" he had seen on the Western Front. Brevet Lieut.-Col. Wavell had monitored the Third Battle of Gaza (Case 33) as Liaison Officer between Allenby and the Chief of the Imperial General Staff in London. And next year, as a brigadier-general, he served on the staff of General Chetwode's XX Corps during Allenby's brilliantly deceptive Megiddo campaign (Case 35).

Having learned deception planning from direct observation and subsequent study of Allenby's two great break-through battles,[47] Wavell experimented with it in his own highly unorthodox inter-war British Army training maneuvers, maneuvers that he personally planned, designed, and directed. Convinced of the value of surprise, which he believed is caused by either mobility or deception or both, Wavell sought to indoctrinate other British officers. In 1931 he published his first of several distinguished books on military studies, *The Palestine Campaign*, which was an immediate success and was made a textbook at Sandhurst and other military schools.[48]

It is relevant that his chief military models were all masters of deception—Belisarius, Marlborough, and Stonewall Jackson. It is doubly relevant that the source he quoted again and again was Colonel G.F.R. Henderson's biography of Jackson, that most deceptive of Confederate generals. His other much admired soldier was Lawrence of Arabia. Early on he concluded that battles were won by unorthodox and deceptive commanders—a view he kept throughout his long career.

Wavell served in Palestine as Commander-in-Chief for six months in 1937-38. This was a time of frequent Arab raids on the Jewish settlements. Here he met and proselytized young Dudley Clarke, a member of his staff, and authorized establishment of the all-Jewish Special Night Squads. Those innovative and aggressive night-fighting ambush units were trained and led by Captain Orde Wingate (Case 14) and included a young Moshe Dayan.[49]

In 1939 at age 57 Lieut.-Gen. Wavell was knighted and appointed Commander-in-Chief, Middle East. After the fall of France and Mussolini's entry in the war in 1940, he put deception theory to effective practice in his rear-guard defense against the over-cautious, semi-competent, but far stronger Italian Army in the Western Desert.[50] Finally, in 1940, December 9th-11th, he proved deception's value by gaining the first British victory of the war at the Battle of Sidi Barrani (Operation COMPASS). Outnumbered 2½-to-1 in combat troops, 3-to-1 in

---

47 Published during WW2 as Wavell, *Allenby* (2 vols. London: Harrap, 1940, 1944).
48 Collins (1948). 85-86, 95, 142, 158, 200, 275; Wingate (1959), 189-204; Connell (1964), 146-184.
49 Moshe Dayan, *Story of My Life* (New York: Morrow, 19760, 45-47.
50 Collins (1948), 268-270.

aircraft, 1½-to-1 in tanks, and a thumping 19-to-1 in artillery, his small Western Desert Force achieved complete strategic and tactical surprise of intent, time, and place. This threw the Italians into full retreat while nabbing 38,300 prisoners, 73 tanks, and 237 guns at a cost of only 624 British casualties.

Several ruses had been used.[51] The original attack plan had envisioned a conventional direct frontal attack on the enemy's center, but Training Exercise No.1 held on D-minus-13 led to a better plan and to Training Exercise No.2. Both rehearsals were portrayed to the troops and to the U.S. Military Attaché as local "training". Meanwhile Wavell's rumor agents in Cairo and Alexandria were busy spreading two stories.[52] First, whispering that the first exercise was merely defensive insurance against a renewed Italian advance. Second, as the official history reported, "Back in the Delta it was not difficult to put about stories that routine reliefs were taking place in the desert and that the British forces were being weakened, and would be weakened still further, to provide reinforcements for Greece".[53] On D -minus-2 Wavell took his family to the horse races in the afternoon and gave a large dinner party that evening in a calculated display of "normalcy".[54] On D-minus-1 RAF bombings covered the real and noisy approach march of the British tanks to their jump-off position,[55] while at Matruh its small garrison force under Brigadier Selby simulated the main attack along the coast, using numerous dummy tanks and a substantial naval bombardment.[56] On D-day, the real assault was preceded by a one-regiment diversion on the eastern flank of the local objective that successfully unbalanced the local Italians.[57]

The arrival in North Africa of Rommel with his Afrika Korps in February 1941 coincided with the decision by London to divert Wavell's best combat units to the unsuccessful defence of Greece. Wavell grossly underestimated Rommel's willingness to take the initiative with numerically inferior forces and Churchill unwisely pushed Wavell into a premature offensive that backfired. At that point, 21 June 1941, having lost confidence in Wavell, Churchill replaced him.[58] Rommel was pleased. At the time he admired Wavell's strategic and tactical moves in both attack and defense and attributed the latter's repeated defeats entirely to the slow and under-gunned British tanks. Later, having faced other British commanders, Rommel judged that "most have a certain

---

51 I have documented each ruse, as most histories give incomplete and, by confusing the later "A" Force ruses, erroneous accounts. See also Whaley (1969). A217-A221.
52 W.G.F. Jackson, *The Battle for North Africa 1940-43* (New York: Mason/Charter, 1975), 53.
53 I.S.O. Playfair, *The Mediterranean and the Middle East* (London: Her Majesty's Stationery Office, 1954), Vol.1, 263.
54 Lewin (1980), 53.
55 Jackson (1975), 53, 56.
56 Jackson (1975), 52, 56.
57 Jackson (1975), 53, 75.
58 An excellent summary of this controversial decision is in Lewin (1980), 98-125.

tendency to think along established lines. The only one to show a touch of genius was Wavell."⁵⁹

General Wavell was packed off as Commander-in-Chief, India. Once again he actively encouraged the practice of deception by his subordinates and—in that new theater of war—personally launched its first deception planning unit and suggested its first deception plan (see Case 15).

CASE 11:
Col. Dudley Clarke, Italian East Africa 1941
A first lesson hard-learned.

> Clarke ... applied the practice of deception with a thoroughness and subtlety never before attempted.
>
> — Col. Noël Wild in Mure (1980). 9

Dudley Clarke, as creator and head of the so-called "A" Force deception planning team in Cairo from late 1940 to its end in 1945 was Britain's most experienced WW2 strategic deception planner. He was also the most consistently successful. Who was he?

Dudley Wrangel Clarke was born in southern Africa in the Dutch republic of Transvaal in 1899 on the eve of the Boer War. Raised in England, the young boy's indoctrination with deception planning and operations came by age 12 when his godfather-uncle, a distinguished amateur magician, Sidney Wrangel Clarke, began teaching him conjuring.⁶⁰ Dudley was in army uniform at age 16 and remained a professional soldier all his life. Throughout his career he was the ideal staff officer, never holding or seeking command and, despite his efforts, never in combat—the perfect military Jeeves. His values were those of a Victorian gentleman, and although he was a handsome man with an eye for the ladies he somehow always lost them to others. Yet such seemingly unpromising material concealed one of the most innovatively deceptive minds in military history.

Clarke was, as his 1974 obituary in *The Times* summed up, "no ordinary man". He was a clear and quick thinker, blunt, respectful of authority but never in awe of it. He had a keen appreciation of the flaws and foibles of himself and of others.

---

59 Rommel (1953), 146, 520.
60 Edwin A. Dawes, *A Barrister in The Circle* (London: The Magic Circle, 1983), 85-87. This is the only published source that even mentions Dudley Clarke's indoctrination to conjuring. It is typical of military and intelligence historians to fail to understand the intimate connection between military deception or deception analysis and such other deceptive arts as magic, practical joking, or confidence games.

He was the complete realist. His friends and colleagues testify to his "puckish sense of humour" and an endearing character "containing a boundless sense of the ridiculous". These were the qualities he brought to the Staff College in 1932 as a student and found his first patron. The Commandant, Lieutenant-General John Dill, was much impressed by the 33-year old lieutenant and gave him support at crucial future moments. And these were the same qualities Captain Clarke brought in 1936 to Palestine where he served, first, as Lieut.-Gen. Dill's Brigade Major and, later, on Lieut.-Gen. Wavell's staff. Wavell became his second patron and taught Clarke his first lessons in military deception.[61]

In 1937 Dill fetched Clarke back to the War Office where he served as the Army's representative on the first-ever team of Joint (that is, inter-service) Planners.

In June 1940, after the outbreak of WW2, Clarke proved his ability to do the unusual by becoming one of the founders of the Royal Marine Commandos, whose name he contributed from his childhood memories of and later readings about the marauding Boer commandos.[62]

Finally, near the end of that year, General Wavell, overburdened by having to act as his own deception planner, had summoned his former aide to Cairo to take over that function. Colonel Clarke reached Egypt on December 18th and began creating the senior deception planning and coordinating staff in the Middle East, which then churned out a succession of largely successful deception operations to baffle the Italians and Germans. Before New Year's Eve he had founded "A" Force, as it was officially known, and headed it throughout the rest of the war.

Initially assigned a single staff officer, Clarke began hand-picking his staff. An early acquaintance, Major Michael Crichton, was plucked away from his desert assignment with the Intelligence staff of a division in 1941 and soon became Clarke's second-in-command.[63] Major Victor Jones and M. Ogilvie-Grant were brought on to set up and run N Section, which handled escape and evasion for M.I.9, initially out of Greece and later for the entire Mediterranean.[64] On September 21st Clarke commandeered Lieut.-Colonel A. C. "Tony" Simonds from SOE to take over as his deputy director in charge of the growing N Section. Simonds had previously served with Clarke under Wavell in Palestine in 1936. He then worked with Wingate and his Special Night Squads in Palestine in 1937 and again with Wingate in Ethiopia in early 1941. Thence he was seconded to set up the Greek section for SOE whence Clarke grabbed him.[65] In May

---

61 Mure (1980), 55-57.
62 Bernard Fergusson, *The Watery Maze* (New York: Holt, Rinehart and Winston, 1961), 48-49; Mure (1980), 60-62.
63 Mure (1980), 102-103.
64 Foot & Langley (1979), 89, 93.
65 Foot & Langley (1979), 89, 185; Mure (1980), 63.

1942, wanting a co-deputy for his growing "A" Force, he shanghaied Lieut.-Colonel Noël Wild. Wild had come out to Egypt as an officer of the crack 11th Hussars. He was noted for his creative imagination and fresh ideas—patterns of thinking learned from his father, a well-known artist and caricaturist.[66]

It is typical of the man that Clarke set up his most secret "A" Force headquarters at No.6 Kasr-el-Nil behind Cairo's fashionable Groppi's cafe in one of Cairo's more popular brothels, whose women continued their illicit business on the top floor while he and the lads conducted theirs on the lower one. Eventually "A" Force expanded, reluctantly taking over the entire building.[67]

Clarke ran the first British "double agents" and with even greater skill (although on smaller scale) than was the case later when this was also done out of London. He devised the idea of entire dummy military units, including whole divisions, corps, and armies. He applied to these bogus units that old and not rare adjective "notional", meaning imaginary, a term still used as jargon by many military deception specialists despite the persistent efforts of typists, editors, and computer spelling programs to have us write "national".[68] Clarke also first conceived the idea of using double agents for strategic deception, doing so since fall 1942.[69]

The planner must decide how he wants his target to react in a given situation. This is a subtle problem, learned by Clarke at the beginning of 1941. As he explained:[70]

> In the first Deception Plan I ever tackled I learned a lesson of inestimable value. The scene was Abyssinia.... Gen. Wavell wanted the Italians to think he was about to attack them from the south in order to draw off forces from those opposing him on the northern flank.
>
> The Deception went well enough—but the result was just the opposite of what Wavell wanted. The Italians drew back in the South, and sent what they could spare from there to reinforce the North, which was of course the true British objective. After that it became a creed in "A" Force to ask a General, "What do you want the enemy to do?", and never, "What do you want him to *think*?"

---

66 Mure (1980), 88-92; Delmer (1971), 24.
67 Mure (1977), 21; Mure (1980), 80.
68 Mure (1980).
69 Delmer (1971) 32-25.
70 Brigadier Dudley Clarke, "Some Personal Reflections on the Practice of Deception in the Mediterranean from 1941 to 1945" (memo dated 6 September 1972), as published in Mure (1980), 274. See also Mure (1980), 9, 81-82; and Daniel & Herbig (1980), 4.

However, as Clarke discovered, "It was surprising how difficult they often found it to produce an answer" to that question. Fortunately, the least deception-conscious of all the commanders that "A" Force served, General Montgomery, was best at answering it. Later, Clarke found that the most successful way of getting Commanders to respond was "by asking them to imagine I had a direct telephone line to Hitler himself, and that he would do anything I told him to do."[71]

By 1944, when "A" Force was at full gallop, it was still relatively small—41 officers, 76 NCOs, and three company-sized operational units These ran all strategic and tactical deception planning and operations, camouflage, and double agents in the Mediterranean Theatre through Cairo HQ and 4 mobile field HQ that moved forward with the Allied armies."[72]

As seen in Case 88, Clarke became instrumental in creating (with "A Force as the model) the first world-wide strategic and tactical deception structure, into which the Americans were soon drawn.

After VE-Day, Clarke remained in Cairo long enough to liquidate "A" Force and write its official story. The HQ building was returned to its original occupants and, as Clarke recorded in the last lines of the official history, "the pounding of the typewriters once more gave place to the squeals of illicit pleasure."[73]

CASE 12:
Lieut. Barkas, 1940-1942
A film director becomes Director of Camouflage in North Africa.

> Indeed, it is a pleasing thought that the greatest and most respected of military commanders have usually been masters of fraud and misrepresentation.
>
> — Barkas, *The Camouflage Story* (1952), 95-96

Geoffrey Barkas had been a young British infantry second-lieutenant in the Great War when he was among the lucky ones to be evacuated from Gallipoli. In the 1920s and 1930s he became a film director who traveled the world with his crew. In 1938 the Great Depression put him "between pictures", so he applied for a job as publicity director of the Shell-Mex petroleum firm. They hired him to manage a touring trade-show called "See How Your Car Works".

---

71 Clarke in Mure (1980), 274.
72 Cruickshank (1979), 19-20.
73 Quoted in Mure (1980), 260.

When WW2 began, Barkas sought useful military service and his recent boss mentioned that his brother, the well-known artist Freddie Beddington, had been appointed by the War Office to create a camouflage organization and was now recruiting. Barkas promptly applied and was interviewed by a Royal Engineers Captain who found that the applicant's only qualification was that he'd had active military service in the previous war. So Barcas was in.[74]

A vexing problem is how to build or rebuild pockets of creativity into an organization without disrupting its normal operations. One common solution is starting from scratch. That was how Barkas did it. Equipped only with his film making experience, a few months primitive learning and practicing camouflage in England, and a commission in the Royal Engineers, he was shipped off to Egypt on New Year's Day, 1941. There he would reinvent the forgotten art of camouflage for the embattled British Army in North Africa.

On arrival he was promptly assigned to the General Staff with the title of Director of Camouflage and three junior officers but no "War Establishment". Now, a War Establishment (W.E.) was to the British Army what the Table of Organization and Equipment (TO&E) was to the American, that essential authorization specifying for each military unit its equipment, personnel, and chain of command. After Barkas spelled out his requirements to the W.E. Committee at Cairo GHQ the Chairman, a lofty brigadier, said "I still don't see how we can pass this establishment as it stands. It has no resemblance to any other unit I've ever come across. What's your real justification?" Barkas' reply, delivered with as straight a face as any high stakes gambler could muster, stands as an inspiration to all mavericks:[75]

> Well sir, as you know, our whole mission [of camouflage] is persuading the army to look and behave as much unlike the army as we possibly can, and I'm sure you'll agree that it is reasonable to apply the principle to our establishment.

After a hushed conference with his committee members the amused Chairman-Brigadier decreed:

> We are going to approve your establishment. Not because we understand it. We don't. But you are the first sponsor to come into this room with an argument that none of us has ever heard before.

Having gotten formal approval to birth his camouflage baby, Barkas's problem was how to keep it alive. Next month (February), to prevent the total collapse of Hitler's Italian ally in North Africa, the Führer sent in Lieutenant-General Rommel and the small but crack Afrika Korps. Now the British forces went

---
74 Barkas (1952), 24-25.
75 Barkas (1952), 102.

from defeat to defeat and their commanders were evidently too frantically preoccupied to even think to draft the camouflage units for combat infantry duty. "Perhaps," as Barkas concluded "we were too small to be noticed."[76]

The pay-off came less than two years later at the decisive Battle of Alamein where even the British commanders acknowledged the extraordinarily cost-effective contribution of camouflage as part of the overall deception plan to the victory over Rommel's Afrika Korps by hiding the main assault units at the real point of attack and drawing Rommel's attention to the diversion created by displaying large dummy forces elsewhere. In announcing the victory at Alamein in the House of Commons on 11 November 1942 a pleased Prime Minister Churchill declared:[77]

> By a marvellous system of camouflage, complete tactical surprise was achieved in the desert. ... The enemy suspected that the attack was impending, but did not know how, when or where, and above all he had no idea of the scale upon which he was to be assaulted.

CASE 13:
Brig. Shearer, North Africa 1941
The Intelligence chief for British Middle-East Command devises a ruse.[78]

Based in Cairo, Brigadier John Shearer was Director of Military Intelligence, Middle East Theatre, from the outset of WW2, serving first under Wavell and then, after 21 June 1941, Auchinleck.

Shearer was one of those rare empathic types who could see things from the viewpoint of his enemy. The previous March 6th he had presented a fictitious "Appreciation of the Situation" as he thought the new Deutsche Afrika Korps commander might see it:[79]

> As a striking force I have full confidence in my own Command. Subject to administrative preparations, I believe that the German Armoured Corps, after a few weeks' training and experience in desert warfare conditions, and unless the British substantially reinforce their present forces in Libya, could successfully undertake the reoccupation of Cyrenaica.

Although his name was not revealed by ULTRA until three days later, this was the true voice of Rommel—or any other blitzkrieg commander. But Wavell rejected Shearer's prescient warning on the advice of his logistic staff who

---

76 Barkas (1952), 107.
77 Barkas (1952), 215-216.
78 Lewin (1978), 168-169.
79 Connell (1964), 384.

believed such an initiative was beyond the enemy's resources.[80] Consequently, Wavell was thoroughly surprised when Rommel struck 25 days later.

That July, during a German air raid a parachutist descended in an open field outside Ramieh in Palestine. A peasant saw him digging holes as if to conceal something. Traced to Jerusalem where he was arrested, he claimed to have deserted from the Luftwaffe because of his Jewish blood. He looked the part and carried a letter of introduction to a family of German Jews in Palestine introducing him as a relative. He was moved to the POW interrogation center outside Cairo where he was kept in a bugged room with other prisoners. Their respectful behavior toward him heightened his captors' suspicions.

Brigadier Shearer now took personal charge of the case. First he ordered that the man's drop zone at Ramleh be searched. This turned up a packet of Palestinian currency, a short-wave transceiver, codes, and a transmission schedule. Faced with this clear evidence of espionage, he confessed that he was the Gauleiter of Mannheim and had volunteered to investigate the possibilities for increased political subversion in Palestine.[81]

The Gauleiter was imprisoned and regular transmissions were begun in his name; and, after a few days, communication was established with the Italian radio center at Bari, Italy. To insure their double agent's credibility, Shearer in coordination with the Director of Security Intelligence Middle East (SIME), Brigadier Raymund Maunsell, had the now simulated Gauleiter transmit "chickenfeed", genuine information about troop movements and similar military activity that they knew the Abwehr was likely to get from its extensive espionage networks in Egypt. Bari soon confirmed that this information was so accurate that it was being sent direct to Rommel. The stage was set for deception.

Auchinleck was planning CRUSADER, his offensive to drive Rommel out of Egypt. It was November 1941 and Shearer, as the "Auk"'s DMI, singlehandedly and without consultation with "A" Force worked up the cover plan for that operation. He decided to deploy their new deception asset, the Gauleiter, for this purpose. Working closely with Maunsell, Shearer devised a false scenario, which the Gauleiter fed to the Abwehr over his radio. Incidentally this would be the world's first radio deception game using a double agent for *strategic* deception. Their scenario acknowledged the British 8th Army buildup in the Western Desert, but reported it was only part of the cover plan for 9th Army's imminent movement north from Palestine to the Caucasus to help the hardpressed Russians protect their threatened and vital oilfields at Baku.

---

80 Jackson (1975), 118-119; Lewin (1978), 160-161.
81 The rather shadowy story of Shearer and the Gauleiter is in Mure (1980). 72-75; and Lewin (1978), 167-168. Brigadier Shearer's memoirs remain unpublished but were used by Mure.

To lend credibility, Shearer and Maunsell arranged for Auchinleck to visit 9th Army headquarters in Palestine.

Subsequently the notional Gauleiter was transferred to "A" Force control where he continued as a major radio double agent for "Thirty Committee" until November 1943 when the invading Allied armies in Italy seized Bari, thereby closing down the Gauleiter's only radio link.[82]

Case 14:
Capt. Thynne. North Africa 1942
The "new boy" gets his first lesson from the "Master of Deception".

Captain (later Major) Oliver St-M. Thynne joined Clarke's "A" Force deception team in Cairo as a novice deceptionist in March 1942. Soon afterwards he discovered from intelligence,[83] that the German aerial observers had learned to distinguish the dummy British aircraft from the real ones because the flimsy dummies were supported by struts under their wings. When Major Thynne reported this to his boss, Colonel Clarke, the "master of deception", fired back:[84]

> "Well, what have you done about *it*?"
>
> "Done about it, Dudley? What could I do about it?"
>
> 'Tell them to put struts under the wings of all the real ones, of course!"

Of course? Hardly. A commander with a straightforward mind, having recognized a telltale flaw in the dummies, would have ordered the camouflage department to correct it. But Clarke's devious mind instantly saw a way to capitalize on the flaw. By putting dummy struts on the real planes while grounded, enemy pilots would avoid them as targets for strafing and bombing. Moreover, it might cause the German photo-interpreters to both mislocate the real RAF planes and underestimate their numbers.

---

82 Mure (1980), 71, 110, 229. For more on the so-called Gauleiter's murky story see Holt (2004), 40n & 864.

83 Although David Mure does not give the source of this intelligence, it was probably the German Air Force ULTRA or possibly ISOS, the British intercepts of German Military Intelligence (the Abwehr), which they were reading along with the better known ULTRA. On the GAF codebreaking see F. H. Hinsley, *British Intelligence in the Second World War*, Vol.1 (London: Her Majesty's Stationery Office. 1979). The ISOS codebreaking was first made public in full detail in a later volume of the same British official history, Hinsley, Vol.III (1981).

84 Mure (1980), 98.

CASE 15:
Col. Peter Fleming, Operation ERROR, Burma 1942

General Sir Archibald Wavell arrived in India on 11 July 1941 to take up his new assignment as Commander-in-Chief. The one-eyed but quite perceptive general brought with him only Lieut.-Col. Bernard Ferguson as his Military Secretary and one of his two ADCs, the equally one-eyed Second-Lieutenant Alexander "Sandy" Reid-Scott of the 11th Hussars. Wavell began working up plans for the British invasion of Iran, which took place in August. Japan's entry into WW2 in December and her rapid expansion into Southeast Asia revived Wavell's need for a deception planning team. In February, from Java, he signaled the CIGS, General Sir John Dill, "Should be glad of Peter Fleming as early as possible for appointment to my staff." At this time Wavell intended that Fleming work in Java under Sir George Sansom, the distinguished Japanologist then serving in Intelligence. Dill complied and Fleming stopped over a week in Cairo, taking the occasion to dig through the "A Force files for clues to his new assignment."[85]

Peter Fleming, 34-years old when he arrived in India, was the older, wiser, and then much better known brother of Ian Fleming. Born into a wealthy upper-class Scottish banking family and educated at Eton and Oxford, Peter soon learned to practice deceit to protect himself from an increasingly eccentric and domineering mother. He grew to become a noted explorer, famous author, prominent editorial writer for *The Times*, and handsome husband of British stage and film star Celia Johnson. Shy and a model of understatement, he concealed his brilliant, witty, and independently unorthodox mind from all but his few close friends.

When WW2 erupted Peter Fleming was too old and too unusual for platoon command in his regiment, the Grenadier Guards. Instead he was marked for unconventional service, being recruited into M.I.(R), the secret branch of the Military Intelligence Directorate planning to set up guerrilla warfare units in such exotic places as China. His flair for deception first blossomed in M.I.(R) in an proposal for floating an ingenious bit of disinformation designed to have "an auspicious effect in the United States. He proposed fabricating a lengthy memorandum ostensibly written by leaders of the Japanese Black Dragon Society outlining "Japan's dishonourable intentions towards American naval bases in the Pacific....", recommending that "Publication might be effected by planting the document on an American foreign correspondent of repute." This interesting but outlandish plan fortunately aborted.[86]

---

85 Duff Hart-Davis, *Peter Fleming* (London: Cape, 1974), 263; Connell (1969), 211.
86 Quoted in Hart-Davis (1974), 216.

Then during the German invasion of Norway in 1940, he was flown in heading a 6-man reconnaissance party and soon coopted as ADC. by General Carton de Wiart, "that legendary, admirable character [who had] only one eye, only one arm, and—rather more surprisingly—only one Victoria Cross."[87] During the Battle of Britain later that year he was assigned to organize and lead "stay-behind" resistance units in southern England to sabotage and harass the soon expected German invaders. When that prospect lessened, SOE sent him in early 1941 to Cairo to recruit a thousand-man Garibaldi Legion of guerrillas among the many Italian POWs. This scheme fizzled when the Italians declined to volunteer for another hitch of fighting, but he did recruit the attention of Wavell who admired his elegant mind and cavalier attitude. Accordingly, Wavell sent Fleming and his band of SOE buccaneers off to Greece to organize resistance and sabotage against the invading German forces.

By the time Colonel Fleming arrived in Delhi in late March 1942 Java had fallen, so Wavell made him his director of deception for the India-Burma theater. Wavell outlined a plan after dinner with his Military Secretary, Bernard Fergusson, and Fleming. He told his two guests he wanted to revive "the Meinertzhagen ploy" and retold that famous but mis-credited exploit (Case 26). When their meeting broke up at 1 a.m., Wavell and Fleming had the outline of Plan ERROR.[88]

Accordingly, Fleming prepared a set of fake documents indicating British strength in India to be growing much faster than was the case. These were placed in Wavell's own dispatch case. On April 29th Fleming left Delhi. Having as yet no staff of his own, Wavell lent him his 24-year old ADC, Capt. Reid-Scott. First they visited the Burma commander, General Sir Harold Alexander, at his forward HQ at Shwebo. Alexander approved their plan and informed them that his forces would soon withdraw behind the Irrawaddy, blowing the bridge linking Sagaing and Ava. Fleming had originally planned to leave the faked documents at Mandalay airfield; but, as the Allies were already pulling out of the city, a new site would have to be found. Alexander provided them with a brand new Ford V-8 staff car, a Jeep, and a sapper booby-trap expert. Reid-Scott's diary explains the plan:[89]

> The idea was that the Chief [Wavell] had just paid a hurried last minute visit to the Burma front and had had a car accident the car skidding going to fast around a corner and then the Japs being close upon our heels we had been obliged to evacuate the car in a hurry and leave most of his kit including his letter case containing a lot of faked information actually written by

---

87 Quoted in Hart-Davis (1974), 224.
88 Hart-Davis (1974) 264-266.
89 As quoted in Connell (1965), 211-212.

the Chief; for instance there were "Notes for Alexander" saying how there were going to be 2 armies in Burma, how large our air strength was becoming and also about a new secret weapon! Perhaps that would make the Japs windy.

From Shwebo, Fleming and his two helpers drove forward to the west bank of the Irrawaddy at Sagaing where the local commander, Maj.-Gen. D. T. Cowan, was headquartered, arriving there on the evening of May 3rd. Cowan also gave his approval, described an ideal place for the "accident" just 400 yards across the Sagaing-Ava bridge, which was due to be blown within the hour. Cowan also explained that while he did not believe the Japanese to be too close he was concerned that the local Chinese troops might find the abandoned car and loot it before the Japanese arrived. To deter this he immediately put out a radio warning to all units that the area just beyond the bridge had been booby-trapped.[90]

Fleming and Reid-Scott drove the staff car across the bridge followed by the sapper in the Jeep. They soon found Cowan's suggested location, made appropriate skid-marks, and shoved the car with its faked papers over a 30-foot embankment. Unfortunately the car simply rolled down and stopped quite undamaged some thirty yards away, its engine still running; so Fleming and Reid-Scott climbed down, shut off the engine, let the air out of one front tire, punctured the other, and threw stones to break the lights and windshield. Fleming reported that: "The car … was clearly visible from the road.… Being in good condition and the right way up, it (a) is more likely to attract the enemy than most of the wrecks he finds along the roads of Burma. (b) has the appearance of having been abandoned in a hurry."[91] Satisfied, the three men drove back around 10 p.m. in the Jeep over the bridge, which was with some delay finally blown spectacularly an hour and a half later.[92]

It was a lovely plan, executed with great attention to detail by both Wavell and Fleming. It showed that Wavell had not lost his touch at deception; and it was a useful training exercise for Fleming, particularly as he had to improvise the last-minute switch of the scene of the crime from the airfield to the bridge. Both realized too late that their ruse had two serious discrepancies that might have raised serious doubts; but, happily, Chinese Intelligence later reported that the Japanese had indeed believed they had "captured" important documents indicating Wavell's defenses in India to be stronger than supposed.[93] Although

---

90 Connell (1965), 212.
91 Quoted in Hart-Davis (1974), 267.
92 Connell (1969), 211-212, based mainly on the diary of Reid-Scot (1918-1960); Hart-Davis (1974), 266-268, based mainly on Fleming's official report.
93 Hart-Davis (1974). 269. Lewin (1980), 173, mistakenly concludes that ERROR was a complete failure. See Whaley, *When Deception Fails: The Theory of Outs* (FDDC, August 2010), Case 2.7.1 (Operation ERROR).

ERROR had "succeeded" to this degree, it is ironic that—contrary to British expectations—India was never on the Japanese agenda for conquest. Even Burma had only been a last minute addition to guard their flank in South East Asia.

Fleming continued to practice deception in that theater of war, gradually honing his talent until in 1944 he achieved a decisive success in Operation CLOAK (Case 56).

CASE 16:
Maj. Orde Wingate, Palestine 1938
The modern Gideon rediscovers the night ambush and teaches Dayan and other future Israeli generals.

Let's back up to look at another of Wavell's protégés, the extraordinary Orde Wingate. Like T. E. Lawrence and Richard Meinertzhagen before him, Wingate was a charlatan, a con man whose connivings and deceptions were directed more at his superiors, friends, and allies than against the common enemy.

Captain Wingate was posted to Palestine in 1937 and assigned to the Intelligence staff. Humorless and an Old Testament religious fanatic, he quickly mastered Hebrew and as quickly adopted the cause of Zionism. Wingate and Wavell first met, appropriately, at a family lunch in Rehovath at the home of Chaim Weizmann, the then President of the World Zionist Foundation and future founding President of Israel. When Wavell left Palestine next year:[94]

> I carried away in a corner of my mind an impression of a notable character who might be valuable as a leader of unorthodox enterprise in war, if I should ever have need of one.

Small wonder that Wavell called Wingate that "odd creature" yet would put him to good use on two occasions in the looming war.

Before handing over his Palestine Command to General Haining in early 1938, Wavell had authorized Wingate to create, train, and command the all-Jewish Special Night Squads to defend the Jewish settlements in the countryside. Wingate now proceeded to coopt Hagana members into these small intelligence-cum-police-cum-night combat patrol units to fend off Arab raids. He worked closely with Efraim Dekel who officially was the Jewish Agency liaison with Wingate but who was, in fact, the chief of the Hagana intelligence service, "Shai".[95] One of the Hagana who gained experience in the Special Night Squads and accompanied Wingate on night ambushes was an obscure

---

94 Field-Marshal Earl Wavell, *Soldiers and Soldiering* (London: Cape, 1953), 101.
95 Efraim Dekel, *Shai: The Exploits of Hagana Intelligence* (New York: Yoseloff, 1959).

young sabra farmer named Moshe Dayan.[96] Dayan would later say: "Every Israeli soldier is a disciple of Wingate. He gave us our technique."[97]

In addition to Dayan, other later prominent Israelis who trained under Wingate in the Night Squads were Yigael Allon, Teddy Kollek, Avram Yaffé, and Avram Akavia.[98]

Wingate's open pro-Zionism became a growing embarrassment to the "neutrality" favored by the British Mandate politicians in Palestine. Accordingly, in 1939, he was recalled to London and put into anti-aircraft work. But he was not forgotten by Wavell.

CASE 17:
Lt.-Col. Orde Wingate Improvises a Ruse, Ethiopia 1941

Next year, in late 1940, Wavell summoned Orde Wingate to Cairo and gave him instructions to restore the exiled Emperor Haile Selaissie to the throne of Italian-occupied Ethiopia. To do so Wingate created his personal "Gideon Force"—some 50 officers & men. It was a mixed group of officers and men, mainly British (including Tony Simonds) but with 20 Israelis (including Avram Avakia as his adjutant) who had previously served with Wingate in the Palestine Night Squads. Gideon Force was the first of the famous WW2 long-range penetration groups.[99]

On 18 Jan 1941 Lt.-Col. Wingate personally escorted Emperor Haile Selassie, following 5 years in exile, across the Sudanese border back into his Ethiopia. Wingate immediately planned several ambushes of the Italian forces. All proved unsuccessful, but Wingate always blamed his failures on the incompetence or disloyalty of others. In fact, he had simply too often trusted the word of others, particularly local chieftains, whom he had little justification in trusting in the first place.

Wingate's only successful ruse against the Italian enemy was a chance opportunity that he instantly improvised upon. This occurred on April 5th when Wingate personally reconnoitered the small Italian fort on the hilltop of Debra Marcos to confirm the rumor that it had been deserted or test his suspicion that it was a trap. Wingate, traveling in two trucks, was accompanied only by a small bodyguard and the *Christian Science Monitor*'s Italian-speaking America journalist, Edmund Stevens. They found that the fort was deserted—

---

96   Moshe Dayan, *Story of My Life* (New York: Morrow, 1976), 45-47.
97   Quoted in Robert J. Donovan, *Israel's Fight for Survival* (New York: Signet, 1967), 83.
98   Bernard Fergusson, *The Trumpet in the Hall* (London: Collins, 1970), 173.
99   Leonard Mosely, *Gideon Goes to War* (New York: Scribner's, 1955); Christopher Sykes, Orde Wingate (London: Collins, 1959).

evidently quite recently, judging from an unfinished meal and scattered papers. As Stevens would recall:[100]

> As Wingate and I entered the building, a telephone rang.
>
> "Who could that be?" asked Wingate.
>
> I replied that Gideon Force was not plugged in to any telephone exchange here. I could only be the Italian line connected with the Blue Nile crossing.
>
> "You better take the call," said Wingate, "as you speak Italian."
>
> "But what should I say?"
>
> "Tell them you are the Italian doctor [who had recently deserted to Wingate], and that the British have taken Debra Marcos and are headed for the Blue Nile crossing."
>
> I took the call and transmitted this information to the Italian switchboard operator, speaking from one of the Nile posts. He was appalled.
>
> "Who should I tell this to?" he shouted at the other end.
>
> "To your commanding officer," I replied. "And my advice to you, if you value your skin, is to pack up and get going."
>
> The deception worked. The Italians abandoned their Blue Nile defensive positions [including two forts] and made for the crossing.

Exactly a month later, May 5th, the East African Campaign ended with Haile Selassi's triumphal return to the Ethiopian capital of Addis Ababa. Next February, Wavell, now C-in-C India, requested Major Wingate's posting to Rangoon. There, at Wavell's instigation, he formed and led the Chindit guerrilla-like Long Range Penetration Groups until his death in an airplane crash the following year.[101]

---

100 Cheryl Heckler, *Accidental Journalist: The Adventures of Edmund Stevens, 1934-1945* (Columbia, MO: University of Missouri Press, 2007),158-159, quoting Steven's unpublished memoirs. See also Anthony Mockler, *Haile Selassie's War: The Italian-Ethiopian Campaign. 1935-1941* (New York: Random House, 1984), 358.

101 Connell (1965), 203, 258-264, 270.

CASE 18:
Maj. Ralph Ingersoll, OVERLORD and FORTITUDE 1943-44
A devious American journalist is ordered to found a deception planning team and learns the ruses of war.

Ralph Ingersoll played a brief but significant role as a US Army deception planner in Europe during WW2. His story is valuable mainly because it is one of the more fully documented accounts of a junior officer's introduction to and development in this arcane art.

Ingersoll was a wealthy American entrepreneur, New York society celebrity, womanizer, innovative professional journalist, and publisher of the left-wing New York tabloid, *PM*, in 1942 when he was drafted into the US Army. As a staff officer he had the opportunity to observe US planning and operations in North Africa at close hand. In July 1943 Captain Ingersoll joined the staff of Brig. Gen. Daniel Noce, the US Army G-3 (Plans and Operations) in London, and was made privy to the British plan for OVERLORD, the cross-Channel invasion of Hitler's "Fortress Europe."[102]

When he discovered that all hope for the great plan's success was contingent on gaining the element of surprise at the beachhead, Ingersoll was appalled. He immediately warned Noce in a memo that "To think its preparations could be disguised would be to assume one could camouflage an elephant by painting its tail white."[103] At this point Ingersoll knew nothing of military deception.

Neither did General Noce. A few days later Noce called in Ingersoll and explained:

> Ralph, Jakie [Lt. Gen. Jacob L Devers, CO of all US forces in England] has just gotten a silly request from down the street. The Limeys are up to something they call very hush-hush. They want a 'very special' personal representative to go out to some damn castle and be told what they are going to do. Get yourself a car and go see what it's all about.

At the castle outside London, Ingersoll learned for the first time that the British were planning a most secret and comprehensive organization to hide OVERLORD'S real objective from the Germans.[104]

Within weeks Noce was ordered to establish a "Special Plans Section" in his 6-3 branch and personally assigned Ingersoll to head it. "Special Plans" was the British cover name for deception planning, so Ingersoll discovered that he had been tasked to help paint the elephant's tail. Major Ingersoll—his majority

---
102 Hoopes (1985), 264-276.
103 Hoopes (1985), 276.
104 Hoopes (1985), 276.

given to put him on a level with his British counterparts—founded, initially with only a sergeant typist/driver, the American's special plans section. The only relevant talent the 42-year old Ingersoll brought to this highly specialized task was an ingrained "genius at deviousness" acquired through his civilian background.[105]

Noce soon recognized the section needed more clout to deal with the British and American brass; and I suspect that Ingersoll's undisguised and arrogant Anglophobia may have been an even more weighty factor in Noce's mind. In any case Noce assigned one of his regular planners, 32-year old West Pointer Lt. Col. William A. "Billy" Harris, as chief of the section. They were soon joined by 33-year old Dartmouth sociology professor Capt. H. Wentworth "Went" Eldredge as Intelligence Officer. The final member to make up this small team was Lt. Col. Clarence "Clare" Beck, an infantry battalion commander with amphibious assault experience in the North African invasion.[106]

Ingersoll often sat in for Harris on Joint Security Control (JSC), the Anglo-American inter-service cover-plan committee chaired by British Army Lt.-Col. David Strangeways who had trained in deception with Dudley Clarke's "A" Force at the Battle of Alamein. By September it met regularly. Ingersoll now had a forum to express his continued skepticism about the ability of deception to produce the factor of surprise that was deemed essential to the success of OVERLORD. In one memo to the committee he again pushed his elephant theme, likening any attempt to conceal such a huge undertaking to "putting a hooped skirt and ruffled pants on an elephant to make it look like a crinoline girl." However, Ingersoll was learning his new craft. As they bluntly put it in their post-VE Day official report, Harris, Ingersol, and Eldredge admitted that:[107]

> During the summer of 1943, the undersigned officers entered deception operations in the United Kingdom with grave misgivings as to their value. By the fall of '43, in fact, their mood was so critical that they successfully destroyed the first Cover plan proposed for Operation OVERLORD—by means of a staff study prepared for General Devers.

However, by this time, instead of wanting to junk all deception, their criticism was directed toward *improving* the deception plan. By the end of November the Britons on Strangeway's committee had begun to accept the Americans' suggestions. And on the 25th at Norfolk House, they found approval for their recommendation calling for "a diversion in the Pas de Calais area" by a simulated build-up in East Anglia of the notional First U.S. Army Group. This

---

105 Hoopes (1985), 278.
106 Hoopes(1985), 276-277; Verbatim Report (1971), 2, 14-15.
107 "Report to the Joint Security Control", 25 May 1945, as quoted in Hoopes (1985), 280.

FUSAG ruse would place "principal reliance on ... radio counter-measures, display of dummy landing craft and ... release of information by what is known as 'special means' [i.e., double agents]."[108] The fact that the crucial influence was probably Col. Dudley Clarke who was simultaneously presenting a similar plan at higher level (the LCS) does not discredit the American's input.

Ingersoll was now a convert. One British psywar expert later wrote that "with Ingersoll it was love at first sight, and he became one of the foremost American exponents of the art of deception."[109] Professor Eldredge told Ingersoll's biographer that:[110]

> Any problem, he would just think a bit and come out with something. This was damn irritating for a college professor. He was always three moves ahead of you. I'd say: 'Shut up for a moment and let me think.' But I'll say one thing; he was out to win this war for the United States. Ingersoll was the trickiest, most elusive person I've ever dealt with. I've never met anyone who was such a bright guy who was such a goddamned liar. He'd say anything to get what he wanted.

Eldredge had also earlier characterized Ingersoll to me as the most imaginative member of their small team, a lively gadfly bubbling over with ideas for deception. True, most of his ideas were wildly impractical and these were quickly rejected by his team-mates. According to Eldredge, the team worked well together. They simply overlooked Major Ingersoll's monumental ego that led him to presume he was the real chief of section and Colonel Harris a mere figurehead. They valued his enthusiasm as a goad to keep trying harder to work up schemes as devious as Ingersoll's but more practical.[111]

Ingersoll noticed that the British Army used wood to fabricate their dummy tanks, trucks, and guns. By careful carpentry and painting, they could not be distinguished from the real at even at fairly close.[112] Ingersoll later recalled:[113]

> Watching them being put together, it amused me to think of them as toys and thinking of them as toys put an idea into my head: Why couldn't they be manufactured as such—as inflatable toys? Why not make heavy rubber ones which could be blown up by compressed air?

---

108 Hoopes (1985), 277.
109 Delmer (1971), 119.
110 Hoopes (1985), 278.
111 Recollections of H. Wentworth Eldredge, as he reported to me in conversations in early 1973 when he was a Professor of Sociology at Dartmouth.
112 Cruickshank (1979), 194-195, summarizes the types and quality of British dummies used in England in fall 1943.
113 Hoopes (1985), 278.

Believing that such rubber dummies could be mass-produced, he put the idea to Gen. Noce. Two days later Ingersoll flew to Washington to convince the Pentagon. There a meeting was set up with rubber manufacturing experts, and Ingersoll claims it took him only two hours to sell the feasibility of his idea for "life-sized rubber toys of war."[114] Within two weeks after Ingersoll's return to London, Noce informed the section that their rubber dummies were already in production.[115] Sometime early next year (by late March), the first batch were delivered—to the 23rd Hq Special Troops, then setting up and training in Camp Forrest, Tennessee. These were rubber dummy M-4 tanks, each of which fit in a single bag, weighed 93 pounds, and could be inflated and moved by one man.[116] The American pressurized rubber dummy tanks (soon joined by similarly constructed trucks, guns, and small aircraft) were a considerable improvement over the British models.[117]

While honing his deception planning skills, Ingersoll was also learning to revise his civilian skepticism about the US Army. Working and sharing posh London quarters with Gen. Noce, he became converted to the view that the professional army:[118]

> ... was practical and soundly conceived to make the best of its inherent liabilities—the vanities, the ambitions and laziness, the meanness and the cruelty, that plague all mankind. Dan Noce was not the only professional soldier who was to demonstrate to me how effective our World War II army could be, but he was the first.

When in January 1944 SHAEF was created, Eisenhower took over in London from General Devers who, together with Noce, packed for the Mediterranean; and their headquarters staff was dissolved. On Devers' recommendation, Gen. Omar Bradley took the Special Plans Section under his command.[119] For the rest of the war it received as much understanding and support from him as it had from Noce and Devers. The preparations and planning for D-Day now increased their pace.

In their official after-action report, Brig. Gen. Harris, Lt. Col. Ingersoll, and Maj. Wentworth Eldredge summed up their section's D-Day work:[120]

> By the completion of the various FORTITUDE deception operations [which covered the assault landings in Europe], the

---

114 Hoopes (1985), 278. Also BW interview with Ingersoll; and *Verbatim Transcript* (1971), 80, for confirmation by Baumer and Eldredge.
115 Hoopes (1985), 279-280.
116 *Official History of the 23rd Special Troops* (1945), 3.
117 Cruickshank (1979), 195-196.
118 Hoopes (1985), 282.
119 Hoopes (1985), 286-287.
120 "Report to the Joint Security Control", 25 May 1945, as quoted in Hoopes (1985), 280-281.

undersigned were completely convinced of the effectiveness of strategic deception as an offensive weapon. The FORTITUDE operations had the dual mission of achieving surprise in the invasion [by concealing the time and target area] and of rendering a decisive number of enemy divisions ineffective following the establishment of the initial beachhead—by pinning them away from the battle area for a minimum of thirty days. These large objectives were achieved.

It is the final appreciation of the undersigned that Cover and Deception is a weapon of very great value. It is doubtful if another can be named which can do the enemy more damage with the expenditure of less personnel and material resources.

With D-Day under their belt, Harris' Special Plans Section rejoined Bradley's Twelfth Army Hq on the Normandy beachhead. Col. Beck left to take command of the 1st Infantry Regiment and Maj. Ingersoll began casting about for some other staff assignment; like many other OVERLORD-FORTITUDE strategic deception planners they presumed their services were no longer needed. They were wrong, now being switched to tactical deception and reassigned to Montgomery's headquarters, working directly under Col. Strangeways who now headed deception for Monty's British 21st Army. They began moving into France. Then, when Bradley replaced Montgomery as commander of Allied forces in France, Harris' Special Plans Section went back to Bradley's U.S. 12th Army.[121]

The 23rd Hq Special Troops were brought over to Normandy and launched its first deception operation against the Germans on July 1st. This operation was officially titled ELEPHANT,[122] obviously in good-humored honor of Ingersoll's earlier doubts about the value of deception.

Eldredge and the others found "that Ingersoll was great fun to be with" despite his trouble-making eccentricities. Among his more valued contributions were his self-appointed chores of preparing the nightly martinis and providing local French women.[123]

---

121 Hoopes (1985), 299-300.
122 *Official History 23rd* (1945), 7-8.
123 Hoopes (1985), 300.

On August 19th, Eisenhower decided to unleash Patton for his famous and controversial[124] long eastward streak. This would leave Bradley's southern flank virtually undefended, so Bradley called on his Special Plans Section to give cover. Ingersoll explained that, "We can put a whole [dummy] corps just south of it, sir. All I will need is a company of infantry with real guns—to keep infiltrators out of the areas where we'll be setting up."[125] Accordingly, part of the 23rd went to Patton's Hq where, when Patton began moving east, they remained to simulate, instead of the promised corps, a single left-behind division. This hocuspocus division was a combination of inflatable rubber dummy tanks, appropriate loudspeaker sounds, and the misleading chitchat of the 23rd's crew of radio operators. The 23rd was left to defend itself with its own rifles plus some local French Resistance fighters, the infantry company Patton had promised having failed to materialize. Patton's liaison officer later explained: "The general says to tell Ingersoll that his boy scouts would have learned more about what a real war is like if they had been shot at."[126]

We shall meet Ingersoll once more (Case 45) when he plays out his last and most inventive deception, the Two Pattons Ruse.

CASE 19:
Dr. R. V. Jones, 1930s-40s
A British physicist evolves the Theory of Practical Joking and teaches the RAF the Theory of Spoof.

Dr. R. V. Jones was a world-class practical joker. He is a pleasure to read and a was a bit unnerving to meet. I have never been certain I believed his plausible explanation of why he was wearing *two* wristwatches that showed the same local time. As a double-check? Like a man who wears both belt and suspenders? But then he'd have needed a minimum of three watches to be reasonably certain which one was off. No, he said apologetically, the second had been a gift from his daughter. Perhaps.

As Professor of Natural Philosophy at the University of Aberdeen in Scotland, Jones has been called "one of the few really brilliant experimental physicists

---

124 Understandably but unnecessarily controversial. Professional and armchair historians bitterly argued the pros and cons of Patton's grand exploit. The pros claimed that his success proved his intuition correct and the risk worth taking. The cons claimed that it was all a lucky fluke, that at any time Patton could have stumbled into a trap. Both factions were wrong; neither risk nor intuition were factors. Patton—with near perfect intelligence of the strength, locations, and future movement orders of all enemy units ahead and alongside his drive—had been taking almost no risk at all. Patton had this ULTRA intelligence and exploited it to the full. Interestingly, Montgomery had the same ULTRA and failed to use it to full effect. Although this key part of the Battle of France has been known in sufficient detail since 1974, I'm not aware that any historian or analyst has so far used this aging data to reassess the Patton-vs-Montgomery legend.

125 Hoopes (1985), 300.

126 Hoopes (1985), 301.

left."[127] During WW2 and since, he has also been a top practitioner, adviser, and theorist on military deception, which he considers neither more nor less than a deadly but intellectually stimulating extension of practical joking as well of certain elements of scientific method. Of all deception planners, he is the only one that has published a detailed record of the evolution of his thinking in this direction.

Jones' theory and practice of deception gradually evolved as a direct result of his early experimenting with practical jokes. It began in the fall of 1935 when Jones was at Oxford University, one year out of his doctorate in physics, as a 23-year old Research Fellow in the Clarendon Laboratories where he had already distinguished himself as a practical joker. At this point the Clarendon staff was joined by a young German physicist, Carl Bosch Jr, son of the Nobel Prize-winning president of the huge chemical firm of I.G. Farben. As young Bosch was also a notorious practical joker, he and Jones quickly combined forces. On the evening they met, their conversation soon turned to a discussion of what tricks one could play with a telephone. Bosch recounted an experiment he had tried two years earlier while he was a research student on the upper floors of a lab that overlooked a block of flats. As Jones recalled:[128]

> His studies revealed that one of the flats was occupied by a newspaper correspondent, and so he telephoned this victim, pretending to be his own professor. The 'professor' announced that he had just perfected a television device which could be attached to a telephone, and which would enable the user to see the speaker at the other end. The journalist was incredulous, but the 'professor' offered to give a demonstration; all the pressman had to do was to strike some attitude, and the voice on the telephone would tell him what he was doing. The telephone was, of course, in direct view of the laboratory, and so all the antics of the pressman were faithfully described. The result was an effusive article in the next day's paper and, subsequently, a bewildered conversation between the true professor and the pressman.

Jones added that, "Bosch and I then happily discussed variations on the telephone theme and ultimately I said that it ought to be possible to kid somebody to put a telephone into a bucket of water."[129] Jones proceeded to test this hypothesis. His target was a prominent Oxford PhD chemist. Jones began by repeatedly telephoning the PhD and then hanging up when the man

---

127 For a biographical sketch of "the most famous practical joker in the scientific world" see Norman Moss, "The Theoretical Joker," *The Sunday Times Magazine*, 18 February 1973.
128 The background details are in Jones (1978), 23. This quote is from Jones (1957). 195.
129 Quoted from Jones (1978), 23.

answered, thereby inducing the suspicion that his phone might be out of order. Jones next confirmed this false hypothesis by now phoning him under the guise of a Cockney telephone company engineer who persuaded him to engage in an increasingly ludicrous series of "tests" that culminated in the final "corrective measure" when the gullible PhD put his instrument in a bucket of water.[130]

In 1938 Jones left Oxford for the Air Ministry where he began to adapt his practical joking to military deception. His first memorandum on deception to the Royal Air Force included his "Theory of Spoof". This memo, dated 10 January 1942, had a profound effect on the Anglo-American aerial war against Germany. It offered the bright insight: "No imitation can be perfect without being the real thing...."[131]

Occasionally throughout the war Jones had troublesome thoughts of Carl Bosch Jr who had left Oxford in 1936 to return to Germany. He was concerned that Bosch might be his "opposite number" as a deception planner. Jones reasoned that, "If so, he would know all my weak points; and he was such an expert hoaxer that he might easily have misled us." Fortunately for Jones, the German armed forces in general made no systematic use of scientific intelligence and only tapped Bosch's talents on special problems, few of which overlapped Jones' work.[132]

Completion of his theory came only after the war as a direct consequence of his appointment in 1946 to Aberdeen University as Professor of Natural Philosophy, a chair whose most eminent earlier occupant had been Sir James Clerk Maxwell. There Jones soon learned that Maxwell had himself been a formidable practical joker. Struck by this delightful coincidence and recalling that other top physicists (Newton, R. W. Wood, George Gamow) shared his fancy for practical joking, Jones "began to wonder whether there might be some connection between the two activities."[133] Stimulated by this newfound insight, Jones combined it with his own experience as both a pre-war practical joker and a wartime scientific spoofer of the enemy to develop his Theory of Practical Joking, which he first published in 1957.[134] Here Jones argues that practical jokes and hoaxes work for the same reasons that military deception plans work. Both involve "induced incongruities" where by presenting false evidence the deceiver lets the victim "build up an incorrect but self-consistent world-picture", thus causing him to take actions that are incongruent with reality.

---

130 The full story is told in Jones (1978). 23-26. Other versions are in Moss (1973), 44; and Jones (1957), 195.
131 R. V. Jones in his "D.T." paper of 10 January 1942. See also Jones (1978), 288.
132 Jones(1978), 28-29, 502-503, 531; and Jones (1957), 196.
133 Jones (1975), 10.
134 R. V. Jones, 'The Theory of Practical Joking—Its Relevance to Physics", *Bulletin of the Institute of Physics* (Jun 1957), 193-201.

Jones illustrates his theory with two examples. First, his early telephone hoax described above. Second, by the occasion when the target was the German Navy in 1943 when Jones and his colleagues persuaded them that their then alarmingly high rate of U-boat losses was due to a fictitious airborne infrared detector. The real device (an improved radar) went unsuspected for several months while the Germans frantically developed an anti-infrared paint and hastily recoated their U-boat fleet. The paint was superb; it would have camouflaged the U-boats—if the British had been using an infrared detector.[135]

In 1957 Jones restated his theory as "no model can be perfect unless it is an exact replica of the original—and even then the perfection is spoilt by the fact that now two exist where there was one before."[136] This seemingly simple insight has enormous practical value for all detectives of deception. Let's listen while our theorist spells out this implication:[137]

> The ease of detecting counterfeits is much greater when different channels of examination are used simultaneously. This is why telephonic hoaxes are so easy—there is no accompanying visual appearance to be counterfeited. Metal strips [dropped from one aircraft] were most successful [at simulating an entire fleet] when only radar, and that of one frequency, was employed. Conversely, the most successful naval mines were those which would only detonate when several kinds of signal, magnetic, hydrodynamic and acoustic, were received simultaneously. A decoy which simulates all these signals is getting very like a ship. From these considerations, incidentally, we can draw a rather important conclusion about the detection of targets in defence and attack: that as many different physical means of detection as possible should be used in parallel. It may therefore be better in some circumstances to develop two or three independent means of detection, instead of putting the same total effort into the development of one alone.

If anything, Jones underestimates the power of his concluding point. I would suggest that it holds true in most circumstances. Multiple sensors will almost always prove more effective than a single one, even when each is less precise. The problem is one of both cost-effectiveness and theory.

We shall meet Dr. Jones on two other occasions in this paper where he applies his skills to specific cases.

---

135 Jones(1978), 321; and Jones (1957), 196.
136 Jones (1957), 199.
137 Jones (1957), 199.

CASE 20:
Sun Tzu—The Chinese Tradition of Deception, c. 350 BC - AD 2010

> [I]n Ancient China, the scope for military deception was appreciated by Sun Tzu, who wrote ..., "The crux of military operations lies in the pretence of accommodating oneself to the design of the enemy."
>
> — R. V. Jones, *Reflections on Intelligence* (1989) 110, quoting from the admirable translation by Griffith.

> Make a noise (clamor or feint) in the East, attack in the West.
>
> — *The 36 Stratagems* (c.1644), Chapter #6.[138]

The Huai Hai Campaign ran from Nov 1948-Jan 1949. It was the last of the three great campaigns that began in late 1948 in which the Chinese Communist People's Liberation Army (PLA) under Mao Tse-tung ousted the Nationalist forces under Chiang K'ai-shek from the mainland half of China north of the Yellow River. It was also the largest of the three campaigns, pitting 600,000 PLA regulars (plus 600,000 irregulars and over 5 million civilian laborers) against 920,000 Nationalist regulars. And it was decisive in that it destroyed the last of the National trained regulars together with nearly all of its modern equipment. And left the rest of the mainland open to a series of relatively easy mop-up operations that continued until December 10th when President Chiang fled to Taiwan.

Huai Hai proved the capstone model of the ChiCom's ability to apply the theories of Sun Tzu (Sunzi)—adapting them first to guerrilla war and then transitioning to conventional warfare.[139] To sum up in the words of historian Gary Bjorge (p.269):

---

138 Incidentally, this famous maxim is usually misattributed by Westerners to Sun Tzu, who never wrote it, or sometimes to Mao who only approvingly quoted it. The earliest of many citations I find dates from the 12th or 13th centuries when it appeared in Chang Yü's commentary on Sun Tzu, Chapter 3 ("Offensive Strategy"), Verse 13.

139 Gary J. Bjorge, *Moving the Enemy: Operational Art in the Chinese PLA's Huai Hai Campaign* (Fort Leavenworth, Kansas: Combat Studies Institute Press, 2003). Based on Dr. Bjorge's unprecedented access to the archives and former participants in both Communist and Nationalist China.

The Huai Hai Campaign can be viewed as the product of [Sunzi's] The Art of War meeting 'operational art.' It was operational art with Sunzian qualities or, some might say, operational art with Chinese characteristics. This raises an interesting issue because, given the completely Chinese origin of *The Art of War*, some might argue that the Sunzian operational art that Su Yu and Liu Bocheng displayed represents a Chinese way of war. Perhaps it does. But the more important point to be raised is the high standard for executing operational art that Su Yu, Liu Bocheng, and their fellow commanders set. ...

Sunzi [Sun Tzu]'s view that in war the only constant is change ... refers to the difficulty of staying in step with the enemy. ... Su Yu, Liu Bocheng, and their fellow commanders not only did an excellent job of staying in step with the enemy, but they also were usually a step or two ahead of the enemy. They accomplished this by practicing operational art at the highest level. They accomplished this by being extremely competent professionally. This is another lesson to be learned from the Huai Hai Campaign, especially as the U.S. Army pursues engagement with the PLA.

CASE 21:
Mao's Theory of Asymmetry, 1965

> You fight your way and I'll fight my way. Whatever the military logic, it can be reduced simply to these two sentences. What is "You fight your way"? He seeks me out to fight but I can't be found, thus aborting the fight. What is "I'll fight my way"? We concentrate a few army divisions and brigades, and eat him up.
>
> — Mao, interview with a Palestine Liberation Organization Delegation, March 1965

Mao Tse-tung (Mao Zedong) was a close reader & fervent advocate of Sun Tzu (see previous Case). This was a natural consequence of the coincidence of two biographical circumstances. Initially, as a youthful academic, Mao had been a student of classical Chinese literature—a literature in which Sun Tzu's *Ping Fa* (Principles of War) prominently figured. Then, as a Chinese Communist Party (CCP) official since 1927 when the civil war forced the Party underground with guerrilla warfare as its only viable military mode, Mao quickly rose in the leadership because his asymmetric strategy applied Sun Tzu's principles to guerrilla realities to produce—after much trial and error—the most consistently successful operations against the Nationalist Government. On the other side, the Chinese Nationalist army under Generalissimo Chiang Kai-shek, by keeping rigidly to Western-style "direct" strategic & tactical doctrine, was unable to cope with Mao's flexible rules. In 1949, Chiang and the Nationalists were driven into exile on Taiwan.

CASE 22:
The Warrenpoint Double-Ambush, Northern Ireland 1979

The Irish Republican Army (IRA) had been running rather unsophisticated deceptions against the British until 1979. Their successes had been much more a matter of effective use of the dissimulative half of the deception equation (tight security and other forms of hiding) rather than the simulative half. The Warrenpoint ambush would raise the level of sophisticated deception a notch—and with it a lesson learned for all subsequent ambushes by other terrorist organizations.

The Warrenpoint ambush was a guerrilla assault on British Army forces by the Provisional Irish Republican Army (IRA) on 27 August 1979. It resulted in the British Army's greatest loss of life (18 killed) in a single incident during Northern Ireland's entire era of "The Troubles" (1968-1998). This operation was typical of double-ambushes that used IEDs in that it had two distinct phases:

Phase One—wherein the ambusher selects a section of roadway known to be a frequently traveled enemy supply route and sets a roadside bomb:

On 27 Aug 1997 in the late afternoon at 1640 hours a single 500-pound fertilizer bomb hidden under bales of straw in a lorry parked at the side of main road leading through the small town of Warrenpoint was detonated by remote control as an army convoy of a Land Rover and two four-ton trucks drove past. The explosion caught the rear truck in the convoy killing six members of 2nd Battalion, the Parachute Regiment.

After the first explosion the British soldiers, believing they were also under fire from IRA snipers, began firing across the close-by maritime border with the Republic of Ireland. This response managed only to kill an uninvolved civilian, an Englishman, and injure his cousin. There were conflicting reports of whether the soldiers had actually come under sniper fire or had mistaken the poppings of ammunition cooking off inside the burning Land Rover.

On hearing this explosion a nearby Royal Marine unit alerted the British Army of an explosion on the road and reinforcements from the Parachute Regiment were dispatched to the scene by road. A rapid reaction unit consisting of medical staff and a senior commander Lieutenant-Colonel David Blair, the commanding officer of the Queen's Own Highlanders, together with his signaler, Lance Corporal Victor MacLeod, were sent by Wessex helicopter. Col. Blair assumed command once at the site.

Phase Two—wherein the ambusher has prepared a second event for the real target, the emergency response team:

Exactly 32 minutes after the first explosion, a second bomb—a monster homemade 800-pound fertilizer device, exploded. It had been concealed in milk pails standing against the outer wall of the gate house at the opposite side of the road. IRA scouts had studied how British forces acted after similar roadside bombings and correctly assumed the soldiers would set up their Incident Command Point (ICP) in the nearest structure.

This second explosion completely destroyed the building and killed twelve soldiers—10 from the Parachute Regiment died along with the two Queen's Own Highlanders. Parachute Regiment Major Jackson who'd arrived at the scene soon after the second explosion described seeing pieces of human remains over the area and the face of his friend, Major Fursman, still recognizable after it has been torn by the explosion from his head. Only one of Colonel Blair's epaulettes remained to identify him.

Consequences:

The attack caused major friction between the British Army and the Northern Irish counties paramilitary police, the Royal Ulster Constabulary (RUC). Lieutenant-General Sir Timothy Creasey, General Officer Commanding Northern Ireland, suggested to British Prime Minister Thatcher that internment be restored and liaison with the Republic of Ireland police be left with the military. Instead, RUC Chief Constable Sir Kenneth Newman, insisted that the conventional (since 1975) British Army practice of supplying their garrisons in South Armagh by helicopter gave the IRA too much freedom of movement.

The death of these 18 British soldiers became a significant factor in moving the British government toward accepting greater independence from the Crown for Northern Ireland. This was a notable case where a single act of terrorism had a direct & swift strategic consequence for the IRA, rather than either the usual long-term wearing down tactic of a continuous series of acts, much less the merely annoying "bee-sting" isolated "incident".

CHAPTER 5:
Planners in Specific Operations

> There are men in the world who can make people believe they see things which they do not see.
>
> — H. Rider Haggard, *Allan's Wife* (1889), Chapter 5

This, the longest chapter in Part Two ("The Case Studies"), arrays 42 cases of planners trying to devise deceptions for specific situations.

Case 23:
Gideon's Trumpet, Israel c.1249 BC

> "Do you remember the story of Gideon? How he reduced his army from thirty-two thousand to a mere three hundred men? And how he won by tactics skillfully executed where mere numbers of second-class troops would not have prevailed. It is a wonderful story, and there are germs of big ideas in it. Except that I had to substitute science for divine inspiration."
>
> — Bernard Newman, *The Cavalry Went Through* (1930), 30

Gideon, a respected judge of the Israelites, became their war hero as well when he repelled an invading Arab army. His story, which is known from the *Old Testament* (Judges 68), is worth retelling for two reasons. First, Gideon is the "father" of the night attack, the dummy or "notional" army, and of "sonic deception". Second, his example influenced later deceptive generals, notably A.P. Wavell, Orde Wingate, and some of the creators of the modern Israeli Army.

Gideon mustered only 300 warriors—but they were an elite force, hand-picked from a much larger pool of soldiers. His target was a far bigger force of Midianite invaders. His band was too small to intimidate the Arabs into flight, much less defeat them by any conventional means.

To conceal his army's small number, Gideon ordered a night attack on the enemy camp. To pretend that he'd been heavily reinforced, he ordered his approach march be heralded by blowing as many extra battle trumpets as could be found, each simulating a new unit. To add to this illusion of numbers, he had his few soldiers carry lighted lanterns and bang away on pitchers to simulate the noise of a large force in motion. Thinking they were being attacked by an overwhelming host, the Midianites fled in alarm. Not only had Gideon created an effective dummy army, he had taken advantage of the dark to create this illusion mainly by deceiving the enemy's sense of sound.[140]

CASE 24:
Maj.-Gen. James Wolfe, Quebec, Canada 1759
The commander heeds timely intelligence, devises a battle-winning stratagem, loses his life, and gains immortal fame.

> "Such a choice of difficulties."
> — Wolfe, despatch to Pitt, 2 Sep 1759

Quebec fronts on an open plain and is backed by a formidable bluff high above the St. Lawrence River. In 1759 the besieged French commander, the Marquis de Montcalm, deployed his army to face the open plain, feeling protected by nature to his rear.

The attacking British commander, Major-General James Wolfe, learned from scouts and his own reconnaissance on September 9th that a narrow and somewhat difficult but not strictly impossible goat trail led up the bluff. This indirect approach offered the best chance for a surprise attack. Wolfe decided to take it.

Wolfe and his main force scaled the Heights of Abraham during the night of the 12th-13th. His advance party, disguised as hunters and speaking French, surprised and captured the small enemy guard post at the top. At daybreak, Montcalm discovered the British Army arrayed against him at his rear. Wolfe fought and won the Battle of Quebec on ground of his choice, dying there himself in his hour of victory.[141]

---

140 A modern military analysis of this battle is A. P. Wavell, "Night Attacks: Ancient and Modern", *The Army Quarterly*, Vol.20, No.2 (Jul 1930), 325-329.

141 Stephen Brumwell, *Paths of Glory: The Life and Death of General James Wolfe* (Montreal: McGill-Queen's University Press, 2006), 249-290; Christopher Hibbert, *Wolfe at Quebec* (New York: 1959), 114-133; C. P. Stacey, *Quebec 1759: The Seige and the Battle* (New York: 1959); and B. H. Liddell Hart, *Great Captains Unveiled* (Edinburgh: Blackwood, 1927), 206-274. A well-sourced summary account is, *Wikipedia*, "Battle of the Plains of Abraham" (accessed 11 Aug 2010).

This was Wolfe's first and last military operation involving deception—as deliberately choosing the "impossible" always is. It soon became a classic case study that, as they acknowledged, inspired at least two later commanders: MacArthur (Case 71) and Wavell.

CASE 25:
Lt. Gen. Washington, Yorktown 1781
A commander proves his mastery of the strategic lie.

The Second Continental Congress chose wisely when in 1775 it promoted a 43-year old rebel colonel of militia to lieutenant general and appointed him Commander in Chief of the all-volunteer Continental Army. George Washington was the most experienced military officer in the American Colonies, having commanded and fought with distinction in the French and Indian War.

During the first years of the new war against the British monarchy, Washington demonstrated competence in all the elements necessary for successful command. He dominated the often delicate politics both within the Army and between the Army and the Congress.[142] He mastered the special morale and discipline problems of an all-volunteer army recruited from 13 separate colonies. He ruthlessly weeded out incompetent officers. He developed and treasured a intelligence service far better locally than did the British. He understood the value of reconnaissance. He planned both lures to draw the enemy onto killing grounds of his choice and feints to keep dangerous enemy forces pinned down. He sensed when the time was ripe for either attack or retreat. And was superb at organizing and directing either. He understood the cost-effectiveness of surprise and never attacked unless he believed he had that advantage.[143]

Washington specifically understood how to leak bogus intelligence. For example, his attack plan (later aborted) for New York in 1780 used two ploys to assure a weak defense. First, Nathanael Greene spread rumors of an impending raid along the distant coast of Canada. Second, Lafayette drafted a proclamation requesting Canadian cooperation with a (notional) French fleet and an American force (equally notional) that were converging on Canada. Of Lafayette's document, Washington said simply, "It will get out." He was right. The proclamation was sent for printing to Benedict Arnold who promptly sent a copy to the British Commander.[144]

---

142 Joseph J. Ellis, *His Excellency: George Washington* (New York: Knopf, 2004).
143 Dave Richard Palmer, *The Way of the Fox: American Strategy in the War for America, 1775-1783* (Westport, Conn.: Greenwood Press, 1975), 101, 109, 134, 137, 142.
144 Palmer (1975), 164.

The British Commander, General Sir Henry Clinton, now made a fateful decision based on two assumptions. First, he felt secure in his army's numbers, equipment, supplies, and discipline plus the fact that the Royal Navy had virtual command of the Atlantic shoreline. Second, he judged his 25,000 troops more than a match for Washington's 19,500. Consequently, Clinton began to split his force around New York to open a new campaign to outflank Washington by retaking the southern states. Washington was particularly enraged that Clinton had appointed the recently defected Benedict Arnold to the rank of brigadier and had chosen him to spearhead the new British offensive in Virginia in December 1780.

In response, Washington also began to divide his forces, initially sending Lafayette with 1,200 troops to try to prevent the British from ravishing Virginia. But this was not just a reactive response as Clinton had hoped, because Washington sensed an opportunity to trap and defeat the British invaders, *if he could get the French navy to set up a blockade.* But the local French naval commander did not cooperate. With an apparently secure base in Virginia, Clinton now pumped in reinforcements to the point that General Lord Cornwallis soon commanded a force of 10,000.

By dividing his force between north and south, Clinton gave Washington two almost equally attractive targets to aim at. At this point, two factors favored the insurgent general. First, the two enemy armies were far enough apart that they could not support each other. Second, yet they were close enough that, by operating on his internal lines of communication, Washington could shift his main force against either British force faster than they could reinforce the more threatened half.

Washington also had a secret advantage. He knew he would soon meet with the French admiral of a powerful new fleet, which was on its way from France. If he could persuade Admiral Count de Grasse to patiently blockade Chesapeake Bay rather than go off swashbuckling after the British fleets as the previous French admiral had done, then Washington could set an even bigger and more decisive trap than the one that had earlier failed.

Washington's various deceptions convinced Clinton that New York was the rebel's prime target. Accordingly Clinton concentrated his defenses there. Meanwhile Washington began his secret buildup for a decisive assault well to the south at the Virginia coastal city of Yorktown where Lord Cornwallis lounged in a false sense of safety in numbers.[145]

Then when Washington's stronger army pressed the British defense into an ever shrinking perimeter, Cornwallis surrendered on October 19th. At Yorktown England had lost nearly 10,000 British and Hessian troops—40% of their

---

145 Palmer (1975), 170-178.

entire army in the Colonies. Washington had won a decisive battle at a cost of around only 300 American and French casualties.

Washington was a truly Great Captain, but not one that later generations would either learn from or emulate. The reasons are simple. He left no clear outline of his strategic planning, and most historians of the American War of Independence grossly underrated his overall competence. They tend to see him as either merely lucky or as a master of Fabian strategy and tactics, ever-retreating to preserve his army until the British simply got tired of the chase and gave up. The research by Dave Palmer showed otherwise—that Washington was indeed "First in war." And another more recent study shows that, by applying the same skills and cunning to national politics, Washington also proved himself "First in peace."[146]

I would nominate the campaign that culminated in the decisive Battle of Yorktown as one of the better examples of what John Arbeeny, Fredric Feer, and William Whelan call "Operations-based Deception (OBD)".

CASE 26:
Maj. Gen. Sherman, The March to Atlanta 1864
The Commander plans a campaign of deception by randomizing his left-right options.

In 1864 Yankee General William Tecumseh Sherman made his decisive 180-mile drive to Atlanta. Throughout this advance, Sherman's logistic tail was tied to a single railway line. He had to advance and attack along that line, a fact that the Confederates knew and that he knew they knew. Yet in every engagement but one—a costly frontal attack at Kenesaw Mountain—he surprised the awaiting defenders as to the place of his attack, defeating them each time. Moreover, although he was the attacker, Sherman inflicted larger casualties on the enemy than his own forces sustained. How was this possible?

At each battle, Sherman had only one option, but he exploited it to the full—the old right/left option. Although his line of advance was narrowly constrained, he retained at the spearhead the alternative of attacking either to the right of the railway line or to the left. He literally, as he wrote to General Grant at the time, placed his enemy on the "horns of a dilemma".[147] Right flank or left, he always succeeded in using tactical deception to conceal which side it would be.[148] And having done so he then, to conclude Liddell Hart's imagery, impaled Johnny Reb on the chosen horn. Interestingly, while Liddell Hart modestly

---

146 Joseph J. Ellis, *His Excellency: George Washington* (New York: Knopf, 2004).
147 Sherman to Grant, letter dated 20 September 1864, in William T. Sherman, *Memoirs* (Bloomington: Indiana University Press, 1957), 115.
148 Liddell Hart (1954), 149-153; and Whaley (1969), 129, 136-137.

credits Sherman with this consequent forced-choice,¹⁴⁹ the explicit statement of the concept is original with Liddell Hart. Sherman only very ambiguously implies it. Either he had not fully understood his own great insight or, more likely, simply neglected to state it.

This is a spectacular example of serial induction of misperception of place.¹⁵⁰ Serial deception involves what Liddell Hart, borrowing a phrase from Rugby football, called "'selling the dummy' first one way and then the other".¹⁵¹

CASE 27:
Maj. Gen. Sherman, The March to the Sea 1864
The Commander plays his options of goals.

Having taken Atlanta, Sherman began his 300-mile follow-up drive to the Atlantic that cut the Confederacy in twain. To do so he had a new insight of deception. Liddell Hart expands on and analyses this as follows:¹⁵²

> In this march Sherman developed a new strategic practice. In the Atlanta campaign he had been handicapped, as he realized, by having a single geographical objective, thus simplifying the opponent's task in trying to parry his thrusts. This limitation Sherman now ingeniously planned to avoid by placing the opponent repeatedly 'on the horns of a dilemma'—the phrase he used to express his aim. He took a line of advance which kept the Confederates in doubt, first, whether Macon or Augusta, and then whether Augusta or Savannah was his objective. And while Sherman had his preference, he was ready to take the alternative objective if conditions favoured the change. The need did not arise, thanks to the uncertainty caused by his deceptive direction. ... Once more Sherman took a deceptive line between alternative objectives, so that his opponents could not decide whether to cover Augusta or Charleston, and their forces became divided. Then, after he had ignored both points and swept between them to gain Columbia—the capital of South Carolina and the centre of Lee's best source of supply—the Confederates were kept in uncertainty as to whether Sherman was aiming for Charlotte or Fayetteville. And when in turn he advanced from Fayetteville they could not tell whether Raleigh or Goldsborough was his next, and final.

---

149 B. H. Liddell Hart, *Sherman* (New York: Dodd, Mead, 1929), 315-316.
150 Another example of serial deception is Alexander's Italian Campaign of 1943-45.
151 A general discussion with other examples and references is in Whaley (1969), 136-139.
152 Liddell Hart (1954), 151- 152.

objective. He himself had not been certain whether it would be Gainsborough or Wilmington!

Here Liddell Hart gives the first and clearest statement of "Operations-based Deception." Indeed, Fredric Feer cites this specific case as one of the few clear examples of OBD so far identified.[153]

CASE 28:
Col. Frederick Funston, The Philippines 1901
The future US Army Chief-of-Staff disguises his small column and effectively ends the Philippine Insurrection.

The Philippine Insurrection at the turn of the century was a protracted guerrilla rebellion led by Dictator Emilio Aguinaldo. By 1901, after two years of bitter fighting, it had cost the lives of 4,000 American soldiers with, as we would say today, no light showing at the end of the proverbial tunnel.[154]

Then, on February 8th, American infantry brigade commander Colonel Frederick "Scrapping Fred" Funston received intercepted dispatches from Aguinaldo ordering reassignment of several guerrilla units to his secret headquarters located in one of the least accessible parts of Luzon. Funston recognized an opportunity to end the war by a decapitation operation.

For this operation the diminutive (5'0") colonel picked four other American officers and 85 loyal Filipino troops. He had his Filipinos disguise themselves as guerrillas while he and his officers dressed themselves as American privates and acted the role of prisoners. Funston started out on March 6th for the remote guerrilla camp. Using captured rebel stationery and forging the signature of one of Aguinaldo's most trusted commanders, Funston kept the guerrilla leader informed of the approaching "reinforcements". The impersonators reached the headquarters village on March 24th. At no loss to Funston's small force and only two killed and three wounded on the rebel side, Aguinaldo was arrested. Thus did the war end by a deceptive *coup de main*. Aguinaldo gave Funston due credit, stating, "It was a bold plan, executed with skill and cleverness, in the face of difficulties which to most men would have seemed insurmountable."

Funston returned to the States to receive his nation's highest award, the Medal of Honor. But this was awarded for an earlier act of bravery under fire and not for the cunning deployment of his mock army. Funston had almost singlehandedly won America's only current war, but the moralistic journalists of the time pilloried him for having won it by deceit. Turn-ofthe-century

---

153 Fredric Feer, unpublished draft, 1988.
154 I've based this case study mainly on Frederick Funston, *Memories of Two Wars: Cuban and Philippine Experiences* (New York: Scribner's, 1911), 384-426; and Editors of the Army Times, *The Tangled Web: True Stories of Deception in Modern Warfare*. Washington, DC: Robert B. Luce, 1963), 23-30.

Americans, it seems, accepted the motto "It's not whether you win or lose, but how you play the game." They preferred their heroes to lose by conventional means than win by cunning.

CASE 29:
Winston Churchill creates a dummy fleet, 1914[155]

> "In wartime, Truth is so precious that she should always be attended by a bodyguard of lies."
> — Churchill to Stalin, at the Tehran Conference, 30 November 1943

Three years before the Great War, First Lord of the Admiralty Winston S. Churchill had contemplated his first exercise in martial deception. His idea was a dummy fleet for the Royal Navy to deter the German High Seas Fleet and lure its submarines into traps. When the Great War began in 1914, he launched this interesting scheme. On October 31st, he ordered that:[156]

> It is necessary to construct without delay a dummy fleet. Ten merchant vessels ... should be selected at once. They should be distributed among private yards not specially burdened with warship building at the present time. They are then to be mocked up to represent fast battleships of the First and Second Battle Squadrons. The actual size need not correspond exactly, as it is notoriously difficult to judge the size of vessels at sea, and frequently even destroyers are mistaken for cruisers.
>
> We are bearing in mind particularly aerial and periscope observation where deception is much more easy.... Very little metal would be required, and practically the whole work should be executed in wood or canvas.

He explained: "Even when the enemy knows that we have such a fleet its presence will tend to mystify and confuse his plans, and baffle and distract the enterprise of his submarines. He will always be in doubt as to which is the real and which is the dummy fleet." It would not matter if the Germans did discover that the phantom fleet existed because they still would not be sure which fleet was real and which was false, or at least not in all cases. And

---

155 Churchill (1923, U.S. ed), 308, 550; Churchill (1924), 576-577; Editors of the Army Times, *The Tangled Web: True Stories of Deception in Modern Warfare*. Washington, DC: Robert B. Luce, 1963. (1963). 55-60; Alan Moorehead, *Gallipoli* (New York: Harper, 1956), 122; Admiral Viscount Jellicoe, *The Grand Fleet* (New York: Doran, 1919), 171-172 and photo.
156 Churchill (1924), 576-577.

they would never be sure whether or not the British were continuing to launch phantom battleships and in what numbers.

By his orders ten old passenger and cargo ships were quickly selected and refitting was begun that same month. Although size was not crucial, silhouette was—in order to resemble each specific battleship it was to simulate. Accordingly, they were fitted out with broader decks, and were given greater length, warshiplike bows and sterns, fake fire-control towers, wooden turrets with wooden "Quaker" guns, and the appropriate number of smokestacks, each belching real smoke from small concealed smoke pots. Because merchantmen without cargo ride higher in the water than warships, each was ballasted down with 9,000 tons of stone.

That winter the Royal Navy was supplemented with nine dummy battleships mimicking *King George V, Centurion, Orion, Marlborough, Ajax, Vanguard, St. Vincent, Collingwood,* and *Iron Duke*. Although her namesake had already sunk, Churchill's tenth dummy warship was named Audacious to prevent German naval intelligence from realizing that the real Audacious had been sunk. Thus nine ships mimicked the real and one, the unreal. After these ten were "commissioned", four more liners and freighters were sent to the shipyards for similar conversion.

Although Churchill's simulated fleet of 14 battleships and battle cruisers failed in its prime purpose as a strategic deception to lure the Kaiser's High Seas Fleet out to a fight in the North Sea, it did serve the ends of tactical deception, particularly in the Mediterranean.

In WW2 Churchill attempted to revive his dummy fleet; but, due to shortage of merchant shipping, only three—mere destroyers at that—were created. And, because of their ineffective deployment, they did not prove useful.[157]

CASE 30:
Churchill, The Ostend Demonstration, Holland 1914
The First Lord of the Admiralty as his own deception planner.

On 5 August 1914 the German army opened its first great offensive on the Western Front by a swift wheel through Belgium. Pivoting on Verdun, the wheel turned the French left flank and pressed their center, forcing both back upon Paris. This maneuver increasingly exposed the rear of the German's own right wing to the Channel ports. That area, then held only the easily contained threat of the 65,000-man remnant of the Belgian army and scattered French units. However this was the site of the very problematical reinforcement from Britain. In this race against time the 5-division British Expeditionary Force

---
157 Cruickshank (1977), 12-13.

(BEF) of 90,000 men arrived in complete secrecy between August 9th and 17th.[158]

This monumental failure of the German intelligence services was not corrected until the 22nd and 23rd when astonished German troops finally identified the BEF by contact in battle. The stage was now set for the first stratagem of the war.

At this crucial juncture, on August 24th, First Lord of the Admiralty Churchill adopted the suggestion of Colonel Hankey, his personal friend and Secretary of the War Council, of mounting a diversion at the Belgian port of Ostend to both support the Belgians and lift some pressure off the BEF.[159] War Minister Kitchener and the Belgian Government agreed. So the next day Churchill ordered Brig.-Gen. Sir George Aston to land his 3,000-man Royal Marine Brigade at Ostend the next morning. Churchill's order to Aston explained:[160]

> The object of this movement is to create a diversion favorable to the Belgians, who are advancing from Antwerp and to threaten the western flank of the German southward advance. It should therefore be ostentatious.... The object in view would be fully attained if a considerable force of the enemy were attracted to the coast. You will be re-embarked as soon as this is accomplished.

To add ostentation, Churchill publicly announced in the House of Commons that a British force had begun landing at Ostend.[161] Due to bad weather, disembarkation was delayed a day, until the morning of the 27th.

The Royal Marine demonstration landing was itself shielded by a secondary diversion—a fine case of using a double-echeloned diversion in depth. Thus, to prevent any German naval interference with the vulnerable sealift and landing, the Royal Navy's entire Southern Force, including Admiral Beatty's three swift battle cruisers, made a daring and successful demonstration on the 28th into the Heligoland Bight itself—right in the face of the German High Seas Fleet.[162] Curiously, while Churchill gives detailed and enthusiastic accounts of both the Ostend and Heligoland actions, he does not mention the connection between them, which suggests that the idea of the Heligoland demonstration was probably not his.

On the 31st, after six days ashore and on only one day's notice, Aston's small force was quietly withdrawn. It had more than served its purpose.

---

158 Churchill (1924), 279.
159 Lord Hankey, *The Supreme Command* (London: Allen and Unwin, 1961), Vol.1, 195.
160 Churchill (1923), 335.
161 Churchill, I (1923), 336.
162 Sir Julian S. Corbett, *Naval Operations*, Vol.1 (London: Longmans, Green, 1920), 96, 99-101.

For the remainder of WW1 and as Prime Minister in WW2 after the fall of France and until final victory, Churchill was a firm advocate of surprise and an ever-impatient seeker of the initiative. And he freely lent his voice and clout in enthusiastic support of all willing practitioners of deception.

CASE 31:
Gen. Freddy Mercer, Neuve Chapelle, France 1915
The British 1st Army artillery chief recommends a tactical surprise.

The Great War quickly changed from a war of manoeuvre to trench warfare and, finally, virtual siege warfare. Assaults on prepared, fixed defenses were immensely costly and the few "victories" became measured in mere yards. The element of surprise was forgotten and deception unlearned. The British, French, and German generals misplaced their faith in ever bigger battalions and increased firepower.

To cut the slaughter of over-the-top charges by lines of infantry into the face of massed machine guns and artillery, the generals conceived the tactic of long artillery "preparation" to "soften up" the enemy's defenses. This tactic was ill-conceived, having the ironically self-defeating consequence of teaching the enemy to dig in deeper, alerting him to the place of the next attack, and giving him ample time to shift his reserves to that part of front for the inevitable counterattack.

The notion of doing something to restore the element of surprise originated with General Freddy Mercer, artillery commander of British First Army. Recognizing the problem his own artillery was creating, he came up with a creative solution: cut way back on the artillery preparation—to *only* four days. On February 10th he made this recommendation to the commander of First Army, General Sir Douglas Haig.[163]

Mercer's suggestion was most timely as Haig was currently busy planning the first Allied offensive of the new year. Haig took to the idea but added a creative touch of his own?[164]

> It would, I think, be of more effect to compress the [artillery] fire into a terrific outburst for three hours ... and follow it by a sudden rush of our infantry. This will take advantage of the element of surprise!

Note Haig's naive use of the exclamation point—like a Marquis of Queensbury boxer suddenly discovering the advantage of the "sucker punch". Haig's one bright thought is no reason for us to follow those modern revisionist military historians who attempt to resuscitate his ragged reputation. There was much

---
163 John Terraine, *Ordeal of Victory* (Philadelphia: Lippincott, 1963), 139.
164 Haig, *Diary*, 10 Feb. 1915, as quoted in Terraine (1963), 139.

that a more sharp-witted commander could and should have done by way of deception and surprise, as proved by the likes of Mercer, Swinton, and Allenby.

All was in readiness on March 9th and, with the promise of good weather, the offensive began next morning at 0730 hours along a two-mile wide front with a mere 35-minute artillery barrage. This was immediately followed by the infantry assault (four divisions) while the artillery concentrated on the approach routes of the enemy reserves. The attack achieved complete tactical surprise, winning the German trenches and opening a gaping hole in their front at far fewer British than German casualties. That was the good news.

The bad news was that Haig and his staff had so little understanding of "the element of surprise" that they had planned no follow-through. Consequently on D+1 the German counterattack easily halted the slow British exploitation; and on D+3 the battle ended. The B.E.F. had lost 11,652 men; the enemy roughly the same. The British had gained less than one square mile of Flanders' fields. Still, this was one of the few attacks on the Western Front where an Allied force managed to approach parity in kill-ratios against the German Army.

CASE 32:
Commander Unwin and the Wooden Horse, Gallipoli 1915
A British naval officer draws a lesson from history.

The Allied expedition at Gallipoli was, as all would later agree, a disastrous enterprise, a model of how not to conduct amphibious operations. However, this judgement overlooks the fact that the initial landings did gain tactical surprise through use of several primitive but effective ruses and feints. Typically, though, the precious time thus obtained was frittered away on the beaches by the confusion of untrained troops and the immobility of indecisive commanders—the same syndrome that would plague the American commander following his surprise landing at Anzio in 1944.

Let's examine the one entirely original ruse used. Royal Navy Commander Edwin Unwin was with the large Allied naval covering force as captain of the old gunboat, *H.M.S. Hussar*. Inspired by the nearby site of ancient Troy, Unwin conceived his own version of the Trojan Horse. His notion was to disguise a troopship as an innocent collier and have it beach as if by accident on D-day when it would then disgorge by surprise the entire initial assault wave. Specifically, he proposed converting the 4,000-ton collier *S.S. River Clyde* to a camouflaged troopship.

Unwin's proposal was accepted and its enthusiastic originator assigned to carry it out, handling the collier's refit and commanding it during the assault landing. Refitting involved cutting sally-ports in the steel hull, through which the troops would exit, disembarking down improvised gangways to towed barges laid ship-to-shore, bridging the final yards. The few persons in on the secret began calling Unwin's coopted landingcraft the "Wooden Horse" in honor of its inventor and his Trojan inspiration. It was the veritable prototype of the familiar LST of the next world war.

On D-day, April 25th, *River Clyde* beached as planned and began disgorging its 2,100 troops. However, poor Intelligence had placed them directly in the face of murderous Turkish small-arms fire. In these unexpected conditions, Commander Unwin and Able-Seaman Williams wallowed into the shallow water to position the lighters, rescue wounded, and earn their Victoria Crosses—Williams posthumously. Fortunately the large steel hull sheltered most of the troops until it was safe for them to land next day.[165]

CASE 33:
Lieut.-Gen. Allenby, Third Gaza, Palestine 1917
The new Commander proposes a plan to end stalemate by a surprise attack.

In 1917 the British Army in Palestine had been stalemated by the Turco-German forces for eight months. When the new British Commander, Lieut.-General Edmund "The Bull" Allenby arrived on June 28th from the Western Front, the local Turko-German command did not expect him to bring any more innovation or imagination than his predecessor. They were preconditioned to expect yet another costly and inconclusive British push toward Gaza from the seaward flank. Allenby, however, came with a "prepared mind", one filled with innovative plans centered around the principle of surprise.

Allenby had been born in 1861, the first son of an English country gentleman, into a family without military tradition. Following an easy time at private school, he failed his exams for the Indian Civil Service and, by default, entered the Army through the Royal Military College at Sandhurst as a cadet at age 20. Thenceforward he was known for his quick outbursts of rage and slow but sure problem solving. Although a man of few words, they were clear and laced with wry humor. A giant in height, he was an imposing figure both mounted, standing, or seated. Always self-assured and not easily intimidated but entirely lacking ambition for rank or rewards, he joined no cliques and advanced in the military entirely on his record of competency.

In 1900 at age 29 Major Allenby got his first look at both war and military deception by his participation in Lord Robert's Relief of Kimberley (Case 2) where Col. Henderson had exercised effective deceptions. A decade-and-a-

---

165 Admiral of the Fleet Sir Roger Keyes, *Naval Memoirs*, Vol.1 (London: Butterworth, 1934), 282, 283, 296.

half later, on the Western Front, Allenby was one of the few Allied generals who even tried to imagine beyond the textbook over-the-top, straight-at-'em, hack-and-slash tactics. All he could see from that dreary business was one big butcher's bill after another that bought only perpetual stalemate. As a cavalryman he understood and sought battle by manouever and hated the rnuddled doctrine of trench warfare that prevented this.

By spring 1917 Allenby commanded British Third Army, comprising 22 divisions. He was ordered by Field-Marshal Haig to mount a limited attack along his 11% miles of front as a diversionary action to support the overall Allied spring offensive. Hoping to gain at least enough surprise to prevent the arrival of German reserves before the battle, Allenby and his artillery commander, Maj.-Gen. Arthur Holland, urged GHQ (specifically Haig and his dull Chief of Staff, Kiggell) that they be permitted to cut the then conventional 7-day preparatory artillery bombardment to 48 hours. This bold idea was effectively silenced by immediately reassigning Holland.[166] Even so Allenby gained what Wavell would characterize as "the most successful day's fighting the British forces in France had yet had in two and a half years' warfare."

Now, in June, given independent command in Palestine, the 54-year old Allenby could call his own shots and proceeded to do so. His first decision was to take GHQ out of the lavish indolence of Cairo and, like Rommel and Patton later, move it forward to the austere battlefront. His second act was to hand-pick a small but remarkable staff—a talent he had acquired on the Western Front. From there he summoned Major-General Louis Bols, his old Chief of Staff and put him again in this role. Bols had an "impish sense of humour" that led to more than one practical joke at GHQ. Despite an innate laziness and "weak intellect" that made him easy prey for cunning underlings, Bols was a "gallant, sprightly little man, with a quick sense of humour, whose ready optimism and willingness suited Allenby."[167] And Allenby inherited from his predecessor two others who would prove even more noteworthy: effective deception planner Guy Dawnay and charlatan Richard Meinertzhagen.

Thirty-nine year-old Brigadier-General G.P. Dawnay was a meticulous staff planner. He also had a mind of exquisite deviousness as demonstrated two years earlier when at Gallipoli he had produced the better plans and devised many of the more successful stratagems—both the military deceptions directed against the Turks and the political ones aimed at London.[168] Maj. T.E. Lawrence, who worked well with him throughout that period, summed him up:[169]

---

166 Wavell (1940), 174-175.
167 Wavell (1940), 164-165; Meinertzhagen (1959/1960).
168 For details on Guy Dawnay see Whaley (1969/2007), Cases A38, A93; and Lawrence (1935), 383-384.
169 Lawrence (1935), 383.

> Dawnay was mainly intellect. He lacked the eagerness of Bols, and the calm drive and human understanding of Allenby, who was the man the men worked for, the image we worshiped. Dawnay's cold, shy mind gazed upon our efforts with bleak eye, always thinking, thinking. Beneath this mathematical surface he hid passionate many-sided convictions, a reasoned scholarship in higher warfare, and the brilliant bitterness of a judgement disappointed with us, and with life. He was the least professional of soldiers, a banker who read Greek history, a strategist unashamed, and a burning poet with strength over daily things. During the [earlier part of the] war he had had the grief of planning the attack at Suvla (spoiled by incompetent tacticians) and the [second] battle for Gaza. As each work of his was ruined he withdrew further into the hardness of frosted pride, for he was the stuff of fanatics.

At the time of Allenby's assumption of command, Dawnay was on temporary assignment to Lieut.-General Sir Philip Chetwode, the best of Allenby's three corps commanders. Dawnay had the outline for a grand deception of the enemy and sold it to his chief.[170] Dawnay's plan was typical of him, Lawrence commenting:[171]

> Dawnay was not the man to fight a straight battle. He sought to destroy the enemy's strength with the least fuss. Like a master politician, he used the bluff Chief [Chetwode] as a cloak for the last depth of justifiable slimness. He advised a drive at the far end of the Turkish line, near Beersheba. To make his victory cheap he wanted the enemy main force behind Gaza, which would be best secured if the British concentration was hidden so that the Turks would believe the flank attack to be a shallow feint. Bols nodded his assent.

Chetwode, an old and proven friend of Allenby, then took Dawnay's plan to Allenby. The timing was right, for Allenby had immediately on arrival turned his mind to strategy, which for him had come to include surprise as its essential ingredient. This dictated abandoning the previously unsuccessful pattern of costly frontal assaults against the entrenched enemy defenses at the coast in front of Gaza. The essence of this strategy was to play to the Turco-Germans' presumed preconceptions by launching the battle from an unexpected quarter. Specifically it was designed to envelope the enemy army by a surprise cavalry sweep through its weakly defended left flank in the desert at Beersheba. Therefore, on July 12th, only two weeks after his arrival, Allenby accepted the

---
170 Lawrence (1935), 384.
171 Lawrence (1935), 384.

Dawnay-Chetwode proposal as his plan of attack.[172] When Allenby briefed Wavell, the latter was impressed:[173]

> The plan itself was simple, as are almost all good plans in war: to concentrate a superior force against the enemy's left flank, while inducing him to believe that his right would again be attacked. The Twentieth Corps and Desert Mounted Corps were to form the striking force against the Turkish left, while the Twenty-first Corps kept the enemy's attention fixed on Gaza.

Then, Wavell recalled,[174]

> It was in essentials almost the same plan as Roberts had exploited against Cronje in the relief of Kimberley in the Boer War some seventeen years before; and it is certain that Robert's move had stayed in Allenby's memory, since it was the first big military operation in which he, then a [cavalry] squadron commander, had played a part.

So small wonder that Allenby had been so quick to adopt the Dawnay-Chetwode proposal.

On August 14th Wavell was back in London, presenting Allenby's plan to the Chief of the Imperial Staff. At the end of Lieut.-Col. Wavell's detailed half-hour private briefing General Sir William "Wully" Robertson approved.[175]

Dawnay's value as a planner being evident, he was immediately transferred from Chetwode's staff to Allenby's HQ as deputy chief of staff. There, as Lawrence observed:[176]

> Allenby, by not seeing his [festering] dissatisfaction, broke into him; and Dawnay replied by giving for the Jerusalem advance [Allenby's planned offensive] all the talent which he abundantly possessed. A cordial union of such men made the Turk's position hopeless from the outset.

Of the same age as Dawnay but three cuts lower in rank was Major Richard Meinertzhagen. He'd arrived from London a month before Allenby to become the latter's chief combat intelligence officer. Throughout later years he would claim (falsely) to have swiftly organized and trained a fine behind-the-lines intelligence network using 15 Palestinian Jews (the NILI spies) that, together with POW interrogation, gave highly accurate and nearly complete intelligence

---

172 Wavell (1940), 191.
173 Wavell (1940), 201.
174 Wavell (1940), 201.
175 Connell (1965), 126-127.
176 Lawrence (1935), 383.

on enemy order of battle and dispositions. Perhaps. We know he soon developed a keen appreciation of deception. But he has recently been thoroughly exposed as a charlatan, an impostor who attributed to himself the ideas and actions of others and padded those out with some creative fictions.[177]

If Dawnay was a genuine master of deception, Meinertzhagen was a pretend grand master. He would claim it was he who advised Dawnay to go beyond his mere "negative precautions" (dissimulation) and also give the enemy specific but wrong intelligence (simulation). Dawnay enthusiastically agreed, Allenby also agreed but had doubts, and Bols played his usual yes-man role, so Meinertzhagen and his bag of tricks were let loose (see next Case).[178]

Allenby and Dawnay had correctly read their enemy. The German Middle East theater commander, General Erich von Falkenhayn, was the man whose sole innovation in military science was the invention of a new strategic means to Pyhrric victory—Verdun. The commander of the Palestine front, General Kress von Kressenstein, drew his experience and promotions from two years of easy victories over Allenby's conventionally-minded predecessor. The Germans were particularly unlucky that the eve of the offensive coincided with the arrival of Major Franz von Papen to design the final Turco-German front-line defensive deployments at Gaza. Von Papen had fought opposite Allenby at Vimy Ridge six months before and assumed Allenby would follow the same tactic at Gaza by announcing his attack by *several days* of heavy artillery bombardment.[179]

Von Papen's judgement about Allenby's SOP, which he conveyed to the German and Turkish commanders, was wrong from the start. At Vimy Ridge, Allenby had been refused permission to cut the conventional lengthly 7-day preparatory barrage down to 48 hours.[180] Now, at Gaza where Allenby was his own master, he went to the even further extreme of limiting his massed artillery preparation to a mere two hours to insure local surprise of timing. Gaza was, of course, only the feint; but Allenby wanted even those troops to benefit from the life-saving advantage of surprise.

Having laid out the scenario for surprise attack, Allenby passed the detailed deception planning to Dawnay. His efforts caused the Turco-German command to grossly misinterpret Allenby's deceptive strategy. This had two decisive consequences. First it enabled the British to win their first battle against that

---

[177] Brian Garfield, *The Meinertzhagen Mystery: The Life and Legend of a Colossal Fraud* (Washington, DC: Potomac Books, 2007); and Whaley, *Meinertzhagen's Haversack Exposed: The Consequences for Counterdeception Analysis* (FDDC, 2007).
[178] Lawrence (1935), 384.
[179] Franz von Papen, *Memoirs* (New York: Dutton, 1953), 70, 73, 74. It is characteristic of this future German Chancellor and Hitler's WW2 Ambassador to Turkey that without overtly lying he so edits his account to imply he was blameless at Gaza.
[180] For Vimy Ridge see Whaley, *Stratagem* (1969/2007), Example B11.

enemy. Second, it set the stage for Allenby's second decisive campaign (Case 27) the following year.

CASE 34:
Maj. Meinertzhagen and the Haversack Legend, Palestine 1917
One of Allenby's intelligence officers plagiarizes a real plan and pretends to carry it out—thereby fabricating the celebrated legend of the "Meinertzhagen Haversack Ruse".

Allenby's deception plans and operations for his 1917 battle-winning campaign described above (Case 33) were being closely observed from the sidelines by one of his intelligence officers. This was 39-year old Richard "Meiner" Meinertzhagen, an unorthodox professional soldier who had learned to view the average British commander with amused contempt and ignore their rule books. He was also on the threshold of a lifetime career as a world-class fraud—charlatan, impersonator, plagiarist, hoaxer, fantasist, and, if we believe his story about the streamers of toilet paper at the Versailles Peace Conference, an imaginative practical joker. And, unlike most of that ilk, his ploys were never mere pranks but always played for their ruthless author's advantage.[181] Interestingly, I do not find any evidence of his *practicing* deception in his boyhood memoir, *Diary of a Black Sheep* (1964), other than a general tendency (pp.xx-xxi) toward the indirect approach in order to "by-pass [opposition] and win that way." This suggests that he was much more a fantasizer than an activist.

Born in 1878, the son of a City of London banker, he received a proper young English gentleman's education at Harrow. His dream was to become a zoologist; his father's hope was that he become a banker. Balked at the first and refusing the second, Meinertzhagen secretly joined the British Army as a second-lieutenant in 1897.

Meinertzhagen's mythologizing about himself would begin sometime around 1922, possibly as early as 1920. He was a major in the British Army. But he was well into his 40s and his long but lackluster military career was failing. He didn't like his past. So he began to change it. Bit by bit he successfully fabricated his own myth—one that would until well beyond his death in 1967 at age 90. Meiner created a fictional other self, an alter ego of heroic size, a döppleganger who supposedly acted in every part of the real man's public life as a fearsome warrior, brilliant intelligence officer, and world-class ornithologist and in his private life as a man to be feared, possibly even as a murderer.

---

181 This case is based entirely on the two most comprehensive studies: Brian Garfield, *The Meinertzhagen Mystery: The Life and Legend of a Colossal Fraud* (Washington, DC: Potomac Books, 2007); and Whaley, *Meinertzhagen's Haversack Exposed: The Consequences for Counterdeception Analysis* (FDDC, 2007).

But it is as the great military intelligencer and deception operator that Meinertzhagen is relevant here. Specifically his Haversack Ruse that supposedly broke the World War One stalemate in Palestine, won the Third Battle of Gaza, and opened the path to total victory in the Middle East. In fact, as I recently (August 2010) figured out, the Haversack Ruse had been conceived and planned by Major (Brevit Lieut-Colonel) J. D. Belgrave, a Royal Artillery officer who would become a full colonel in the Reserve until 1942 when retired as over age. He was not Brian Garfield's more famous Royal Flying Corps Captain James Dacres Belgrave, a fighter ace who served only at the Western front until 1918 when shot down and killed in 1918. The officer who rode out to deposit the haversack in no man's land within sight of the Turks had been, as Garfield first proved, Captain Arthur C. B. Neate of the Desert Mouted Corps. Meiner evidently learned of this ruse—or at least of its full details—on September 11th when Capt. Neate stopped by with the bag at Yeomanry Division HQ to confer with Meiner before Neate's ride (on a borrowed horse) the following morning to the front.[182]

Although the real Haversack Ruse had proven rather a fizzle, we can thank Meiner for having made it the stuff of legend—second only to the Trojan Horse. Moreover it was a legend that generated considerable real-world consequences because it would inspire the next two generations of military deception planners to imitate it. Specifically, it inspired Gen. Wavell to produce Operation ERROR (Case 15) and Flight-Lieutenant Cholmondley with Operation MINCEMEAT (Case 49).

Being duped by documents is an embarrassment we intelligence historians and analysts share with other mortals. But the Haversack Ruse is only one sub-type of documents planted to deceive. Prompted in 2007 by H. Richards Heuer to enlarge the data base of military cases where both real plans were lost and false ones planted, I compiled a set of 40.[183] They ranged from Greek and Chinese antiquity to the Vietnam War. Of those 40 cases, 36 involved planting false documents and 5 involved the unintended loss of real ones. These are analyzed below in Tables A & B.

---

182 Neate's key role was first fully documented in a fine piece of research by Garfield (2007), 31-37.
183 Whaley, *Meinertshagen's Haversack Exposed* (FDDC: 2007), 24-29.

Table A: Disposition of Known Fake Haversack-type Deception Plans in History

No.	DISPOSITION		
3	Cancelled	—	vetoed by higher authority
0	Cancelled	—	overtaken by events
7	Cancelled	—	aborted for other reasons
2	Completed	—	unknown result
1	Completed	—	failed with backfire
7	Completed	—	failed
8	Completed	—	partial success
7	Completed	—	full success
35	TOTAL FALSE PLANS		

SOURCE: Compiled from Whaley, *Stratagem* (1969); Whaley, *When Deception Fails* (draft); Whaley, *The Deception Planners* (draft); Howard (1990); Holt (2004).

Seems cost-effective, given that 15 of 25 (60%) of the completed efforts to float false plans enjoyed at least some success.

Table B: Disposition of Known Real Plans Lost

No.	DISPOSITION
1	Unknown effect
4	Disbelieved
5	TOTAL REAL PLANS

Interesting but, given the small sample, inconclusive.

CASE 35:
Lieut.-Gen. Allenby, Megiddo, Palestine 1918
The Commander keeps his own counsel.

After Third Gaza (Case 33), General Allenby lost his chief deception planner, Brig.-Gen Dawnay to the Western Front. And Brevit Lt.-Col. Meinertzhagen had packed off to the War Office in London. But, as Maj. T. E. Lawrence personally observed, "After the Meinertzhagen success [sic], deceptions, which for the ordinary general were just witty hors d'oeuvres before battle, became for Allenby a main point of strategy."[184] Allenby's thinking for this battle was,

---
184 Lawrence (1935), 537.

as always, brief and straight to the point: "Thorough preparation. Deception. Concentration of strength; with strong feints."[185]

Allenby's plan of campaign was, true to his style, entirely his own. He would not disclose it even to his staff until after thinking it through in considerable detail. On August 1st he presented his preliminary scenario. This used his old pattern of feint-cum-deception but reversed the real axis of operations from desert to coast. Then, in late August, he tabled his detailed revision. D-day was only three weeks off. The essence of Allenby's stratagem was to build upon his enemy's preconceptions. He shrewdly and correctly reasoned that his name had become linked by the Germans and Turks with a cavalry thrust against their desert flank, not only from his earlier victory but because Allenby's undisguised strength there had been verified by his two large-scale raids across the Jordan. As Lawrence observed:[186]

> The two raids ... had fixed the Turk's eyes exclusively beyond Jordan. Every move there, whether of British or Arabs, was accompanied by counter-precautions on the Turks' part, showing how fearful they were. In the coast sector, the area of real danger, the enemy had absurdly few men. Success hung on maintaining them in this fatal misapprehension.

Accordingly, Allenby's deception operations were now tailored to reinforce that notion. Much credit for detailed planning, particularly that of the deception, belongs to Allenby's Chief-of-Staff, Major-General Sir Louis Bols. Even more credit is due Bol's intelligent and able deputy, Brigadier-General William "Barty" Bartholomew who proved an "extremely able staff officer" to both Chetwode (until Wavell replaced him as deputy chief of staff) and now to Allenby (also as deputy chief of staff).[187] Wavell, who was present, describes the planning process:[188]

> The details of the plan were worked out at a series of conferences, over which Allenby presided. Those who attended them will not easily forget his almost presumptuous confidence about the issue of the operations, the clearness and incisiveness of his instructions, and his occasional abrupt impatience at some objection or difficulty. It was not his way to be content with half-measures, and this was shown clearly in two aspects of the plan—the arrangements for the break-through on the coast and the measures for the deception of the enemy.

---

185 Quoted in Brian Gardner, *Allenby* (London: Cassell, 1965), 195.
186 Lawrence (1935), 537.
187 Wavell (1940), 211, 245.
188 Wavell (1940), 268.

Allenby's strategic deception was carefully designed to gain both surprise of time and place. To deceive the enemy about the timing of the offensive, an official public announcement was made that a major public event—a horserace—had been scheduled for September 19th, that is, D-day. As for the place of attack it was designed to draw the bulk of the Turco-German forces to the broad eastern (mountain and desert) flank and lock them there while the real attack rolled up the narrow western (coastal) flank. This was a complete reversal of the earlier operation at Gaza. The main elements of this deception of place were the following:[189]

Elaborate measures were taken to simulate the imminent transfer of Allenby's headquarters from his camp in the plains to a hotel in Jerusalem, which was cleared and prepared for it, with offices marked, telephones installed, and so forth. This ruse was enhanced by spreading rumors of a big buildup in the Jerusalem area and inspecting buildings as suitable billets.

Bartholomew arranged to have all condemned tents in Egypt collected, brought to the Jordan valley, and pitched near Jericho to simulate a huge encampment. Smaller camps were set up throughout the valley. The horse lines were filled with 15,000 thousand dummy horses, made of canvas; and sleighs drawn by mules raised clouds of dust at the times when the canvas horses should have been going to water. During the day, battalions (West Indian noncombatant labor battalions) marched ostentatiously into the valley to the dummy camps, returning secretly at night to their real camps in covered trucks. Otherwise the dummy encampments were manned mostly by dummy men. Normal radio traffic was continued from Desert Mounted Corps' former headquarters near Jericho long after it and nearly all its troops had been transferred to the other flank. A new bridge was thrown across the Jordan as if in preparation for a full-scale assault. Further east, Lawrence's agents spread false news that the British cavalry would soon require large quantities of forage in the trans-Jordan Amman district.

Meanwhile, at the western coastal end of the line, the concentration of Allenby's real attack force was being dissimulated. Tight secrecy prevailed. Only a few officers knew it was underway. All movement into the area was at night. No new tents were put up and the old ones out in the open were now double-occupied; but most of the newly arrived troops were simply encamped under cover of the orange and olive groves, whose irrigation channels brought the water for their thousands of horses. Campfires were strictly forbidden.[190]

This concealment was crucial. Bartholomew:[191]

---

189 Wavell (1940), 269-270; Lawrence (1935), 537-538; Connell (1964), 139.
190 Connell (1964), 139.
191 Lawrence (1935), 538.

warned us that ... success would hang on a thread, since the Turks could save themselves and their army, and give our concentration to do over again, by simply retiring their coast sector seven or eight miles. The British Army would then be like a fish flapping on dry land, with its railways, its heavy artillery, its dumps, its stores, its camps all misplaced; and without olive groves in which to hide its concentration next time.

And all this time the RAF flew continuous fighter patrols to keep the enemy from getting too close a look at the dummies in the east or the real build-up under camouflage in the west.

The enemy's spies and aerial reconnaissance reported the highly visible but bogus threat in the east. The Turco-German command bought it and massed fully two-thirds of its limited combat force there (25,000 Turco-Germans facing 25,000 British). When on September 19th Allenby's army struck in the west, it caught the enemy hopelessly off balance (8,000 defenders against 44,000 attackers) and rolled quickly forward 350 miles, not stopping until Turkey withdrew from the war six weeks later. For 5,000 British casualties, Allenby had taken 75,000 prisoners, captured Damascus, and forced Turkey out of the war.

CASE 36:
Major T. E. Lawrence, Arabia 1917-1918
A case of deception and self-deception.

> I wondered if all established reputations were founded like mine, on fraud.
>
> — T. E. Lawrence, 1918

Lawrence of Arabia is one of the grand myths of our century, a myth created by Lieut.Colonel T. E. "Freddie" Lawrence and vouched for by many overly romantic or self-serving writers. First, even his rank and medal (the D.S.O.) were got by fraud—his largely fictitious official report on his role in the Battle of Tafileh on 24-25 January 1918.[192] And his full colonelcy was merely a temporary courtesy granted in October by General Allenby to enable him to travel home in comfort from the war in the Middle East. Yet Lawrence continued to wear his full colonel's badges during the Paris Peace Conference. As usual, no one challenged him.[193] He fascinated listeners and readers alike with tales

---
192 Stewart (1977), 195-196, 198; Suleiman Musa, *T.E. Lawrence: An Arab View* (London: Oxford University Press, 1966), 132-151.
193 Colonel Richard Meinertzhagen, *Middle East Diary: 1917-1956* (New York: Thomas Yoseloff, 1W), 30.

of his multiple bullet and other war wounds, yet neither Meinertzhagen before whom he allegedly bathed nude in 1919 nor the Army doctors who examined him on his reenlistment in 1922 noticed any such scars, only the red weals he had on his chest from having been ignominiously dragged across barbed wire by a rampant camel.[194]

Simply put, Lawrence was a con man whose deceptions were directed more against allies than foes. He risked lies to gain fame and social acceptance among the famous, whose names he freely dropped. Still, he was as his close friend and severest critic, Meinertzhagen, observed, a "very complex and interesting man". Lawrence earns his place in this study of deception planners not so much for what he actually did as for the enormous influence he had on the imaginations of other much more authentic deceivers. Churchill was completely conned by this man who told him only what he wanted to hear, including bad-mouthing Allenby. Liddell Hart, as his authorized biographer, uncritically accepted many of his lies. Wavell, who knew him only slightly, was largely taken in but did spot frequent biased and sometimes outright false claims. Allenby had from their first meeting suspected he was a bit of a charlatan but gave him full support. Meinertzhagen's suspicions were fully confirmed (or so he would claim) in 1919 by Lawrence's repeated private confessions—themselves not always true—in Paris. Meiner's diary noted at the time that:[195]

> He is writing a book on his Arabian exploits and admitted to me that though it purports to be the truth, a great deal of it is fancy, what might have happened, what should have happened and dull little incidents embroidered into hair-breadth escapes. He confesses that he has overdone it and is now terrified lest he is found out and deflated. He told me that ever since childhood he had wanted to be a hero, that he was always fighting between rushing into limelight and hiding in utter darkness but the limelight had always won. And now he is genuinely terrified at his brazen imagination—all to what purpose? He hates himself and is having a great struggle with his conscious. His self-deception filled him with bitterness. Shall he run away and hide, confess his sins and become completely discredited—or carry the myth on into the limelight in the hopes of not being exposed. Poor little man, he's in a ghastly mess and I wish I could help him.

And Lawrence's ravaged mind harbored other crippling fears. He was ashamed by his "littleness", a tiny stature not fitting his heroic ideal. He was ashamed of his bastardy and was terrified it would become publicly known, despite

---

194 Meinertzhagen (1959/1960), 32-33.
195 Meinertzhagen (1959/1960), 30-31.

Meinertzhagen's words of consolation: "I told him that in these enlightened times such things mattered little and that he was in good company for Jesus was born out of wedlock."[196] A masochist, he solicited punishment by flogging—and, ashamed of that, invented the famous fiction of his having been forcefully flogged and buggered in Deraa.[197] He was ashamed of his "accessory deceitfulness" toward his trusting Arabs as emissary of a great power. And he was ashamed that these Arabs had finally seen through his empty promises and so he fled the scene with Allenby's timely permission.[198] Lawrence was all false modesty in writing that:[199]

> I must have had some tendency, some aptitude, for deceit, or I would not have deceived men so well, and persisted in bringing to success a deceit which others had framed and set afoot.

Meinertzhagen concluded: "It is safe to say that Lawrence's Desert Campaign had not the slightest effect on the main theatre west of Jordan."[200] This was true of Lawrence's role during the Battle of Third Gaza in 1917 when Meinertzhagen was still on the scene; but it is far too strong a debunking when applied to his desert campaign the following year. On that occasion Lawrence did make a secondary but very real contribution to Allenby's overall deception plan. As we saw (Case 35), Allenby's strategic deception in 1918 was to portray his main strength in the east by feints and other ruses. To support that notion, Lawrence was given two deception assignments:

His earlier assignment was to have his Arab agents spread news that the British forces in the Jordan valley would soon need very large quantities of forage for their cavalry, enough for Allenby's 15,000 canvas dummy horses that soon replaced most of the real ones there.[201]

Another deception was to threaten the only railway line that linked Turkey and Syria to the front, the railway from Damascus south to Deraa where it then split into two lines, one leading south to Amman, the other west to Haifa. Lawrence's assignment was to threaten the three lines converging at Deraa and, then, cut them and keep them cut during Allenby's offensive. Lawrence did precisely this, his diversionary sideshow helping keep 6,000 Turco-German combat troops of the Turkish Fourth Army, admittedly a demoralized and second-rate lot, tied down on the extreme eastern trans-Jordan flank. This was done with a mounted force that numbered only 1,000 regular soldiers (a mixed force of Britons, Egyptians, Gurkhas, and French Algerians) and 3,000

---

196 Meinertzhagen (1959/1960), 32.
197 The first and conclusive exposé of this monumental lie was by Suleiman Mousa, *T. E. Lawrence: An Arab View* (London: Oxford University Press, 1966), 115-118.
198 See particularly Desmond Stewart, *T. E. Lawrence* (London: Hamilton. 1977), throughout.
199 Lawrence (1935), 552.
200 Meinertzhagen (1959/1960), 28.
201 Wavell (1940), 269.

irregulars (Arabs) with only 8 armored cars; 4 field guns, 25 machine guns, and 2 aircraft.[202]

Two final points are noteworthy about Lawrence's conduct of that operation. First, he preceded Dudley Clarke in the creation of a notional military unit. The Imperial Camel Corps Brigade had been a potent unit in the Sinai and then during the desert offensive the previous year. Now, with little further desert fighting planned, it was broken up. All that remained was a single battalion of 300 men under Colonel Buxton. On July 13th, Lawrence's intelligenceofficer, Alan Dawnay, younger brother of Guy Dawnay, had a bright idea. If Buxton's battalion were lent to Lawrence's small force it might be taken for the entire brigade and "confuse the Turks' reckoning". Bartholomew passed the Dawnay-Lawrence scheme to Bols and Allenby and got their approval.[203]

The second subsidiary ruse was that Lawrence covered his final real attack on the Deraa rail lines by a feint against Amman.[204]

In October in Damascus, while the war raged to the north, the Arabs learned of Lawrence's two-facedness; and, in his final shame, he asked his chief to post him immediately to England. Allenby, annoyed, said merely "Yes, I think you had" but, pleased with Lawrence's cost-effective contribution, gave him full colonelcy to ease the trip home.

Lawrence's real contribution to military history was his articulately argued theory of guerrilla war, which gained undeserved weight by the mythical success that surrounded its author. But this myth gave encouragement and ammunition to such advocates of unconventional—and successful—surprise attack operations as Churchill, Wavell, and Liddell Hart.

CASE 37:
Gen. Von Hutier, St.-Quentin, France 1918
The German Chief of Artillery plans a tactical surprise.

Like Allenby on the Allied side, a German artillery commander had become disillusioned with the conventional lengthy (4 to 19-day) pre-assault barrages on the Western Front. General Oskar von Hutier substituted a short preparation that included a high proportion of gas and smoke shells followed immediately by a rolling ("creeping") barrage that moved steadily forward at about one kilometer per hour just ahead of the first assault wave.

The old method was, of course, more effective at destroying enemy defense positions and killing enemy troops, but that advantage was more than offset

---

202 Major Sir Hubert Young, *The Independent Arab* (London: Murray, 1933), 217-219, 227-233; Wavell (1940), 269, 272; Lawrence (1935), 537-637, for his own often dissembling account.
203 Lawrence (1935), 538.
204 Lawrence (1935), 582, 583, 588.

both by giving the enemy ample warning to bring up reinforcements and by so chopping up the terrain that the attack itself was inevitably slowed. The new "Hutier tactics" were designed to temporarily blind and confuse the enemy observers and gun positions."[205] And they restored the element of surprise and some slight mobility to trench seige-warfare.

Von Hutier and his staff had first experimented with this tactic on a small scale on the Eastern Front at Riga on 1 September 1917. They further battle-tested it in Italy at Caporetto on October 24th. Now, Field-Marshal Ludendotff adopted it for the first time on the Western Front to open Germany's 1918 spring offensive with a major drive on the Somme. This was his plan MICHAEL, known to the Allies as the Battle of St.-Quentin.

The great offensive began on March 21st at 0440 hours with a five-hour bombardment with 6,000 cannon and 3,000 mortars firing gas, smoke, and high explosives at the 40-60 mile of front chosen by Ludendotff for his battle. Then, at 0940, the 32 German assault divisions began their advance under cover of a fortuitous fog and the creeping barrage, which was fired according to a predetermined map-and-time schedule. Although the Allied commanders had—through good intelligence—expected a strong German attack at the approximately correct time and place, they were quite surprised by its size, ferocity, and tactics.[206]

CASE 38:
Marshal Mustapha Kemal, Dumlupinar 1922
The future Atatürk acts as his own deception planner and operator.

> Trickery is one of the most useful things employed in warfare. It is the thing most likely to bring victory.
>
> — Ibn Khaldun, *Muqaddimah* (1377)

Mustapha Kemal had commanded a Turkish division at Gallipoli in 1915 and the Turkish Seventh Army in Palestine in 1918. Ironically, he proved a better student of his more deceptive enemies, Monro and Allenby than he did of his own conventional commanders, the German generals Von Sanders and Von Falkenhayn. Now, in the Greco-Turkish War of 1921 22, he would apply these lessons against the Greek invaders. At this point Kemal was Commander-in-Chief of the Turkish Army.

---

205 Brigadier General Vincent Esposito (*editor*), *A Concise History of World War I* (New York: Prager, 1964), 105-107; Liddell Hart (1954), 205-207; and, for a surprisingly sound summary, *Wikipedia*, "Oskar von Hutier (accessed 3 Sep 2010).
206 For details and documentation see Whaley (1969/2007), Case B18.

After three months of a bitterly fought withdrawal, Kemal finally stopped the Greek advance in September. That fall he set about planning his own offensive, to begin early next year. He planned it in secret together with the Chief of the General Staff, General Fevzi, and the Western Front Commander, General Ismet (later famous as Inönü). The plan was his own and not that of the Soviet Russians whose arms he welcomed but whose offered troops and advisers he declined as politically risky. Specifically, he was annoyed when the Ukrainian Bolshevik general, Frunze, volunteered to draft the Turkish campaign plan during his stay in Ankara in December-January.[207]

CASE 39:
Gen. Hans von Seeckt, Germany 1919
The "disarmed" Commander deceives the arms controllers.

From 1919 through 1934 Germany partially rearmed in defiance of the severe arms limitations imposed by the Versailles Treaty. To avoid provoking military intervention by France and Britain, the Germans systematically used deception to dissimulate their excess strength during this period.[208]

The main architect of this policy of dissimulative camouflage of rearmament was General Hans von Seeckt.[209] Full details of the many ruses employed by Von Seeckt and his successors and allies are available elsewhere.[210]

CASE 40:
Hitler, Europe 1935-38
The Führer plans a bluff in grand strategy.

> "You will never learn what I am thinking. And those who boast most loudly that they know my thought, to such people I lie even more."
>
> — Hitler, August 1938[211]

In 1935 Chancellor Adolph Hitler unilaterally renounced the Versailles Treaty and openly proclaimed Germany's intention to rearm. Henceforward

---

207 Whaley, *Stratagem* (1969/2007), Case A11.
208 Details and analysis are in Whaley, *Covert German Rearmament, 1919-1939: Deception and Misperception* (Frederick, Maryland: University Publications of America, Inc., 1984).
209 A sound biographical sketch is "Hans von Seeckt," *Wikipedia* (accessed 19 Sep 2010).
210 See the earlier part of Whaley, *Covert German Rearmament, 1919-1939: Deception and Misperception* (Frederick, Maryland: University Publications of America, Inc., 1984); and as condensed in Whaley, "Covert German Rearmament, 1919-1939: Deception and Misperception," *Journal of Strategic Studies* (London), Vol.5, No.1 (March 1982), 3-39.
211 Harold C. Deutsch, *The Conspiracy Against Hitler in the Twilight War* (Minneapolis: University of Minnesota Press, 1968), 32, quoting his post-war interview with Halder.

deception was used imaginatively to simulate a much higher degree of German military strength than in fact existed. Hitler's purpose was bluff—to induce the British and French to back down each time he touched his (almost empty) scabbard. This policy of bluff produced bloodless victories in his takeover of the Rhineland (1936), Austria (1938), and Czechoslovakia (1938) and was not "called" until September 1939 when the British and French reluctantly decided to honor their commitment to Poland and go to war.[212]

CASE 41:
Gen. Rojo, The Ebro River, Spain 1938
The Spanish Loyalist Chief of Staff devises a baited attack but forgets its purpose.

The Spanish Civil War was a rehearsal for WW2 in every way except deception. I have examined in detail all major battles in that bitterly fought three-year conflict and find only two that qualify as a deception-aided surprise, the Battle of Barcelona (Case 77) and the Battle of the Ebro, which as we shall see here may not have actually been planned as such.

By summer 1938, the prospects for the survival of the Spanish Republican (Loyalist) Government were dim. The Nationalist (Rebel) Army of Generalissimo Franco was larger, stronger, and once again grinding forward in ponderous offensive. To regain the initiative Premier Negrin called for a major diversionary attack. Accordingly, General Rojo, the Chief of Staff, proposed an attack across the Ebro River to threaten both the Nationalist's lateral communications and their salient to the sea that divided the Republican zone.[213]

Captain Tom Wintringham, the skilled Communist commander of the British Battalion of the XVth International Brigade, provided a professional post-battle analysis of Rojo's strategy. He asserted that:[214]

> The push across the Ebro was "the baited attack," to use Liddell Hart's phrase, in an almost perfect shape. Tactically it was the most advanced thing we had yet done; and strategically it had this very great advantage—that it was completely unexpected.

Strategic surprise was indeed obtained—and for two reasons. First, Franco was preoccupied with his own offensive against Valencia and assumed his enemy would respond in the manner usual to both sides, namely by direct confrontation. Second, the axis chosen by Rojo for his attack did not

---

[212] See the latter part of Whaley, *Covert German Rearmament, 1919-1939: Deception and Misperception* (Frederick, Maryland: University Publications of America, Inc., 1984).
[213] This case is condensed from Whaley, *Stratagem* (1969/2007), Case A14.
[214] Tom Wintringham, *English Captain* (London: Faber and Faber, 19(39), 312 and, generally, on 308-317.

immediately threaten any important military objectives—that would occur only if the first stage succeeded. And that is just what happened. The generally ineffective Nationalist Intelligence Service had failed to give warning. Air reconnaissance had revealed part of the enemy build-up of troops, boats, and pontoons; but the preconception held that the upper Ebro was not a sensible place for attack. The Republicans had scraped together a large 10-division force of nearly 100,000 troops in Catalonia.

On the morning of 24 July, the War Council in Barcelona authorized the attack. The mass crossings of the formidable Ebro began that same night at a quarter past midnight. Tactical surprise was assured by the moonless night, the absence of preparatory artillery fire, and swift execution of the initial assault. The small Nationalist force guarding the long 60-mile stretch of the river chosen for the crossing was overwhelmed by daybreak. It took over two hours for word of the attack to reach the sector headquarters—the 2-division Moroccan Army Corps, headed by General Yagüe. Initial success was complete.

By D + 1 the huge bridgehead covered 115 square miles and over 4,000 Nationalists had been taken prisoner. Republican losses were light. By D + 7 the Republicans held 250 square-miles. Moreover, the "baited" part of the attack had also succeeded. Franco broke off his pressure elsewhere to rush all available forces to contain the new threat. At this point, the innovation of an "indirect" strategy had proved itself. Henceforward, imagination failed.

Captain Wintringham was wrong—the Republican generals did not understand the theory of the "baited attack." Their World War One and Soviet Russian doctrine of direct frontal attack immediately reasserted itself upon the appearance of major opposition. Like Verdun, both sides now began their prodigal commitment of lives to the cauldron at the beachhead. The Communist commander of the Vth Army Corps, Colonel Enrique Lister, proved his Russian military training by ordering that: "If anyone loses an inch of ground he must retake it at the head of his men or be executed."[215] Forced to operate with such an unsuitable "doctrine," the irreplaceable Republican Army of the Ebro was virtually destroyed. It had even failed as an attritional battle— the 115 day fight had cost the Republicans more than twice the casualties incurred by Franco's Nationalists.

---

215 [Note missing]

CASE 42:
Lt.-Gen. Rommel, Mersa el Brega, North Africa 1941 & 1942
The "Desert Fox" twice preempts ULTRA.

> "Mental conception must be followed by immediate execution. This is a matter of energy and initiative."
>
> — Rommel, 1944

On 11 January 1941, with the Italian army in Libya in full flight-before Wavell's small Western Desert Force, Hitler decided to send in just enough German troops to prevent the embarrassment of his Roman ally's imminent eviction from Africa. For Hitler, his priorities focused on the Balkans and Russia as his next victims, North Africa was a sideshow, worth only a holding action. To accomplish this limited aim, on February 6th, Hitler authorized formation of the two-division Afrika Korps and appointed as its commander an outstanding Panzer officer, Lieutenant-General Erwin Rommel.

The future "Desert Fox" came under-armed but mentally well-prepared. In the Great War and in the 1940 blitzkrieg in France he had already learned and practiced the doctrine that the commander who moves first, seizes the initiative with all of its rewards in surprise and an ever-expanding choice of options (Case 6). Consequently he was impatient to attack. Now, in Africa, he would prove adept at pure deception in its classic form of the interplay of simulation and dissimulation.

Rommel flew into the Libyan capital of Tripoli on February 12th, followed two days later by the new Afrika Korps' advance elements, namely part of a reconnaissance battalion and an anti-tank battalion, which within 50 hours was at the front, 500 miles to the east. Acutely aware of his weakness, Rommel immediately decided that:[216]

> To enable us to appear as strong as possible and to induce the maximum caution in the British, I had the workshops three miles south of Tripoli produce large numbers of dummy tanks, which were mounted on Volkswagen and were deceptively like the original.

This was done by setting wooden turrets on cardboard frames fitted over Volkswagen bodies. Other dummy tanks were stationary, mere wood and cardboard mock-ups. By the 21st the first 35 had arrived at headquarters and

---
216 Rommel (1953), 103. This order for dummy tanks was, however, not his "first" order, as stated by Brigadier Desmond Young, *Rommel* (London: Collins, 1950), 115.

an additional 170 were under construction.²¹⁷ At that point the only real Axis tanks in North Africa were the 80 with the Italian Ariete Division.

The first real German tanks off-loaded in Tripoli on March 11th. These were the 120 (60 medium and 60 light) comprising the two seasoned tank battalions of 5th Panzer Regiment of the Fifth Light Division. At 1100 hours Rommel paraded them in front of Government House in the thronged town square. They drove past in seemingly endless numbers because he had them go around the block several times like some operatic "stage army" to fool any enemy spies. Thence straight to the front. There the real light-tank units were "strengthened" by dummy medium-tanks to fool enemy ground patrols and aerial reconnaissance, which it did—the 5th Light Division's war diary noting that "Intercepted enemy radio messages report having sighted medium tanks. This shows that our deception has worked."²¹⁸

Rommel, knowing his weakness and with poor intelligence that grossly overestimated enemy strength and intent, initially expected to fight a defensive battle, although typically a highly mobile and aggressive one to exploit any enemy weak points. On March 19th Rommel was ordered by Berlin to mount a short drive into the British lines, after his full Panzer division arrived at the end of May. However, Rommel set the timetable back. Misled by intelligence, it did not occur to him that it was the British who considered themselves on the defensive. Consequently he saw an urgent need to preempt before they could set up for what he believed would be their final push.

By March 24th, patrols and reconnaissance in strength had disclosed his enemy to be soft at the front and Rommel began to probe forward. At this point he still had only part of one of his two promised Afrika Korps divisions (with its 120 tanks) and the Italian Ariete division (with its 80). Thanks to ULTRA the British knew Rommel's order of battle as well as the orders from Berlin that held his attack until the end of May and assumed he would obey both orders and the logic of weakness. Instead Rommel launched his attack March 31st, a full month early.

The British were totally surprised by the timing, intent, and ferocious style of Rommel's attack. Although Rommel had intended only a spoiling attack, it was characteristic that he was prepared and willing to exceed his ordered goal by exploiting whatever opportunities might develop during the battle. And, as the British were swiftly beaten piecemeal or retreated at each engagement, he quickly changed his spoiling attack into an all-out offensive. Throughout Rommel used tactical deception to apparent advantage—dummy tanks at Agedabia and "dust clouds which were deliberately stirred up by our troops"

---

217 Irving (1977), 68; Mitcham (1984), 65.
218 Irving (1977), 69.

at Mechill.[219] When the First Battle of Mersa el Brega ended 13 days later, Rommel had advanced 400 miles to the Egyptian frontier.

Even the German high command back in Berlin was surprised by the timing and extent of Afrika Korps' offensive. Rommel had achieved the ultimate in security by keeping his intentions to himself until the last moment, preparing for and reserving the options of offense or defense. This was, of course, the very effective method advocated as early as 1732 by the ever-victorious Marshal de Saxe and practiced as recently as Hitler. Hostile Intelligence services have no direct means of penetrating that particular form of security. But the risk of this kind of "private" security when exercised by subordinate commanders is that it can interfere with higher level strategy. In this case Rommel's unauthorized success could not be denied; and so, ironically, Hitler was forced to drain precious resources from his forthcoming Soviet venture.

■ ■ ■ ■ ■

Next, in May 1941, while both exhausted armies jostled for position, Rommel again concerned himself with camouflage measures:[220]

> To disperse the enemy artillery fire, we installed dummy tanks—mainly in the sector held by the Brescia [a weak Italian infantry division]—and these did in fact soon draw heavy fire from the British artillery. Unfortunately, the troops had no idea of how to use such devices, which must be kept continually moving and not left standing for a fortnight on the same spot. I made repeated visits to the front to try to inculcate in the troops some up-to-date ideas in position warfare appropriate to the conditions they were facing.

■ ■ ■ ■ ■

Forced back by 11 January 1942 to his original starting point on the Cyrenaican-Tripolitanian border by Cunninghams's Operation CRUSADER, Rommel seemed even less fit to counterattack than 10 months earlier in the First Battle of Mersa el Brega. Yet he proceeded to replay the earlier scenario with similar success. Again he expected a British attack, again he moved as quickly as possible to preempt, again kept his plans secret from his officers, allies, superiors, and the enemy. On the 20th, sensing the time was ripe, he decided to go next day and arranged for his Quartermaster to post up orders during the night in every Road Maintenamce Depot in Tripolitania, orders for

---
219 Rommel (1953, 120; Carell (1961), 18.
220 Rommel (1953), 134.

a dawn attack that same morning.[221] And, as before at the Second Battle of Mersa el Brega, Rommel enjoyed similar success, driving the British back (250 miles) with heavier losses (100 British tanks to Rommel's 30).

CASE 43:
Lt-Gen. Rommel, Gazala, North Africa 1942

> Deception measures of all kinds should be encouraged.
> — Rommel, "Rules of Desert Warfare" (1943)

The Battle of Gazala was fought in the Western Desert from 26 May to 15 June 1942. It would become a classic case of surprise achieved by a deception-enhanced "indirect" approach ". By that time Rommel had taken the measure of his British enemy. This included specific insights about his opposite number, British General Wavell. These clues Rommel had gleaned from a translation of Wavell's pamphlet, *Generals and Generalship*. That booklet was based on a series of three lectures that Wavell had given at Cambridge University in 1939 on the eve of the war. It accurately portrayed its author's thinking and priorities about combat planning priorities. Rommel kept a copy in his pocket, which he reread, and closely annotated throughout the North African campaign. This is a case of "knowing one's enemy" that probably reinforced Rommel's natural tendency to work within his opponents' deliberately slower planning & preparation cycle and thereby launch preemptive attacks.

And by this time Rommel had also gained a clear grasp of the value of deception, which he later distilled in a key paragraph in his paper titled "Rules of Desert Warfare."[222]

> Concealment of intentions is of the utmost importance in order to provide surprise for one's own operations and thus make it possible to exploit the time taken by the enemy command to react. Deception measures of all kinds should be encouraged, if only to make the enemy commander uncertain and cause him to hesitate and hold back.

During April Rommel had taken particular personal interest in creating new simulative deception assets. He inspected a tank-repair company, which was then temporarily busy disguising trucks as tanks. He also had a Luftwaffe workshop prepare a prototype device to his specifications. This strange

---
221 Rommel (1953), 180-181.
222 Rommel (1953), 200.

invention was a truck mounting an aircraft engine whose propeller faced to the rear. His headquarters diary recorded that "The C in C is delighted with this design and orders ten such trucks from the Luftwaffe." He planned to use these vehicles to create moving clouds of dust to simulate the movement of a large panzer unit.[223]

By April 15th he already had the outline of his plan:[224]

> We are going to use decoy tactics to cause the enemy to switch the bulk of his forces up [north] to Gazala. ... The killer blow is going to be dealt to them in the south.

On May 12th he explained his detailed plan to a gathering of all his senior commanders:[225]

> Our job is to lure this British field army as far west as possible. We're going to achieve this by creating an impression that we are not going for an outflanking move to the south so much as a frontal break-through in the north. This will oblige the enemy to move up his armor. This is why each phase of our attack is staggered—the first feint by our forces will lure them up to the Gazala end of their line. That will begin at about 2:00 p.m. on X day. Our main force will go in around here [pointing to the desert end of the British line] at dawn the next day.

Although greatly outnumbered by the British forces, the German-Italian force broke through. On 14 June the British began a headlong retreat—the Gazala Gallop—that ended with the encirclement and fall of Tobruck on the 21st and an advance through Mersa el Brega. Too exhausted to press on to Cairo, Rommel stopped to regroup at Alamein. Hitler, having failed to grasp the strategic value that a conquest of Cairo and all Egypt would represent, skimped on reinforcement's for his almost triumphant general. Instead General Rommel had to settle for the baton of a field-marshal.

■ ■ ■ ■ ■

The front now stalemated for several months, the British nervously secure in their Alamein line while both exhausted armies refitted for the next battle, Alam Halfa (Case 45). On July 5th, the British, taking advantage of a German replacement effort, launched a small attack with 40 armored cars and tanks that opened a wedge in the line. The only available blocking force was a single German artillery battery. It stopped the British advance with its last few

---

223 Irving (1977), 162.
224 Quoted in Irving (1977), 162.
225 Quoted in Irving (1977), 164.

rounds; and Rommel, as he says, "immediately gave orders for the extensive use of decoys, including dummy tanks and 88-mm A.A. guns, to take away British taste for further attacks."[226] I don't know that these dummies deterred the British—but they did not renew the attack.

CASE 44:
Hitler, Russia 1941
The Führer plans a strategic deception.

BARBAROSSA, the German invasion of the Soviet Union on 22 June 1941, is a case where surprise was the direct consequence of a closely orchestrated and very large-scale German deception operation, indeed the largest of its kind ever planned or attempted until that time. These became the ultimate shield of secrecy, misleading enemy intelligence about Hitler's intentions after all other details of the BARBAROSSA plan had leaked out through the faulty German security system.

In this case Hitler personally sketched the outline of the deception. It was then planned in detail by the High Command (OKW) and coordinated closely with the Nazi propaganda, diplomatic, and other organizations.[227]

CASE 45:
Brig. De Guingand, Alam Halfa, Egypt 1942
Monty's Chief of Staff devises a ruse.

> We were very "deception minded" in those days.
>
> — De Guingand (1947), 151

Colonel Francis "Freddie" de Guingand, a professional staff officer, first appeared in Cairo in December 1940 where he was assigned to the Joint Planning Staff at Wavell's GHQ. He was promoted brigadier when he succeeded Brig. Shearer as Auchinleck's Director of Military Intelligence at the end of February 1942. Then in late July he was moved up to become Chief of Staff, first to the "Auk" and then in early August, after the latter's relief, to Montgomery with whom he remained until the end of the war. His first job for "Monty" was to oversee the preparations to repel Field-Marshal Rommel's next attack, which was expected in a few weeks.

---

226 Rommel (1953), 250.
227 For the security leaks see Whaley, *Codeword BARBAROSSA* (1973) throughout; and for the deception elements see particularly Chapter 7 and Appendix A.

De Guingand was involved in an amusing non-military deception curtain-raiser. During the late preparatory stage, Prime Minister Churchill stopped off on his return from Moscow to visit Montgomery at his Eighth Army HQ on the desert coast on August 19th. As De Guingand describes it:[228]

> It was found that there was no brandy in the mess, and so an A.D.C. was sent into Alexandria to buy some. A local product was found, and to drink this, one had to have a cast-iron stomach, and a very good head. I'm afraid a little deception was tried out—we were very "deception minded" in those days—and the liquor was poured into an empty bottle bearing the labels of a well-known French brand!

They were very "deception minded" indeed. Alam Halfa had been planned as a holding operation only, buying time for Eight Army to reinforce and train for its own big offensive, LIGHTFOOT, which Montgomery had already scheduled for late October.

In addition to the overall deception plan, Operation SENTINEL,[229] devised by Colonel Clarke's "A Force, Brigadier De Guingand now made his personal contribution, a plan to lure Rommel's armored spearhead into a trap. As he would recall:[230]

> We always produced "going" maps which were layered in colours to show the type of desert in so far as it affected movement. We knew the enemy had captured many of our maps and was making use of them. At the time of [our] retreat to Alamein no "going" maps existed of the area to the rear of our positions. These we produced after we settled in.

Putting together his knowledge of the mapping procedure, interrogation reports that the enemy was using these maps, and the certain expectation of an attack by Rommel, De Guingand planned a trap:

> I, therefore, decided to have made a false "going" map which would link up quite correctly with the maps already in enemy hands, and then to falsify a particular area to suit our plans. The area I selected, in consultation with our Intelligence staff, was one south of Alam Halfa. Due south of the highest point [Hill 132 on Alam Halfa Ridge] was a area of very soft sand. As we appreciated the enemy would make for this ridge I thought that by showing this bad area as good going, the enemy might be

---

[228] Major-General Sir Francis De Guingand, *Operation Victory* (London: Hodder and Stoughton, 1947), 151. And, in general, see also H. O. Dovey, "The False Going Map at Alam Halfa," *Intelligence and National Security*, Vol.4, No.1 (Jan 1989), 165-168.
[229] Cruickshank (1979), 25-26.
[230] De Guingand (1947), 146-1 48.

tempted to send his tanks around that way. It would also give him a shock if he were making for El Hamman, for instead of a "good gallop," he would find himself wallowing in deep sand.

De Guingand had been blessed with almost perfect intelligence on Rommel's intentions and preparatory redeployment. As Rommel saw it:[231]

> ... only small British forces lay in the southern part of the front. Our reconnaissance consistently reported that only weakly mined defenses existed in the south, which would be comparatively easy to penetrate. These positions were to be taken in a night attack by the German and Italian infantry, and the enemy thrown back by armoured formations following immediately behind. Then in a headlong thrust to the east [bypassing Alam Halfa Ridge], the Afrika Korps and part of the Motorized Corps were to win through before morning as far as the area south-west of [the coastal town of] El Hammam [sic], 25 to 30 miles from their starting point.

De Guingand's plan now became operation:

> We had this map secretly printed in very quick time by the energy of an old associate of mine in the M[ilitary] I[intelligence] Directorate in Cairo—Stuart-Menteith. Then we plotted with 13th Corps to have it "captured" by the enemy. In the south, light forces were continually patrolling around the enemy's minefields, and so it was arranged that a scout car should get blown up on a mine, and that the crew should be taken off in another truck. Left in the scout car were soldier's kits and the usual junk, whilst stuffed away in a haversack was an old and dirty "going map" (the fake) covered in tea stains, but quite readable.

To assure feedback on this first stage of the operation, a follow-up patrol was sent out next morning. It reported back to De Guingand that "The car had been ransacked ... and the map had disappeared." Quite true. The German troops in the southern sector had heard nighttime activity in the minefield and sent a patrol to check. With the help of Very Flares to illuminate the minefield they found an abandoned British scout car, obviously wrecked on a mine, with bloodstains on the ground, and various bits of gear including an officer's map case. De Guingand's doctored map—creased and worn and stained with tea-cup rings—was closely examined at Rommel's Forward Headquarters. After checking with their own charts, Rommel's staff were satisfied that it was both

---

231 Rommel (1953), 273.

genuine (because it matched their proven information) and valuable (because it added new information).[232]

The Battle of Alam Halfa began on the moonlit night of 30/31 August when Rommel launched his main attack in the south. He soon realized that "The assault force had been held up far too long by the strong and hitherto unsuspected mine barriers (150,000 mines], and the element of surprise, which had formed the basis of the whole plan, had been lost."[233]

As De Guingand had anticipated, Rommel now changed his plan:[234]

> With the British armour now assembled for immediate action, it was impossible for us to continue with our wide sweep to the east, as our flanks would have been under a constant threat .... This compelled us to decide on an earlier turn to the north than we had intended. The objective of the attack was now set as Hill 132 for the Afrika Korps ....

Wheeling north toward Hill 132, the German armor immediately slowed, struggling through De Guingand's patch of soft sand. Subsequent prisoner interrogation disclosed that the falsified map had led these tanks to the spot, tripling their fuel consumption. De Guingand also soon learned (from ULTRA) that Rommel personally attributed his defeat to fuel shortages. "So", as the perpetrator of this ruse modestly concluded, "it looks as if it probably helped."[235] De Guingand's conclusion was later confirmed by Rommel's own account "Due to the heavy going, the Afrika Korps' petrol stocks were soon badly depleted and at 16.00 hours we called off the attack on Hill 132."[236]

Two weeks later, Maj.-Gen. Ritter von Thoma, the disgruntled commander of Afrika Korps, was captured in no-man's land, possibly a deserter. Talking freely in Montgomery's mess, he confirmed that the false going map had had its intended effect.[237] Here was an example case where the old "Meinertzhagen Haversack Ruse" (Case 34) worked.

CASE 46:
"A" Force, Plan BERTRAM, Alamein, Egypt 1942

Plan BERTRAM was the deception plan for LIGHTFOOT, Lieut.-Gen. Montgomery's decisive Battle of Alamein. It was the most sophisticated and largest-scale deception run up to that time by the Allies in WW2 and would not be surpassed by them in either cunning or magnitude until the Normandy

---
232 Paul Carell, *The Foxes of the Desert* (New York: Dutton, 1961), 254-255, 258.
233 Rommel (1953), 277.
234 Rommel (1953), 277.
235 De Guingand (1947), 148.
236 Rommel (1953), 278.
237 Winston S. Churchill, *The Second World War*, Vol.4 (London: Cassel, 1951), 490.

D-Day BODYGUARD/FORTITUDE ruses two years later. As Major Mure recapped:[238]

> Plan Bertram was ... the complete blueprint of all the plans that were to come. Here the ingredients of strategic deception—bogus order of battle, double agents' reports, misleading W/T [radio] traffic, concentrations of bogus landing craft were to be combined for the first time with the tactical measures—camouflage dummy tank and artillery formations, sonic devices; and, combined for the first time, they worked like clockwork.

The preliminary deception plan was personally designed by "A" Force chief Dudley Clarke in accord with "Monty's" original battle plan. Following his usual procedure, Colonel Clarke designed it to express what his Commander would want the enemy to do and not merely think:[239]

1) To relax his state of immediate vigilance, in favour of a policy of reorganization and reinforcement.

2) To make faulty dispositions, especially to denude his defenses to the north to enable an initial penetration to be made there deep enough to neutralize the effect of 'the devil's garden', the complex of minefields stretching the whole length on the restricted and entirely 'cover-less' front.

Now, in late September, Clarke had to fly off to Washington to brief the American JCS on "global deception" (Case 79), leaving the final planning to his able deputy, Lieut.-Col. Noël Wild.[240] On October 6th Montgomery made a major planning change for his LIGHTFOOT battle, which was scheduled to open the great Alamein campaign that would start on October 23rd.[241]

At Montgomery's Eighth Army headquarters during this redesign phase of the battle, Col. Charles Richardson was chief of plans (G.S.O.1 Plans) and Col. David Strangeways was chief deception officer, liaising with "A" Force. Wild now had to coordinate with these two and suitably readjust the deception. This was readily done and the operation was success.[242]

---

238 Mure (1980), 142.
239 Mure (1980), 132.
240 Delmer (1971), 31-32; Mure (1980), 142.
241 Mure (1980), 131, 139; Delmer (1971), 32.
242 Holt (2004), index; Whaley, *Stratagem* (1969/2007), Case A35; Barkas (1952), 179-216.

CASE 47:
"A" Force blows its camouflage, Alamein, Egypt 1942

> A most elaborate campaign of deception had successfully misled the enemy's Intelligence.
>
> — Tedder, RAF C-in-C, Middle East

Thinking along the lines of Col. Clarke's ruse with the aircraft-struts (Case 12), the "A" Force overall deception plan BERTRAM (see Case 46) for the Battle of Alamein included an ingenious double-bluff. This subordinate Plan MUNASSIB is important as a very rare example of deliberately blowing a camouflage operation to the enemy.

As part of its big effort to simulate a major buildup on the deep desert flank, the "A" Force Camouflage Section erected bogus artillery positions on a large scale, then let German aerial reconnaissance discover these by deliberately faulty placement of camouflage netting. After the enemy discovered the bogus nature of these positions, the camoufleurs gradually introduced real guns under perfect camouflage. Thus the Germans were taken by surprise when their southern front erupted in a real battle. It was, of course, only a diversionary attack but one that the enemy initially mistook for the real one.[243]

CASE 48:
Wing-Commander Winterbotham, ULTRA Security 1942
A security officer plugs a breech of security with a ruse.

RAF Wing-Commander Frederick W. "Freddie" Winterbotham had been an S.I.S. (M.I.6) intelligence officer since 1929, working mainly against Nazi Germany. In 1939 he became Deputy Chief in charge of ULTRA security and dissemination and held that position throughout the war. A cheerful, highly conscientious officer, he does not come through in his three memoirs as particularly bright or innovative. But he did produce one very bright and deceptive thought.[244]

Throughout Rommel's 1942 campaign in North Africa, his greatest continuing shortage was fuel for his tanks and trucks. Enough was being shipped from Italy and Greece; but the problem was that so few of the transports were getting through. The RAF and particularly the Royal Navy were wrecking a terrible toll on this Axis shipping. For example, 70% were lost in March, 44%

---

[243] Barkas (1952),196, 206; Young & Stamp (1984), 73-74; Mure (1980), 141; Holt (2004), 243, 829.

[244] For general autobiographical background see F. W. Winterbotham, *Secret and Personal* (London: William Kimber, 1969) and F. W. Winterbotham, *The Nazi Connection* (London: Weidenfeld & Nicolson, 1978).

in October, and 26% in November. Rommel personally, and the German and even the Italian staffs, soon realized that this was more than British blind luck; they were sure it was the work of spies, Italian traitors. The British were indeed being tipped off to these sailings—port and time of departure, course to be taken, port of destination with expected arrival time, and contents of each ship. But the source of this vital intelligence and the subsequent high score was due almost entirely to their ULTRA readings of the German and Italian military communications that gave all these details.[245]

To prevent the Axis allies from even suspecting their systematic security leak through ULTRA, security SOP dictated that no action of any kind ever be taken that could have been based exclusively on that source. Maritime operations posed a special problem with its own deceptive solution. For each enemy target vessel or convoy whose movements were discovered from ULTRA it was deemed necessary to direct a spotter aircraft to its approximate position. Then, only if the spotter radioed a sighting and was presumably seen, were the nearby warships or bombers sent in to attack. This was a clever ruse but a ruthless one; because the unwitting aerial observers were sent on virtually suicidal flights, their radioed sightings, which necessarily gave their own position, immediately attracting nearby land-based Luftwaffe fighter aircraft to destroy them.

Now, during Rommel's long retreat to Tunisia following his defeat at Alamein in early November 1942, an incident occurred that risked the ULTRA secret. As Winterbotham describes it:[246]

> After about the third of these desperation convoys had been sunk without trace a dense fog came down when the next one to go out had not long left Naples. Quite obviously an aeroplane couldn't be expected to see or be seen by the convoy through a thick fog. Malta left the operation as late as possible in the hope that the fog would clear, but as the convoy was nearing the African coast, action had to be taken. It was unfortunate, from Ultra's point of view, that the RAF and the Navy turned up in a dense fog in exactly the right spot at the same moment and sank the ships, and not before one of them had reported this rather strange occurrence. This made Kesselring [the German commander in the Mediterranean theater] really cross and also a little suspicious. He sent a signal to the Abwehr, the German Military Security Service in Berlin, asking them to investigate these strange circumstances which pointed to some leakage about the sailings of his precious convoys.

---

245 Lewin (1978), 266; F. W. Winterbotham, *The Ultra Secret* (New York: Harper & Row, 1974), 79-80.
246 Winterbotham (1974), 80.

At this delicate point, Winterbotham intervened by reinventing a neat counterintelligence switch on the old agent provocateur ruse.

> I took the precaution of having a signal sent to a mythical agent in Naples in a cypher which the Germans would be able to read congratulating him on his excellent information and raising his pay. I can imagine the Naples waterfront was not a happy place for a while, but we could not afford to let up and the ships continued to fail to reach Rommel. Eventually the matter died down, no doubt because the Abwehr could not get any further with it. We did hear some time later that the Italian admiral in charge of the port had been relieved of his job on suspicion of himself giving the information away. It was reassuring to know that the idea we were reading their signals had not occurred to them.

CASE 49:
Flight Lieutenant Cholmondeley, Sicily 1943
An RAF intelligence officer with Twenty Committee cooks up
MINCEMEAT.

The Allies decided at the Casablanca Conference in January 1943 that their next target would be Sicily. It was now Deception's job to convince the Germans, specifically Hitler, that the real target was either Greece or Sardinia or both. Several stratagems were played to this end.

The overall deception planning was the responsibility of Col. Dudley Clarke's "A" Force in Cairo. However, in London, the LCS and Twenty Committee contributed one plan. This was Plan TROJAN HORSE, which was later renamed MINCEMEAT, and became world famous after the war as "The Man Who Never Was."[247]

Ironically, or so I have been told, TMWNW came about as a kind of practical joke. Some members of LCS, having free time and wishing to help out, began to wonder just how far the Abwehr could be pushed. Noting that the Abwehr had swallowed most of the simple deceptions employed up to then, they thought it a good opportunity to test the limits of the enemy's gullibility. "A" Force was already laying on its full array of stratagems and ruses, and LCS thought why not try out one of its own. What, after all, was there to lose?[248]

The original inspiration for MINCEMEAT lay in the memory of Major Ronald Wingate, Executive Director of the LCS. As a Middle East expert, he recalled

---
[247] The most accurately and comprehensively detailed account is Macintyre (2009). Second best is Smyth (2010).
[248] BW conversations with Prof. H. Wentworth Eldredge, early 1973.

the old so-called Meinertzhagen Haversack Ruse (Case 34) and proposed that a similar ploy be used to plant false documents on the enemy."[249]

Wingate's proposal was passed along to Twenty Committee to see what, if anything, could be done along these lines. Fortunately, the members had already given the matter some thought, although it had aborted ("When Deception Fails", Case 1.5.1.1). It had been Flight-Lieutenant Charles Cholmondeley's suggestion to parachute a dead body equipped with radio set, which, if German Intelligence tried to play it back, would be known for the deception it was, thereby enabling the British to play their own secret game. It aborted for purely technical reasons. Twenty Committee also recalled that a potentially serious compromise of Allied plans had occurred the previous September when a British courier carrying real plans had been lost at sea, recovered by the Spaniards, but both body & plans returned without evident tampering.

Combining Cholmondeley's scheme and the French courier fact, the Admiralty representative on Twenty Committee, Lieut.-Commander Ewen Montagu, suggested "Why shouldn't we get a body, disguise it as a staff officer, and give him really high-level papers which will show clearly that we are going to attack somewhere else [other than Sicily]."[250]

There was one final problem about "Major Martin". The body, which had died following long exposure, looked like what it was—the corpse of a man who in life had been unathletic and unhealthy, hardly fitting the image of a Royal Marine officer. Montagu's finest moment came when queried by a senior officer on this point. Montagu squelched this objection by saying, "He does not have to look like an officer—only like a staff officer."[251]

CASE 50:
Field-Marshal Alexander, Italy 1943-45
The Commander encourages deception for an entire campaign.
General Sir Harold Alexander had been the new British Army field commander in Burma for less than two months when on 30 April 1942 he received his first indoctrination on deception, at least in a combat situation. Col. Peter Fleming had come out from Delhi to explain and get permission for Operation ERROR (Case 15). In the midst of retreat Alexander had little time but listened closely, quickly understood, approved, and provided logistical support.[252]

---

249 Interview with R. Wingate as reported in Brown (1975), 279-280, 522-523.
250 Montagu (1954), 25.
251 Montagu (1954), 30.
252 Connell (1969), 211; Hart-Davis (1974), 266-267.

In August Alexander took over as C-in-C Near East Command at the same time that Lieut.-Gen. Montgomery got the subordinate command of Eighth Army. Alexander soon met Col. Clarke and discovered "A" Force and its extraordinary deception capabilities. Although he did not personally contribute to the subsequent deceptions, Alexander henceforward became an enthusiastic supporter of his deception planners. After the war he declared that Clarke had "done as much to win the war as any other officer".[253]

With the Allied landings in southern Italy in September 1943, Field-Marshal Alexander got command of a second army, the U.S. Fifth in addition to British Eighth. Although each had its own tactical deception capabilities, with two armies to deal with, Alexander henceforward coordinated their overall strategic planning, including their deceptions. His chief deception planner was Colonel Michael Crichton, seconded to Alexander's HQ in Italy from "A" Force HQ in Cairo where he had learned his skills as co-Deputy Director under Dudley Clarke. Crichton had first met Clarke in 1925 when both were lieutenants. Early in WW2 he served in the Western Desert on the Intelligence staff of 7th Armoured Division, working closely with the Long Range Desert Group. Then in 1941, Major Crichton joined "A" Force where his empathy and wry humor were well appreciated.[254]

As Alexander's two armies began their slow advance up the narrow, difficult spiny boot of Italy in the face of determined German resistance, it was his chance to "sell the dummy" left and right of the central mountain chain. For each new offensive he exercised the deception-covered alternatives of either jumping off from his right flank (east coast) with British 8th Army or from his left (west coast) with U.S. 5th Army. He also had the subsidiary alternative of an amphibious "end-run" on either coast. Throughout the long campaign Alexander employed both sets of alternatives with greater or lesser success but, with one exception,[255] always gaining at least some significant degree of surprise, as measured by thy less than optimum concentrations of enemy troops that opposed most of his main attacks.[256]

CASE 51:
Lt. Cmdr. Douglas Fairbanks Jr, Operation ROSIE, Genoa, Italy 1944
An American movie star steps off the screen to found the Navy Seals and lead them in deceptive battle.

---

253 Mure (1980), 38.
254 Mure (1980), 48, 102-103.
255 See Whaley, *When Deception Fails* (FDDC, 2010), Case 3.2.3.
256 Jackson (1967), which gives a battle-by-battle account of Alexander's surprise-through-deception strategy.

Seven weeks following the main Allied landings in Normandy in June 1944, a secondary but large-scale landing (3 U.S. and 7 French divisions, plus a British brigade) offloaded from 330 ships onto the French Riviera on August 15th. As usual at this time, it was shielded by an elaborate deception plan—both strategic and tactical.[257]

The U.S. Eighth Fleet in the Mediterranean was given the naval part of the Genoa deception plan. This was the task of the fleet's deception officer, 34-year old Lieutenant Commander Douglas Fairbanks Jr.

First, to separate this fighting sailor from his celebrity image as movie star and son of a movie star, let's look at the opening words of the demobilization citation he received in 1945 from the Secretary of the Navy, James Forrestal:[258]

> Commander Fairbanks assisted materially in the original development of tactical deception and diversionary warfare, conducting research and developing the operating procedure of numerous special devices. He recruited and organized volunteer technicians in the first 'beach-jumper' unit with a special school for their training.

A movie actor is not a bad choice for a deceptioneer. Actors, particularly cinema actors are at least marginally involved in one of the major arts of illusion. Actors like Fairbanks are surely more promising recruits—all other things being equal—than, say, MBAs or PhD political scientists.

With only two gunboats, four PTs, and a command ship, Fairbanks steered toward Genoa, noisily simulating a large task force and landing 67 commandos near Cannes at 0140 hours. Although the commandos were captured, Radio Berlin credited Fairbanks with the command of "four or five large battleships."[259]

CASE 52:
Dr. R. V. Jones, channel deception for "Gee", 1942
The RAF deception planner camouflages a navigational device.
In March 1942 the RAF introduced its first synchronized radio-pulse navigational system to guide their bombers from bases in Britain to targets in Germany. This system, called Gee, superficially resembled the Luftwaffe's Knickebein beam navigational system, which the Germans knew the British had recently mastered.

---

257 Whaley (1969), A41 0-A-41 3; Cruickshank (1979), 165-169.
258 Brian Connell, *Knight Errant: A Biography of Douglas Fairbanks, Jr.* (Garden City, NY: Doubleday, 1955), 145.
259 B. Connell (1955), 155, 160-173; Fairbanks in Young & Stamp (1989), 167-168; Samuel Eliot Morison, *History of United States Naval Operations in World War II*, Vol.11 (Boston: Little, Brown, 1957), 250.

To delay German efforts to fathom Gee's simple electronic secret and thereby immediately be able to jam it, Dr. R. V. Jones devised an ingenious two-part deception scheme. First he simulated a navigational device called Jay that worked on the German's own Knickebein beam principle, thereby hoping to flatter the enemy into mistaking a decoy for a sincere imitation. Second, Jones simultaneously dissimulated Gee to make it seem the same as Jay. Gee's disguise was both electronic (to fool the German radar stations) and physical (mislabeling the actual components so that any recovered from downed bombers would be mistaken for an ordinary radio transceiver).

Jones' German counterparts were so well duped by Gee that they wasted five months trying to discover an appropriate counter-measure—two months longer than even the most optimistic British estimates had allowed.[260]

CASE 53:
Dr. Jones versus the V-Bombs, England 1944
The deception planner diverts Luftwaffe Intelligence.

In 1944 the Luftwaffe's V-1 campaign against London pumped in 2,340 of these "Flying Bombs", killing 5,500 and seriously injuring 16,000. A subsequent operations research analysis showed that casualties would have been as much as half again as many except for the enemy's persistent misperception that most hits were overshooting the intended aiming point, Tower Bridge at the geographical center of the city. In fact, most bombs were falling short, onto the less densely populated southern suburbs.[261]

To adjust range, the Germans depended on individual time-and-place bomb reports from their spies in London. Unknown to them, all these agents were under British control.

Dr. R. V. Jones conceived and designed a scheme of plausible agent reports by keeping the hits consistent with any German photo-reconnaissance evidence but faking their timings. This induced the Luftwaffe to steadily readjust their real aiming point ever further short of their intended one, ending up four miles south.[262]

Jones' plan was begun in coordination with Twenty Committee, specifically two of its members: Flight-Lieutenant Charles Cholmondeley, the R.A.F. representative; and Sir Findlater Stewart, the Home Defence Executive representative.

---

260 Price (1977), 98-104; Jones (1978), 217-222.
261 Jones (1978), 423.
262 Irving (1965), 250-252, 255-258; Delmer (1971), 203-214; Jones (1978), 420-424; Jones (1989), 133-135; and Montagu (1978), 158-161.

The operation nearly aborted when it came to the attention of the Cabinet. However, Jones proceeded as if he was unaware of this potenial snag.[263]

Had Jones been playing with lives? Yes, but in patriotic disregard for his own personal interests. As he explained:[264]

> The episode had forced a choice on me personally, for my mother and father lived in Herne Hill very near the mean point of impact of the flying bombs. By trying to persuade Wachtel to keep it there, I knew I was increasing the risk to them; but I also knew that they would never have wanted me to do otherwise, and so the deception went ahead.

CASE 54:
Maj. Ingersoll and the Battle of the Bulge, France 1944
Wherein an American ex-publisher improvises the "Two Pattons Ruse"[265]

Improvisation of a deception plan in its extreme form was thrust upon Major Ralph Ingersoll during the critical Battle of the Bulge. It was December 1944 and the German army had just broken through the Allies' weak point in a surprise attack. One measure of this surprise was that Col. William "Billy" Harris was away on other matters. Harris headed Gen. Omar Bradley's 12th U.S. Army Group's "Special [that is, deception] Plans Section". So, at this crucial moment, the Section's command devolved upon Maj. Ingersoll.

On December 19th General Eisenhower went to Bradley's rear HQ at Verdun to meet Bradley and Patton and decide on a strategy. Ingeroll was present at the momentous 11 A.M. meeting. Battle-eager Lt. Gen. Patton assured Eisenhower and Bradley that he could rush his powerful Third Army north and stop the enemy advance. Patton's two senior commanders were doubtful because of the immense logistical problem but recognized that desperate measures were needed. So they unleashed Patton.

Urgency demanded that Patton's elaborate movement orders to his corps and division commanders would have to go out over his radio nets "in clear" (uncoded), despite the certainty that the German signals intelligence teams would overhear.

Everyone involved knew it was too late to mount any conventional deception operation to cover this counterattack. Nevertheless, General Bradley turned to Major Ingersoll and asked, "Is there anything you and your people can think

---

263 Jones (1978), 421-422.
264 Jones (1989), 135.
265 BW interview with Ralph Ingersoll, 12 May 1973. See also Roy Hoopes, *Ralph Ingersoll: A Biography* (New York: Atheneum, 1985), 304; and Whaley & Bell (1982), 379-381, where—misled by Ingersoll's exaggerations—I dubbed this the "Five Patton's Ruse". Ingersoll's memory had evidently improved his original deception plan.

of to throw the Germans off—about where they [Patton's divisions] are going to strike?" Ingersoll replied "Yes, sir. We can do"—he hesitated—"something." Bradley was momentarily silent before simply ordering, "Then do it."[266]

Ingersoll later told me (and still later his authorized biographer) that the idea had come to him in a flash. To me he explained what had inspired him. Realizing during the meeting that time would be too short for any conventional deception, he had been trying to think of some alternative. His mind lit on the recent example of the vast confusion to German military intelligence engendered on D-Day by the unintentional scattering of the two American and British airborne divisions.[267] With this thought in mind, Ingersoll suddenly conceived—indeed invented—the unprecedented ruse of The Two Pattons.[268] He personally codenamed the operation KODAK because he intended that it confuse the enemy by giving them a "doubleexposure".[269]

The only resource available to Ingersoll was Special Plans' operational deception unit, the 23rd Headquarters Special Troops. It was too late for their usual panoply of visual and sound spoofs. Radio deception working alone would have to do the job. Accordingly 19 officers and 20 enlisted men were detached from the 23rd's Signal Company, rushed forward, and dispersed among advance units of Patton's Third Army. An additional 11 officers and 205 EM provided support further back. It was, as the official history called it, "a big (29 sets), loose radio show".[270]

These radio operators normally spent their time simulating "notional" (fictitious) U.S. Army units in a largely successful effort to dupe the enemy to waste precious resources by either advancing or retreating from these phantoms. But now, for two days, December 22nd and 23rd Ingersoll had them imitate two real units—the 80th Infantry Division and the 4th Armored Division that were spearheading Patton's advance. The 23rd bogus radio show was timed to start when these divisions' radio nets began broadcasting "in clear".

The real 80th was getting ready to jump off due north from Luxembourg, and the real 4th was preparing to roll up from Arlon to effect its historic relief of the 101st Airborne Division trapped in Bastogne. "The 23rd mission was to show ... the presence of the 80th Infantry and 4th Armored Divisions slightly northeast of Luxembourg and in position to forestall any German plans of extending their counterattack southwest through Echternach".[271]

---

266 Hoopes (1985), 304.
267 See Whaley, *When Deception Fails* (FDDC, Mar 2010), Case 2.1.3.
268 Elsewhere I dubbed this the "Five Patton's Ruse", an error corrected by reading the recently declassified official history of the 23rd Hq Special Troops. In my interview with Ingersoll he had, as Eldredge warned me, exaggerated.
269 *Official History of the 23rd Headquarters Special Troops* (1945), 23.
270 *Official History 23rd* (1945), 23, and also Enclosures I and V.
271 *Official History 23rd* (1945), 23.

In effect they presented German intelligence with two General Pattons, each approaching the Bulge from a slightly different direction. Of course, the Germans quickly understood that a radio game was being played against them, but they were still dazzled by the two fake divisions advancing eastward of the two real ones. In the event, the Germans were able to keep track of only one of Patton's several advancing divisions. All others were either lost entirely on the German battle maps or, worse, mislocated. Consequently Patton was able to gain substantial tactical surprise that helped him break the back of the Wehrmacht's last offensive.

Long after the war, I interviewed Ingersoll about his role in military deception. The Two Pattons story—unpublished at that time—emerged only as an afterthought when Ingersoll said apologetically that, while proud of his improvisation, he did not class it as "deception", which he defined as making the victim certain but wrong. Instead he chose to make the enemy merely uncertain, confused, and hope for the best. Ingersoll's unique ruse does indeed fit one category of deception, the one called "Dazzle" in the Bell-Whaley typology.[272] That is the least ideal category—the ideal being, what I have called, making one's enemy "certain, decisive, and wrong." True, it was a desperate measure provoked by a desperate situation, precisely the type of rare circumstance where magician Rick Johnsson's Too Perfect Corollary applies.[273]

CASE 55:
Lt. Col. Truly, Crossing the Rhine, Germany 1945
An American deception liaison officer concocts a tactical cover plan.

Operation VIERSEN was the last, most extensive, most sophisticated, and one of the two most successful of the 21 operations conducted by Gen. Bradley's deception unit. It was conceived, planned, and coordinated by Lt. Col. Merrick H. Truly, the 23rd Headquarters Special Troops liaison officer with the G-3 section of Lieutenant General Simpson's U.S. 9th Army, which was attached at that time to Field-Marshal Montgomery's 21st Army Group.[274]

An Infantry "regular", Truly had joined the 23rd back in the States on 20 January 1944 as Executive Officer. He held that position until October 30th when he was switched to liaison duty. The 23rd had begun detaching some of its officers to work directly with the units they serviced to assure tailoring their deceptions to fit the precise needs of these units and to win the cooperation of

---

272 Whaley (1982), 184.
273 For a full account of the Too Perfect Principle see Whaley, *When Deception Fails: The Theory of Outs* (FDDC, Aug 2010).
274 *Official History of the 23rd Headquarters Special Troops* (1945), 29, and Enclosure I; and Holt (2004), index under "VIERSEN".

their commanders in such matters as radio silence and removing the identifying patches and markings from all uniforms and vehicles.

Truly's assignment was to give cover to the assault troops spearheading Monty's long planned prestige crossing of the Rhine. The real crossing was to take place opposite Wesel and would be undertaken by two crack infantry divisions, the U.S. 30th and 79th. Truly's plan, Operation VIERSEN, would have the 23rd simulate a full-scale build-up for a crossing at a different point. Its "notional" (fictitious) divisions deployed nearly 400 rubber vehicles and radioed information implying heavy road traffic while engineer units built real bridging equipment.

On the night of March 23rd, while Montgomery slept and Churchill, Eisenhower. Field-Marshal Alanbrooke, and General Simpson watched from the near shore, the two assault divisions crossed with only 31 casualties. The enemy had been completely surprised. The G2s of 9th Army and both divisions agreed that the deception had worked. It would be the 23rd last operation of the war.

CASE 56:
Col. Fleming's Operation CLOAK, Burma 1945

As seen above in Case 15, Colonel Peter Fleming's "D" Division had, for several reasons, much difficulty selling deception to the Japanese forces in Burma. However his last major effort was both his finest job and the most successful.[275]

Beginning in late 1944 Mountbatten began his final offensive—Operation CAPITAL—to drive the Japanese from Burma. The crucial phase would be the difficult river crossing of the wide Irrawaddy. Detailed planning and command of this phase—Operation EXTENDED CAPITAL—was in the hands of the 14th Army under Lieutenant-General Sir William J. Slim.

Accordingly, in mid-December 1944, Gen. Slim began planning his great offensive to cross the Irrawaddy River and cut off the Japanese forces in northern Burma. The overall deception plan had, as usual, two elements: a strategic plan to mask his intent to cross that river[276] and a tactical one (Plan CLOAK) to conceal the specific point of crossing. The details were developed by Fleming's "D" Division back in Delhi.

As his army neared the Irrawaddy, Slim assumed, correctly, that the enemy would realize that his next move would be to cross the river. They would also station a light screen of garrisons and patrols—to act as a detection tripwire—

---
275 Hart-Davis (1974), 285.
276 Major-General S. Woodburn Kirby, *The War Against Japan*, Vol.4 (London: Her Majesty's Stationery Office, 1965), 173-174, 181, 255.

along their lengthy river-bank. Moreover they could, and would, deploy their main force as mobile reserves able to quickly descend on and destroy the British beachhead before it could consolidate. Nevertheless, Slim achieved a strategic surprise by his crossing on 13 February that so disrupted the Japanese strategy that they were forced into complete withdrawal from their generally favorable defensive positions along the river. He achieved surprise only because of a most successful, comprehensive deception plan.

Slim's 14th Army deception plan was the key to surprise and victory. Knowing that the Japanese expected an offensive, expected it soon, and expected it to involve only a single main crossing at one point, Slim wisely concentrated his effort to mislead his enemy about the site of his real crossing at Nyaungu.

The 14th Army used the same sort of comprehensive, carefully coordinated deception operation first used by Montgomery at Alamein (Case 46), namely camouflaged bases, covert deployments, counterfeit units, fake radio traffic, and a premature feint attack to draw the enemy's reserves to the wrong end of the battle-line. Each unit, from corps to division, had its own part to play and was responsible for designing and carrying out its own deception operations synchronized and coordinated with the general plan. The key was CLOAK, the specific deception plan devised by IV Corps to mask its crossing. Plan CLOAK is reproduced in its entirety below in Appendix C.

The degree of surprise is measured by the fact that with approximate parity in unit strength—5 divisions in British 14th Army to 5 divisions in Japanese Burma Area Army—along the active portion of the Irrawaddy-front, the British were able to concentrate and move 2 divisions and 1 brigade across at a point where the Japanese mustered only a single under-strength regiment.

The operation had been a complete success. The commander of Japanese 15th Army, Lt. Gen. Katamura had gotten only incomplete, conflicting, and false intelligence on the various movements of his enemy's units. Specifically, he had no intelligence on the whereabouts of IV Corps and concluded that two of its four divisions had taken such heavy casualties that they had been withdrawn from further operations.[277]

Plan CLOAK has the curious distinction of being the first Allied deception planning document to have been published complete in its original form. On the surface it is astonishing that it appears in the official British history published in 1965, long before any of the Allies even acknowledged the details of deception. However, CLOAK'S cover had already been blown by the newly independent Government of India in its own official history of the war.[278] After

---

277 Kirby, Vol.4 (1965), 186, 189.
278 P.N. Khera & S.N. Prasad, *The Reconquest of Burma, June 1944-August 1945*, Vol.2 (Calcutta: Combined Inter-Services Historical Section [India & Pakistan], 1959), 260, 499-502.

all, it was Indian 7th Division that had been the principal unit involved in the deception, and key members of the staff would have been witting. At any event, this document is sufficiently interesting for the light it throws on the way the planner thought through and wrote out a plan that it is reproduced below in Appendix B. It also proves that the British wrote out their deception plans in the same way and with the same format as if they had been real plans, which is exactly what several of their top planners argued should be the case.

CASE 57:
Brigadier Yadin, Palestine 1948
The Israeli Director of Operations remembers Liddell Hart In the nick of time.

With their northern front now secure and a cease-fire on the east, the new Israeli Army concentrated for its final offensive in the south—Operation AYIN (or HOREV as it is also known). Its goals were specified in the directive of 10 December 1948 to be nothing less than the final defeat of the Egyptian forces and their expulsion from southern Palestine. On that front, 5 Israeli brigades faced 4 Egyptian, three of which were clustered along the coast and only one inland. All preparations were to be completed on December 16th. Zero hour was set originally for the night of the 20th/21st; but, at the last moment, was put off one night because of intense rain. This December 10th directive was issued by Brigadier Yigael Yadin, the Director of Operations.

Yadin revealed immediately after the war that AYIN had been planned and coordinated at the center by himself in conscious emulation of Liddell Hart's general strategy of "indirect approach" and specific principle of "alternative goals", including the ruses and diversions that can be played with the latter.[279] Moreover, AYIN was also specifically conceived as a replication of Allenby's brilliant Third Battle of Gaza (see Case 33), which Liddell Hart had cited as a prime example of indirect approach using alternative goals.[280]

Yadin's plan was to capitalize on the Egyptian expectation that the main attack would be directed at the coast. To do this he mounted a convincingly large attack on the night of December 22nd to take hill 86 astride the Egyptian coastal road to Gaza. The one Israeli brigade assigned this mission was able to keep the three Egyptian coastal brigades fully occupied on the coast throughout most of the operation.

Even when the Israeli battalion was driven off Hill 86 on the afternoon of D+1, the ruse was only enhanced. The Egyptians found a copy of the operation order of the Hill 86 attack on the body of the slain battalion deputy commander. This

---
279 Yadin (1949/54).
280 Colonel Netanel Lorch, *The Edge of the Sword: Israel's War of Independence, 1947-1949* (New York: Putnam's, 1961), 408.

order, which concealed its diversionary nature from friend and foe alike, only confirmed for the Egyptians that the Israeli offensive was indeed aimed at the coast.[281]

Moreover, the initial Israeli airstrikes and naval bombardment concentrated on the coast. The deception now even extended to the Israeli press, which joined the Egyptians in presuming the Israeli objective was to isolate and then role up the Gaza strip.[282]

Meanwhile, the real Israeli attack was to be mounted 50 miles inland with a drive from Beersheba to Auja and thence fanning out through the Negev to take the Egyptians far to their rear. After a 24-hour delay due to flooding, this attack launched on December 25th.

Yadin's new-found philosophy proved so successful that it prevailed throughout the final phases of the campaign. The Israelis fully exploited their fluid follow-through by improvising ever new diversions in keeping with the alternative objectives principle, thereby "selling the dummy" right and left along their axis of advance. Operation AYIN ended on January 7th as a decisive victory that ended the first Arab-Israeli war. Moreover this 16-day campaign brought success for no greater casualties than the Israeli's costly previous indecisive campaigns. The Israeli Army was beginning to master the art of deception.

CASE 58:
Col. Haney, Guatemala 1954
The CIA's field director invents "token insurgency".

The CIA's main covert mission in 1954 was to overthrow the Communist-leaning Guatemalan Government of President Jacobo Arbenz Guzman. This task fell in the jurisdiction of the so-called Plans Division, i.e., covert operations. Plans was headed at that time by 45year old Frank Gardner Wisner.

Wisner had been with OSS as mission chief in Istanbul during WW2 and in Germany afterwards. Following a brief return to law practice, in 1948 he joined the newly formed CIA where he succeeded Allen Dulles in 1951 as DDP, the CIA Deputy Director heading the Plans Division. Wisner was not only in charge of the Guatemala operation but has been plausibly credited as being its main deception planner.[283]

Albert Haney, a powerful six-footer married to a wealthy heiress, resigned in 1940 from his career as a businessman in Chicago to join U.S. Army counterintelligence. Assigned to the Panama Canal Zone, he gained a

---
281 Lorch (1961), 411-412.
282 Lorch (1961), 413.
283 Author's recollection of conversation in 1969 with Richard M. Bissell Jr, author of the official CIA history of the operation and Wisner's successor in 1958 as DDP.

reputation for his ability to control Axis agents there. Haney apparently preferred the world of espionage to the business world for, after the war and to his wife's dismay, he joined the newly formed CIA. Haney was assigned to Ecuador and Chile, where they lived according to his wife's expensive tastes. In 1951 Haney was reassigned to Seoul, South Korea. The irate wife refused to follow and quickly divorced. The Korean War was underway and Colonel Haney was assigned to create and direct behind-the-lines guerrilla operations. He recruited as his aide "Rip" Robertson, a CIA paramilitary instructor who had been working on Saipan. With Haney's approval, Robertson, an ex-college football star, took pleasure in going with his Korean guerrillas into enemy territory. These operations were sufficiently effective to win Haney further kudos from the agency.[284]

Haney invented a remarkable new type of stratagem, one that Dr. Ernst Halperin has dubbed "token insurgency" and what I later came to call "simulated guerrilla warfare". The plan was conceived as pure deception: to break Arbenz's will by convincing him that an irresistible U.S.-backed force had invaded Guatemala and was about to topple his regime. The necessary "stage" army was provided by an ill-trained rabble of some 150 Guatemalan emigres nominally led by the CIA'S stooge, the incompetent Colonel Carlos Castillo-Armas. Critics of this operation have missed the point that lack of training and leadership qualities were irrelevant to this band's real mission.

The fact of U.S. backing was made plain to Arbenz by a handful of U.S. war-surplus pilots and planes and the colorful semi-public maneuverings of Ambassador John Puerifoy. Simultaneously, the legal fiction of non-involvement was preserved by the translucent cover of ex-U.S. Army "advisers" and American "volunteer" pilots flying planes "sold" to the fully cooperative Nicaraguan Government while Ambassador Henry Cabot Lodge lied to the UN Security Council on D+2 that:[285] "... the situation does not involve aggression but is a revolt of Guatemalans against Guatemalans" and categorically denied U.S. support of the rebels.

Amidst a fanfare of publicity, the insurgent band "invaded" on June 18th, then just 6 miles across the Nicaraguan border immediately and quietly bivouacked. Yet a calculated, propaganda campaign had the world's press reporting the insurgents' advance to success after success. To hide the sham of this "invasion" two essential steps were taken. First, all journalists were excluded from the "front"; and, second, the radio communications of the

---

[284] Stephen Schlesinger & Stephen Kinzer, *Bitter Fruit: The Untold Story of the American Coup in Guatemala* (Garden City, New York: Doubleday, 1982), 109. Most of the Schlesinger-Kinzer information on Haney and his Guatemala planning came from an unpublished manuscript, "Spymaster's Odyssey: The World of Allen Dulles" by Richard Harris Smith.

[285] *New York Times*, 21 June 1954, p.3. The U.S. State Department had earlier made similar disavowal of U.S. involvement. See New York Times, 20 Jun 1954, p.1.

1,700-man Guatemalan Army were monitored and false messages fed back into the channels. Meanwhile the few real military acts were also primarily psychological—sweeps over the capital by CIA planes, which dropped only leaflets on D-day but soon added some noisy but light and selective bombing and straffing. (An attempt to knock out the pro-Arbenz radio tower failed.) The CIA's phantom guerrilla army suffered one KIA, a courier.

The effect of this giant hoax was to so confuse or, rather, selectively mislead President Arbenz that he was unable to make appropriate much less effective military or political decisions. Moreover, those few and belated decisions he did make were dysfunctional, serving only to discredit him with the general public, the middle class, and the army. On June 27th, after 9 days of watching their panicked President, the army finally moved on its own, forcing Arbenz' resignation and seeking a solution acceptable to the U.S.

In retrospect this operation as actually run implies that Wisner had meticulously and consciously planned it. His successor as DDP, having read the official post-mortem on Operation SUCCESS, is not so sure. Richard M. Bissell Jr has disclosed his impression that, while Wisner's plan was a good one, he had more-or-less cobbled it together on a hit-or-miss basis, working more instinctively than with conscious rationality.[286]

CASE 59:
O/C Eamon Timoney, Northern Ireland
The IRA'S Officer Commanding Derry plans a diabolical ambush.

Eamon J. Timoney is a small, wiry Irishman with a wry wit and quick mind. He had been a railway worker in Northern Ireland. A member of the IRA, he served as Officer Commanding (OC) for County Derry during the "Troubles" in Northern Ireland in the 1950s. Although officially a "terrorist"—a label my friend does not deny—he was, in fact, a deception-minded guerrilla thinker of excellence. IRA resources at that time were slim indeed; few trained men with obsolescent weapons, short even on such simple terror weapons as dynamite—and old, unstable dynamite at that. IRA operational planning was not noted—neither earlier, then, nor later—for clever deception. Its deceptive SOP was almost exclusively limited to simple covert ambush. Eamon was about to think differently.

Mr. Timoney and his small IRA team highjacked a moving freight ("goods") train and derailed it. Clever. But that train wasn't the target, only the lure. The real target was the "breakdown train" that would be sent to fix the damage. Timoney, as an old railway man himself, knew the Irish rail line had only one of these pieces of equipment capable of handling a derailment. Destroying

---
286 Interview with Bissell by Halperin and Whaley.

it would cause maximum inconvenience. But, bad luck for them, they were unable to attack the relief train.[287] Consequently, because Timoney's invention of the "double ambush" had aborted, it did not become part of the lore of terrorist tactics, a bit of field craft that would have to wait for the Warrenpoint Ambush of 1979 (Case 22).

Timoney next turned his planning from railways to shipping, where he again saw a vulnerability that could be exploited with his small resources. He noticed that the passage into a local harbor had a very narrow choke-point and figured that one medium sized ship sunk at that point would block the entire harbor for a considerable time. This plan aborted when Timoney was accidentally "lifted" in a random police raid and then identified as IRA. He spent the next few years in Crumlin Road Prison where he took a correspondence course in accounting. After serving his sentence, Timoney emigrated to the USA to pursue his new profession of accountant and become a citizen.

In 1979 I was co-manager of a counterterrorist role-playing game directed by Dr. Robert H. Kupperman at Georgetown University's Center for Strategic and International Studies. The three teams, particularly the terrorist team, comprised most of America's top experts on counterterrorism plus the Israeli Prime Minister's senior expert. Unknown to the players, Eamon Timoney was hidden away in the game administration as a most efficient Message Center Chief. During the two days of play, he routed the several hundred messages passed by the two playing teams (terrorist and U.S.) to the Control Group. Reading these messages as they crossed his desk, Timoney was surprised to see how slow the teams were to recognize each other's vulnerabilities and to exploit these through either action or deception. He frequently called me aside, saying "Look here, why don't they consider doing X?" In each case, to the credit of the American experts, one player or another did eventually suggest the point; and the team would then discuss and decide to do just what Timoney had anticipated by an hour or two. To me this was a dramatic demonstration of the difference between the thinking of the field operator and that of chairborne "experts." Or, perhaps, Timoney simply had the most deceptive mind present—certainly it was the quickest.

CASE 60:
Maj.-Gen. Dayan and the Sinai Campaign, Egypt 1956
The Israeli Chief of Staff plans a strategic surprise.
Having given a detailed analysis of this campaign (Operation KADESH) elsewhere, I refer the reader to that study.[288]

---

287 BW conversations with Timoney, New York City, 1979.
288 Whaley, *Stratagem* (1969/2007), Case A63.

CASE 61:
Defense Minister Dayan and the Six-Day War, Israel 1967
Dayan does it again at the level of grand strategy.

Having given a detailed analysis of this campaign elsewhere, I refer the reader to that study.[289]

CASE 62:
President Anwar Sadat, Israel 1973
A President plans a strategic surprise.

> The fox has many tricks, and the hedgehog has only one, but that is best of all.
>
> — Erasmus, *Adaaia* (1500)[290]

Until 1973 the israelis had proved themselves the leading masters of surprise-throughdeception in the Near East. Now the Israeli fox was about to meet an Egyptian hedgehog. During the months preceding Yom Kippur, Israeli political and military leaders and senior Intelligencers viewed Egyptian President Sadat's "rathers" as falling strictly within the following range: ideally to conquer all Israel, minimally to recover the humiliating territorial losses of the 1967 Six-Day War. Assessing these extreme cases, the Israelis concluded that Egypt lacked the military capability to achieve either goal. Moreover, they assumed that Sadat accepted this limitation. Therefore an attack was most unlikely, despite the enormous political pressure on Sadat to act. And, at worst, no such attack in depth could succeed.

Sadat had a different viewpoint. Although, as a former Egyptian Army colonel, he fully appreciated his military limitations, the intensity of politics was such that he felt he must do *something* dramatic to restore the honor of Egyptian arms and at least embarrass Israel. A very *limited* but still *moderate value* target was available—recovery of the east bank of the Suez Canal and *nothing more*.[291]

The Israelis failed to appreciate that Sadat would even contemplate such a limited payoff. Their failure to see this limited goal was also closely linked to their similar misperception of Egyptian capabilities and tactics. The Israelis expected—100% expected—that Egyptian attack would involve a medium-to-

---
289 Whaley, *Stratagem* (1969/2007), Case A66.
290 Erasmus based his maxim on the even more famous one of Archilochus (early 7th Cent. BC) as his Fragment 103: "The fox knows many things, but the hedgehog knows one great thing." This latter version is often attributed to Tolstoy, but he had merely quoted it with approval.
291 J. Bowyer Bell, "National Character and Military Strategy: The Egyptian Experience, October 1973". *Parameters*, Vol.5, No.1 (1975), 6-16. See also Frank J. Stech, "Political and Military Intention Estimation: A Taxonomic Analysis—Final Report" (Bethesda, MD: Mathtech, Inc., November 1979), 178-211.

long range armored drive, as per prior Egyptian practice and its adopted Soviet doctrine. Accordingly they deployed for their own armored counterattack to catch the enemy in motion and, as ever before, smash him.

Sadat, however, having opted for a limited goal, needed only to get his army across the Canal, secure the approaches by advancing to shallow depth no greater than 20 miles, dig in, and hold. His prime weapon was thus not armor but infantry. And the Egyptian infantry, being peasants not Bedouins, like the hedgehog. "knew one great thing—how to dig in and hold. The Israelis had overlooked their own prior experience that Egyptian infantry could hold and not run *when dug in*.[292]

For the first time, the Egyptian general staff used many and fairly sophisticated deceptions, both strategic and tactical, to support this operation, hoping to enhance the element of surprise.[293]

CASE 63:
Col. Robin Olds, Operation BOLO, Vietnam 1967

The North Vietnamese thought their nimble MiG-21 interceptors were ambushing the usual bomb-laden F-105 Thunderchiefs. Instead they were counterambushed by Col. Robin Olds and his Wolfpack, flying the new F-4 Phantom II.

Source:

Walter J. Boyne "MiG Sweep," *Air Force Magazine*, Vol.81, No.11 (Nov 1998), heavily edited verbatim text with supplementary information from other sources, particularly *Wikipedia*, "Operation Bolo," "Robin Olds," and "Ella Raines" (all accessed 22 Aug 2010).

Overview

On 2 Jan 1967, with its aircraft losses in Vietnam rising, the United States Air Force (USAF) resorted to an elaborate combat sting. This mission, called Operation BOLO, was an electronic Trojan Horse. It was designed to hide the hard-hitting F-4 Phantoms of the USAF's 8th Tactical Fighter Wing (TFW) within a radar signature that simulated vulnerable bomb-laden F-105 Thunderchiefs (Thuds). Despite adverse weather and a some operational surprises, the "MiG Sweep" did what it was designed to do, namely sucker the MiG-21s of North Vietnam into a counter-ambush with Phantoms rigged for dogfighting.

---

292 Bell (1975).
293 Colonel Trevor N. Dupuy, *Elusive Victory: The Arab-Israeli Wars, 1947-1974* (New York: Harper & Row, 1978), 391-392.

Background

Until the latter part of 1966, MiG aircraft had not posed as great a threat to USAF strike forces as the Surface-to-Air Missiles and anti-aircraft fire. Ironically, the introduction of the electronics countermeasures (ECM) pod on the F-105s changed this. Because this ECM pod was effectively neutralizing the enemy radar controlling their anti-aircraft SAMs and flak, the resilient North Vietnamese responded by concentrating their MiG fighters to preying on the highly vulnerable F-105s which were specifically configured as bombers.

Operating under ground control, and making maximum use of both cloud cover and the almost benevolent American rules of engagement, the enemy aircraft were effectively employed. The MiGs, especially the later model MiG-21s armed with heat-seeking missiles, sought to attack the bomber sorties and force them to jettison their bombs before reaching their targets. The MiGs mission was successful if the Thuds were forced to drop their bombs prematurely, but they also tried to score kills wherever possible.

As in World War Two and the Korean War, the US Air Force mission in the Vietnam War was to gain air superiority, destroy the enemy air forces, and conduct long-range bombing operations. The mission of the North Vietnamese was to defend their key targets by intercepting the incoming American bombers.

There were other parallels with WW2 & Korea. To achieve the air superiority mission, the American fighters had to have a long-range capability and still be able to defeat the enemy fighters over their own territory. What the Mustangs and Sabres had done in their wars, the F-4 Phantom II (F-4C) was required to do in Southeast Asia. Flights of F-4s, carrying a mixed ordnance load of bombs and missiles, would be sandwiched in between Thud flights at four- or five-minute intervals. Then, if the F-105s in front or behind were attacked, the F-4s would drop their bombs and try to engage. If they were not attacked, the F-4s would drop bombs right along with the Thuds.

A final, tragic parallel is the price paid to execute the missions that were often laid on for statistical rather than tactical reasons. Flying Phantoms and Thuds was dangerous work. As a single example, by late 1967, more than 325 Thuds had been lost over North Vietnam, most to SAM missiles and anti-aircraft gunnery.

The North Vietnamese air force (NVAF) consisted of slow but heavily armed and maneuverable MiG-17s and a handful of modern delta-wing MiG-21 Fishbeds. The MiG-17s were semi-obsolete but still effective in their defensive role. (The MiG-19 did not enter service with the North Vietnamese air force until February 1969.)

The MiG-21 was roughly half the size of the Phantom and was designed as a high-speed, limited all-weather interceptor. It could carry two cannons and two Atoll infrared homing air-to-air missiles which had been developed from the USAF's Sidewinder. At altitude, the MiG-21 could outfly the F-4 in almost all flight regimes. It had spectacular acceleration and turning capability. At lower altitudes, the F-4s used their colossal energy in vertical maneuvers that offset the MiGs' turning capability, for they lost energy quickly in turns at low altitudes. The MiG-21s operated under tight ground control. They typically sought to stalk American formations from the rear, firing a missile and then disengaging. If engaged, however, its small size and tight turning ability made the MiG-21 a formidable opponent in a dogfight.

The Phantom had been originally designed as a fleet defense aircraft. But it proved to be versatile in many roles, including reconnaissance, Fast Forward Air Control, Wild Weasel, bombing, and air superiority. They were armed only with missiles, although gun pods could be fitted.

The air war in Southeast Asia had grown progressively intense, and 2 Dec 1966 became known as "Black Friday" when the USAF lost five aircraft and the Navy three to SAMs or anti-aircraft fire. Air Force losses included three F-4Cs, one RF-4C, and an F-105; the Navy's were one F-4B and two Douglas A-4C Skyhawks.

These heavy losses to ground fire were accompanied by the marked increase in MiG activity during the last quarter of 1966. Because the politically dictated American rules of engagement prohibited airfield attacks on enemy airfields, the aircrew of the 8th Tactical Fighter Wing (TFW) were determined to blunt the enemy's efforts by luring the MiGs into air-to-air combat and then destroying them. But the reluctance of the MiG-21s to engage did not mean that the North Vietnamese pilots were lacking in either courage or skill. At the time, the US estimated that there were only 16 MiG-21s in the theater, and the enemy chose to deploy this precious resource only in ambushes against weaker aircraft rather than risk dogfights with the powerful and more numerous Phantoms.

A New Boy with a New Concept

Col. Robin Olds arrived on 30 Sep 1966 at Ubon airbase in Thailand to take command of the somewhat demoralized 8th TFW "Wolfpack." He immediately recognized that he was the proverbial "new boy on the block." Son of Maj. Gen. Robert Olds, one of the most influential generals in the Army Air Corps, Col. Olds was West Point football star and World War II double ace—with 12 confirmed kills of German fighters during two tours in Western Europe. However, his ace status was undercut among his superiors among the Air Force brass by his reputation as a maverick. He had often argued forcefully against contemporary Air Force training. He was an outspoken advocate of intensive training in the arts of war he had learned in Europe. Unable to get into the Korean conflict, he had continued to press for training in strafing, dive-bombing, and other conventional warfare techniques at a time when US fighter aircraft were being adapted to carry nuclear weapons and fight a nuclear war. His advice, though not well received, was a realistic forecast of what would be required for war in Southeast Asia.

Moreover, Olds did not initially particularly impress his peers and subordinates. Being as yet unblooded in the new style of all-jet air combat was one factor. Many also openly resented that at age 44 he had surpassed them in speedy promotions and a chestful of combat decorations. And standing six feet two while flaunting a striking non-regulation waxed handlebar moustache, he looked more like Hollywood's concept of a combat commander than your typical Air Force career officer. This last judgment was, at least in part, because he had not married the stereotypically approved young "girl next door" but mature & sultry retired film star Ella Raines, two years his senior.

Olds Sells His Idea for an Ambush

Olds knew he would have to prove himself to the combat-hardened veterans of the 8th as a leader in their war. He hoped to use his past experience & beliefs in a scheme that would confirm his present status. He had first presented his idea for a MiG ambush to Gen. Hunter Harris Jr., Pacific Air Forces commander. Harris ignored him.

Olds then sought out the commander of 7th Air Force, Gen. William W. "Spike" Momyer. It was in early December 1966, at a cocktail party in the Philippines, that Olds approached Momyer. After a few polite remarks, Olds said, "Sir, the MiGs are getting pesky" and went on to describe possible ways to bring them to battle. Momyer's expression of disinterest didn't change. He moved away, leaving Olds thinking he had blown a good opportunity.

However, Momyer had listened after all, and a week after their first conversation, Olds was called to Saigon to discuss the concept of tricking the MiGs into combat. Momyer told Olds to develop a plan.

Olds Plans a Luring Ambush

By 13 Dec, Olds was working closely with four top veterans of the 8th, striving to develop his idea. The planning group included Capt. John B. Stone, Lt. Joe Hicks, Lt. Ralph F. Wetterhahn, and Maj. James D. Covington, a wing staff officer.

In brief, Olds' concept called for the F-4s to simulate F-105s, and Olds gave his planners specific guidelines to work by. Central to the concept was that, while no North Vietnamese airfields could be attacked, the MiGs would be prevented from landing—flights of Phantoms would orbit above the airfields, cutting off MiG escape routes to China. Olds hoped either to engage the MiGs in combat and destroy them in the air or, by denying them access to any airfields, cause them to run them out of fuel and crash.

It was a perfect combination—Olds providing the overview and the major decision elements, and the younger officers, more experienced in the theater, breathing life into a concept. The team worked long hours to develop key details on force structure, refueling points, and altitudes, ingress and egress routes, radio communications, flak suppression, electronic countermeasures, and all the many other details the mission required.

The planners determined that, if the MiGs engaged in combat, their endurance from takeoff to landing would extend only for about 55 minutes. F-4 flight arrival times were set five minutes apart to ensure maximum opportunities for engagement. The group planned for a concerted strike by a "west force" of seven flights of F-4s from the 8th at Ubon and an "east force" made up of five flights of F-4s from the 366th TFW at Da Nang AB, South Vietnam.

Everything hinged on getting the MiGs airborne, where they could be destroyed. But luring them into battle would not be easy, for the North Vietnamese often declined to attack if they thought the weather would seriously impair the bombing accuracy of US attacking aircraft. They also had several advantages. All of the targets were in the midst of the most heavily integrated air defense system then in existence. Local geography and the self-imposed rules of engagement under which American forces operated had severely reduced the F-105s' options in their strategic Operation Rolling Thunder missions that were intended to break the enemy's will to resist. The number of approach routes was limited, as were the targets permitted to be attacked.

The Pod Deception

Olds took these factors into account and called for a plan that depended upon a basic deception. The strike force would imitate the route, altitude, speed, and radio chatter of a normal F-105 mission. However, the force would comprise not bomb-laden Thuds but rather F-4s, each armed with four Sparrow and four Sidewinders missiles. Maj. Gen. Donavon F. Smith, chief of the Air Force Advisory Group in Vietnam, suggested the Phantoms carry the QRC-160 radar jamming electronic countermeasures (ECM) pod that only the Thuds typically carried.

Simply acquiring these ECM pods was a logistic effort that extended all over Southeast Asia and all the way back to the United States. It was the first of a series of events that involved many separate elements of the Air Force.

Preparation & Coordination

Also at play was another factor, one that Olds hoped would be the key factor in success. The first three flights entering the combat area would have "missile free" firing options. For a few precious minutes, the Americans would know exactly where all friendly aircraft were. Any other aircraft could be assumed to be hostile and be fired upon without visual identification. This gave many advantages, including surprise, isolation from counterfire, and, most of all, time to let the missile do what it was designed to do under the most favorable conditions, without excessive g forces to trouble the missile systems.

On 22 Dec in Saigon Col. Olds briefed his immediate superior, Gen. Momyer, commander of the 7th Air Force. At this point the plan was assigned the code name, Operation BOLO, after the cane-cutting machete which doubled as a Filipino martial arts weapon. Sharp and deadly, the bolo did not seem like a weapon until the victim is drawn in too close to evade. This was the plan's intent—to draw the MiGs in too close to evade Olds' Phantoms after they uncloaked.

Otherwise, Momyer accepted Olds' plan without a change. Execution was set for 1 Jan 1967. The force would contain 96 fighters—56 F-4s, 24 F-105s, and 16 F-104s. This airborne force also would include KC-135 tankers, EB-66s electronic countermeasure-support aircraft, EC-121 Big Eye surveillance aircraft, and rescue teams.

Eight days after he briefed Momyer, Olds canceled all leaves at his 8th TFW and postponed the New Year's Eve party. Because of the tight security imposed by Olds, the pilots assigned to fly the mission scheduled for 1 Jan were not briefed until 30 Dec. Then, bad weather moved in, and it was obvious that the mission would not be flown as scheduled. Most thought it probably would not occur on 2 Jan either. The party was reinstated for the evening of 1 Jan—a mistake, for soon the mission was reset for the morning of 2 Jan. Olds reluctantly agreed to go forward, despite the probability of bad weather, because the necessary ECM jamming pods were "on loan" to him for only seven days.

Normally, the computers at 7th Air Force generated the code words assigned to flights, targets, and routes. Because timing was so critical, however, code terms for Operation BOLO were picked according to an improvised and thereby unusual rule. Accordingly, the seven Wolfpack flights were now assigned the names of American-made automobiles—Ford, Rambler, Lincoln, Tempest, Plymouth, Vespa, and, coyly, Olds—with mission commander Olds himself leading Olds Flight. Olds was dismayed by this obvious breach of security. He rightly felt that the flights should have been given code names similar to those routinely used by the F-105 flights. But it was too late for him to correct this unnecessary incongruity in what he had hoped would be a near seemless F-105 disguise of his F-4s.

An his pre-mission briefing Olds told his pilots to use first names for their radio calls. As further cover, all MiG airfields were identified by the names of US cities. Thus Phuc Yen, northwest of Hanoi, was called "Frisco," while Gia Lam, south of Phuc Yen, was "Los Angeles."

It had required a massive Air Force-wide effort to bring BOLO into being. The entire 8th TFW's energy was thrown into overcoming last minute problems, with the support troops working all night long. A typical glitch involved the sway braces on the F-4C. They were located differently than on the F-105, and the shell of the ECM pod had to be reinforced in order to fit well.

However, as the aircraft rolled for takeoff, the long days of nonstop planning, the assembly of resources, the intense training of munitions crews, crew chiefs, pilots, and backseaters now began to condense into a 13-minute dogfight. The historic battle would be fought in a slice of sky that ranged from 10,000 to 18,000 feet in altitude and within a 15-mile radius of Phuc Yen airfield.

BOLO Airborne

Olds carefully simulated the F-105 flight profile, flying a fluid-four formation at 480 knots until reaching the Red River. At that point, he accelerated to 540 knots and assumed the ECM pod formation. This was similar to the standard fluid four but with a separation of about 1,500 feet. The aircraft would weave up and down, and the combined effect of the pods was to jam the enemy acquisition radar.

The force maintained this Thud feint for a full three minutes after the Olds Flight arrived at its target. By that time, Olds expected the North Vietnamese to have realized what they were dealing with. Olds arrived over Phuc Yen at 1400 Zulu, exactly on schedule, but he was disconcerted to find that the MiGs were not airborne. There was a complete undercast, with tops at about 7,000 feet; and the enemy ground controllers had delayed the MiG takeoffs by about 15 minutes. Olds had no way of knowing this and had to contemplate calling the mission off for the inbound flights.

He passed over Phuc Yen airfield to the southeast and then made a 180-degree turn to the northwest. The first sign of enemy activity proved sterile as Olds 3 picked up and then lost a bogie moving swiftly in the opposite direction. Knowing that Ford Flight, led by his longtime friend Col. Daniel "Chappie" James Jr., was due over the target, Olds now canceled the missile-free option and made another 180-degree turn.

The Dogfight

Ford Flight entered the battle area exactly on time and simultaneously with the belated arrival of the first MiG-21s popping up into sight from the undercast. Ford 1 called out a MiG-21 closing up behind Olds' Flight. Olds turned to throw off the MiG's aim and attacked another MiG that appeared in his 11 o'clock position, low and a little over a mile away.

It was Olds' first trip to the Hanoi area, and his first engagement with a MiG. With his backseater, Lt. Charles Clifton, he set up for a Sparrow attack as he closed to get positive identification. When he saw the silver delta shape of the MiG he fired two Sparrows and a Sidewinder—but both missed. Olds then spotted another MiG—they were appearing everywhere now—and used the Phantom's power and energy to vector roll behind it. This time he fired two Sidewinders and the first hit, blowing the MiG-21's right wing off. He did not think the pilot ejected. One MiG down.

1st Lt. Wetterhahn, one of the key planners, had been disappointed to be flying as Olds 2, but in the course of Col. Olds' own attack Wetterhahn was able to slide behind a MiG-21. Working with his GIB (the Guy In Back), 1st Lt. Jerry K. Sharp, he salvoed two Sparrows. They lost sight of the first one, but the second Sparrow caught the MiG just forward of its stabilizer and blew it up. Two down.

Olds 4 saw a MiG-21 tracking Olds 3 and experienced some difficulty getting a solid tone on his Sidewinder before firing. But his missile guided perfectly, striking just forward of the MiG's tail and sending it spinning into the undercast. Three down.

The next MiG fell to Ford 2. Two MiGs had closed on Ford 3 and 4, overshot, then pressed an attack on Ford 1, overshooting him as well. The MiG broke into a hard left turn, and Ford 2 rolled to wind up at the MiG's six o'clock position. He fired a Sidewinder that guided up the MiG's tailpipe, blowing it up. Four down.

Rambler Flight had arrived exactly on time, to find itself in the midst of the MiG melee. One of the main BOLO planners, Stone, was flying as Rambler 1. Over Phuc Yen, he detected two MiGs, 4,000 feet below and two miles away. Uncertain of his lock-on, he fired three Sparrows. The second missile struck the MiG's wing root, and the pilot ejected. Five down.

Rambler 2 had been on Rambler lead's wing all through its combat maneuvers. Just after Rambler 1 scored, Rambler 2 locked on to a MiG-21 and fired two Sparrows. The second missile hit the MiG in its wing root, the debris damaging Rambler 2 slightly. The enemy pilot ejected and Rambler 2 saw his parachute open. Six down.

Rambler 4 locked on to a MiG-21 and tracked it carefully, pulling no more than 4g's, and fired two Sparrows. Rambler 4 lost sight of the first missile but managed to track the second from launch to impact. It struck the tail section. So swiftly did the parachute appear that Rambler 4 later speculated that the pilot had ejected when he saw the missile coming. That made seven MiG-21s down. It was the last confirmed victory of the day.

Rambler 4 locked onto a second MiG and fired four Sidewinders. They saw the first two detonate just below the enemy's tailpipe, with the last two tracking well, but then Rambler 4 broke off on hearing "F-4C, I don't know your call sign, but break right." The radio message had been meant for Stone in Rambler 1, but their abort caused Rambler 4 to claim only a probable. Rambler 3 also claimed a probable.

Suddenly, the MiGs were gone, and the four (out of seven) remaining Wolfpack flights (Lincoln, Tempest, Plymouth, and Vespa) arrived to find the action was over. The seven flights of 366th Tactical Fighter Wing out of Da Nang, had flown up the coast to a point off Haiphong, evaluated the weather, and elected not to participate in the western part of the mission. Operation BOLO was over.

Assessment

Seventh Air Force was elated with the Wolfpack's results. Twelve Phantoms had engaged 14 MiGs and shot down seven, with no losses. (The Vietnamese later admitted to five MiGs lost with all five pilots having ejected safely.) The only sour note was that BOLO had aborted before the surviving MiGs could be prevented from landing before their fuel ran out. The 15 minute delay in getting the MiGs airborne meant Olds's Wolfpack Phantoms were running low on fuel and the poor weather caused the 366th Phantoms to abort their airfield interdiction role.

It is worth noting that of the 14 crew members (2 per Phantom) who scored victories, only one had ever seen a MiG in air combat before. And Olds had only seen MiGs at a distance. The Phantom crews, despite their relative inexperience in combat and their lack of dissimilar aircraft combat training, used vertical maneuvers to put themselves in firing position.

For dogfighting, the Phantom proved clearly superior to the MiG-21, and the Sparrow and Sidewinder missiles had proved themselves highly effective weapons. Only 10 Phantoms had fired their missiles. Eighteen Sparrows had been launched; of these, only nine guided, but these nailed four MiGs. Twelve Sidewinders had launched, seven guided correctly, and they destroyed three MiGs.

The ECM radar-jamming pods had apparently worked very well, although the presence of MiGs in the combat area undoubtedly inhibited both missile and anti-aircraft fire. Only five SAMs were spotted and a light burst of 85 mm anti-aircraft fire seemed to be aimed at random.

The battle proved beyond doubt the importance of the largely unsung GIB, the Phantom's backseaters, who locked the radar on the target and who, despite the continuously changing g forces, kept their heads on a swivel watching out for enemy aircraft and SAMs.

The battle had proved Olds to his men. He made sure that all who participated in Operation BOLO, whether in the air or on the ground, received full credit for their contributions. Finally, the general effect of BOLO on Air Force morale was positive, in Southeast Asia and the US. And Operation BOLO became the most often cited example of a successful USAF aerial operation during the entire Vietnam War.

A Deceptive Dividend

The surviving MiG force retaliated during the next two days, 3 and 4 Jan, by attacking the daily photo reconnaissance missions by a USAF RF-4 aircraft. These attacks inspired 7th Air Force planners to improvise a simplied version of Col. Olds' original deception.

So, on 5 Jan, two fully armed Phantoms flew in sufficiently close formation to simulate the single radar blip of that day's expected RF-4 reconnaissance plane. But this drew no enemy response. But next day, when the pair of Phantoms repeated this maneuver, they were rewarded by being bounced by four MiGs. The Phantoms shot down two of the North Vietnamese aircraft,

This meant that a total of 9 of the enemy's original 16 MiG-21s had been shot down within a single week. The MiG-21s now went through a three-month stand-down, during which both the North Vietnamese and their Russian suppliers studied the lessons of the battle.

CASE 64:
Jody Powell and the Iranian Rescue Mission, Iran 1980
An amateur reads Bodyguard of Lies and meddles in an ops plan.

> According to Jody Powell, the secret preparations
> for the Iranian rescue mission were partly inspired
> by Allied intelligence tricks in World War II.
> — *New York Times*, 4 May 1980

The late Jody Powell was Press Secretary throughout his old friend and boss Jimmy Carter's one-term tenure (1977-1981) as President of the United

States. It was during their watch that the Iranian Hostage Crisis began in embarrassment and peaked in catastrophe. It had begun on 20 Jan 1980 when Iranian Islamic students seized the U.S. Embassy in Tehran, taking hostage 53 Americans. It ended 444 days later on 24 Apr 1981 when the secret Iran-Contra negotiations swept Ronald Regan into the Presidency. Three months into this ordeal a secret Pentagon special forces-type rescue attempt had ended on 24 Apr 1980 in immediate and highly visible complete failure.

One back story that contributed to this amateurish failure involved a study of WW2 deception operations. In 1975 British journalist Anthony Cave Brown had published his *Bodyguard of Lies*, the first detailed account of the hugely successful British deception operations that culminated in the 1944 Allied D-Day landings and breakout in Normandy. It became a best-seller in the USA.

In mid-March 1980 during the early planning stages for a joint Pentagon-CIA rescue operation Jody Powell read a copy of Brown's *Bodyguard*. It was a revelation for him; and he immediately began praising its advocacy of military deception to all who would listen.[294] Powell would later admit that his reading of Anthony Cave Brown's *Bodyguard of Lies* inspired him to devise lies to the White House press corps suggesting that any possible military action to recapture the hostages being held in the U.S. embassy in Iran would not take place before mid-May 1980 when, in fact, the operation was set for late April. Here is a fine although generally overlooked case of the old "It's Later Than You Think" type of deception ploy.

Unfortunately, this input would have a small but dysfunctional role on Operation EAGLE CLAW, the catastrophically failed American attempt in 1980 to rescue the hostages being held in the seized U.S. Embassy in Tehran. Powell's naive grasp of deception operations only compounded the already poorly thought-through plan. Too complicated, weakly coordinated, and un-rehearsed, it had been designed to fail.[295]

---

294 Steven R. Weisman, "How Jody Powell Misled Press on U.S. Aim in Iran," *The New York Times*, 2 May 1980. See also comment on the editorial page, "Historic and Weighty Lies", *New York Times*, 4 May 1980; and Jody Powell, *The Other Side of the Story* (New York: Morrow, 1984).

295 For the details of that case study see Whaley, *When Deception Fails: The Theory of Outs* (FDDC, Apr 2010), Case 2.3.9.

CHAPTER 6:
Selling the Commander

> "For by wise counsel thou shalt make thy war."
> — *Proverbs* 24: 6

> The task before him of explaining this thing to his unimaginative senior was sufficiently hard without prejudicing himself in the other's eyes by any misplaced levity."
> — Col. E.D. Swinton (writing as "Ole Luk-Oie"), 'The Second Degree,' *Blackwood's Magazine* (Mar 1908)

This section examines the deception planner as salesman. Having come up with a plan, how does he then sell it to his boss or convince his allies? We have already seen a few examples of deception sales-craft (Cases 2, 37, 49, 54, 63). But now we shall look at this specific job, so necessary in getting plans off the drawing board and into operation.

CASE 65:
Gen. Odysseus, Troy 1183 BC
A wily warrior convinces his reluctant heros to use a ruse.

> *Timeo Danaos et dona ferentes.*
> I fear the Danaans (Greeks) even if they bring gifts.
> — Virgil, *The Aeneid* (19 BC), Book 2

The most famous ruse in military folklore is the Trojan Horse ploy. It was celebrated by Homer, Virgil, Apollodorus of Athens, Dictys of Crete, and Dares the Phrygian. The story may seem trite today, but it conceals a subtle theme, first introduced in the legend around AD 350 by Quintus Smyrnaeus in his *The Fall of Troy*. This theme is that of the Greek Commander, Odysseus, trying to sell his deception plan to conventionally-minded soldiers.

The situation in 1183 BC was that the Greeks had spent ten costly years in their cruelly fought siege of the Trojan capital. There seemed no possibility of a breakthrough. At that point the prophet Calchas assembled the weary Greek chief and heroes and told them, "Stop battering away at these walls! You must devise some other way, some cunning stratagem." At first none could suggest a suitable plan. Then the ever wily Odysseus spoke up. He proposed, "If Troy is to fall to guile, then let us fashion a great horse in which our mightiest warriors shall hide in ambush."

Odysseus explained his daring plan. They would place the Horse outside the city walls, burn their camp, embark, and sail away—but only just over the horizon to await developments. Meanwhile, their secret agent, Sinon, would explain to the astonished Trojans that the Greeks had given up and had left the Horse as an offering to appease the goddess Athena for having looted her sacred image from the city. The Trojans could then be expected to drag the Horse into their city as a victory trophy. That night, while they slumbered, drunk and gorged from the celebration, Sinon would light a signal fire to summon back the Greek fleet while the 30 hidden warriors would slip from the Horse to spread havoc and open the city gates.[296]

Calchas approved this scheme. But Neoptolemus, the blond "battle-eager" son of Achilles, was disgusted. He argued, "Brave men meet their foes face to face! Away with such thoughts of guile and stratagem!." On and on he ranted, denouncing deception as unworthy of heroes. In traditional terms, he was of course right and very Greek. It was not the Hellenic fashion to cheat in war. Their reputation before gods and men would suffer. The weary soldiers, however, hungered more for victory than for further futile heroic displays; and so they voted for Odysseus' plan.

Accordingly, they built their "great horse of guile". And, as Odysseus had predicted, the Trojans took the lure and the Greeks took the city. But, as Neoptolemus foresaw, this ruse earned a new reputation for his people—ever after, and in lands and languages then unknown, the unwary have been advised, "Beware of Greeks bearing gifts".

Legend? Yes. Sheer fiction? Perhaps. But this tale has enough plausibility to have inspired generations of military deception planners. Indeed, the next most famous deception operation, "The Man Who Never Was", began with the title Plan Trojan Horse. And Commander Unwin's creative ruse at Gallipoli (Case 32) was unofficially dubbed "The Wooden Horse".

---

296 Col. Frank Stech at the MITRE Corporation has recently suggested the plausible scenario that the Horse may have been deliberately made tall enough that the Trojans would have had to partly dismantle the main gate, rendering it more easily breached by the Greek attackers.

CASE 66:
Gen. Manstein, The Ardennes, France 1940
Selling the Führer.

Plan YELLOW was the German design for the assault against the West, through Holland and Belgium and France. The French High Command fully expected the offensive through the Lowlands to outflank the Maginot Line. However, they had drawn several false conclusions from their similar experience in the Great War, anticipating the main attack all the extreme northern flank. They also accepted the assurance of Deuxième Bureau's *A Comprehensive Study of the Polish Campaign* that, "The type of warfare used by the Germans in Poland was related to a peculiar situation. ... Operations on the Western Front will be very different." The French were convinced that the Ardennes forest was impenetrable terrain for the German armor and so only a thin screen of 12 mediocre French divisions was assigned to that 95-mile wide sector in the center of the line.[297]

This was a correct reading of the German's original version of Plan YELLOW, which had been proposed by the Army High Command (OKH) and approved by Hitler and the Supreme Command (OKW). The German General Staff had, like their French counterparts, looked at their maps and decided that the Ardennes forest was impenetrable by German armor. However one Army General Staff officer thought otherwise. He would convince Hitler and change the entire plan.

General Erich von Manstein had become convinced that that a surprise breakthrough could be made with a concentrated drive straight through the Ardennes forest with 44 divisions, including all but one of his Panzer divisions.[298]

Accordingly, on May 10th, the Wehrmacht launched its great offensive through the Ardennes with nine of its ten Panzer divisions spearheading 35 infantry divisions. Despite parity across the front, all the French had to stop them here were 12 low quality infantry divisions. Surprise backed by overwhelming strength won a quick breakthrough, unleashing the "expanding torrent" of the German blitzkrieg.

---

297 See Whaley (1969/2007), Case A21.
298 Whaley, *Stratagem* (1969/2007), Case A21. Manstein's autobiography is Field-Marshal Erich von Manstein, *Lost Victories* (Chicago: Regnery, 1958).

CASE 67:
Capt. (USN) Francis S. Low, The Tokyo Raid, 1942

A submarine officer solves an aerial problem and sells his plan to the bosses.

During the four months after Pearl Harbor, the Japanese Home Islands felt secure from retaliation. It was inconceivable they could be reached by any existing American aircraft. All US air bases were far beyond range, and the US Navy's aircraft carriers had only short-range, single-engined dive and torpedo bombers. Japan's screen of offshore picket ships and medium-range air patrols would give ample warning to sink any American carrier so foolish as to come close enough to launch, much less recover, its short-range planes. The Japanese were therefore astonished on an April morning in 1942 when the sacred homeland was hit by a squadron of US Army Air Corps twin-engined, medium range bombers. A pin-prick, yes; but an embarrassment to the victim and a much-needed morale booster for the perpetrator.

Fifteen days after Pearl Harbor, on 22 December 1941, President Roosevelt first stated his desire for an ASAP bombing raid on the Japanese Homeland to his Army, Army Air Corps, and Navy chiefs, Gen. Marshall, Gen. Arnold, and Adm. King. King, as usual, immediately passed on this new requirement to his staff.

On January 10th Roosevelt reiterated this desire, but his military chiefs had so far come up empty. Admiral King returned to the Navy Building and reminded his staff of the presidential tasking. Around 8 PM King left the Navy Building for the Washington Navy Yard and *Vixen*, the ex-German yacht berthed there, which served as his flagship, second office, and quarters shared with key staff members. The admiral then had dinner and retired for the evening. At that point his Operations Officer, Captain (USN) Francis S. "Froggie" Low, waited a few minutes before deciding to speak alone with his commander, a stiff man whom few of his staff found easy to talk with. Low was a submariner and not an airman, but thought he might have accidentally stumbled upon a solution to the Japan bombing problem. Low knocked at King's cabin and was invited in.[299]

"Yes, Low, what do you want?"

"Sir, I've got an idea for bombing Japan I'd like to talk to you about. I flew down to Norfolk today to check on the readiness of our new carrier, the Hornet, and saw something that started me thinking. The enemy knows that the radius of action of carrier aircraft is limited to about 300 miles. Today, as we were taking off from Norfolk, I saw the outline of a carrier deck

---

[299] Lieutenant Colonel (USAF) Carroll V. Glines, *Doolittle's Tokyo Raiders* (Princeton, NJ: D. Van Nostrand Company, Inc., 1964). 13-14, as seemingly based on Low's own recollections.

painted on the airfield which is used to give our pilots practice in taking off from a short distance."

"I don't understand what you're getting at, Low."

"Well, Sir, I saw some Army twin-engine planes making bombing passes at this simulated carrier deck at the same time. If the Army has some longer-range planes than our Navy fighters—maybe a medium bomber like the B-25 or B-26— and if they could take off in the length of a carrier deck, then it seems to me a few of them could be loaded on a carrier and be used to bomb Japan. It would be a mighty big surprise to the Japanese and would certainly build up the morale of the American people."

King was silent a full minute, and his intruder expected the usual rebuff. Finally his boss said simply, "Low, you may have something there. Talk to Duncan about it in the morning." As an afterthought King added, "One thing, Low. Don't tell anyone else about this".[300]

Duncan was Captain (USN) Donald B. "Wu" Duncan, King's Air Operations Officer. The next morning, Duncan heard Low's idea and how he had conceived it by "fortuitous association". Low posed two questions:[301]

As I see it there are two big questions to be answered: first, can such a plane—a land-based twin-engine medium bomber— land aboard a carrier? And secondly, can such a plane, stripped down to its absolute essentials, and loaded with gasoline and bombs, take off from a carrier deck? If either one or both questions can be answered affirmatively, we may have a whole new concept of operation to go on.

Duncan answered "definite negative" to the first question—landing was out. But he said he would have to work on the second—take-off might be possible. Told of King's insistence on total secrecy, Duncan worked alone, collecting the necessary data and calculating the conclusions. Five days later he had a 30-page handwritten analysis. This indicated that the B-25 was the only feasible aircraft, if it could be trimmed in weight and fitted with extra fuel tanks; that *Hornet* was an appropriate carrier; that Army pilots would require special training; and that, as a surprise naval approach and air attack was essential, the tightest possible secrecy must prevail. He informed Low, and the two officers briefed King who instructed them to check it out with General Arnold. King

---

300 Glines (1964), 14-15.
301 Glines (1964), 15.

also told Duncan that, "if this plan gets the green light from Arnold, I want you to handle the Navy end of it."[302]

The next day, January 17th, Duncan and Low briefed General Henry H. "Hap" Arnold. The Chief of the U.S. Army Air Corps was enthusiastic and assigned the Air Corps side of this joint mission to Lt. Col. James H. "Jimmy Doolittle, an MIT PhD in aeronautical engineering and world-famous test-pilot. Doolittle agreed that with modifications and special crew training the B-25 might work.[303] The mathematics seemed OK, but Duncan arranged a field test. On February 2nd two production model B-25's manned by experienced crews were successfully launched from the 500-foot deck of *Hornet* while it cruised at only 10 knots into a 20-knot wind. Duncan was now satisfied that a combat-laden modified B-25 could make a carrier take-off. Doolittle completed the necessary modifications.[304]

Doolittle put his 16 B-25 medium bombers on *Hornet*. But, while *Hornet*'s 770-foot long flight deck could just manage to launch such unprecedentedly large planes, it could not recover them. Therefore Doolittle's squadron planned on a one-way flight over Japan and on to improvised emergency landing-fields in Nationalist China. In fact, all 16 aircraft ran out of fuel and crashed or were ditched. Lt. Col. Doolittle, expecting a courts martial was awarded the Medal of Honor and promoted two grades to Brigadier General.

Interestingly, although *Hornet* was reported by Japanese picket ships, the event was not entirely "self-revealing". The Japanese Army, wedded to its preconceptions, assumed the twin-engined bombers must have originated from some land base. Only Admiral Yamamoto accepted this early intelligence as meaning carriers and launched an all-out off-shore search—unsuccessful, as *Hornet* was long gone.[305] The Japanese learned the truth of the matter only later from papers recovered from one of the B-25s that had crashed in Japanese held territory.[306] Both Low's innovation of medium bombers operating from a carrier and Duncan's dual invention of one-way bombing and from sea-to-land hit the enemy with complete surprise of tactical style.

Captain Low's success in selling this idea to King is instructive and even somewhat surprising considering the admiral's generally negative attitude toward surprise and deception. For example, in his rejection in 1943 of a study recommending that the U.S. build midget surprise-attack submarines, King penciled in the remark: "The element of surprise has been dissipated.—

---

302 Glines (1964), 18.
303 Glines (1964), 24-27.
304 Glines (1964), 33-36.
305 Layton (1985), 386; Hiroyuki Agawa, *The Reluctant Admiral: Yamamoto and the Imperial Navy* (Tokyo: Kodansha International,1979), 300-302.
306 Samuel Eliot Morison, *History of United States Naval Operations in World War II*, Vol.3 (Boston: Little, Brown, 1957), 389-398.

IJK."³⁰⁷ At that point, U.S. Navy policy on surprise was felt fulfilled defensively by its large-scale harbor defense program. Its potential in offensive operations was overlooked in the confident reliance on overwhelming numbers of ships and planes. Surprise and its tools had become viewed as "weapons of despair of the have-not nations, ... not for us."³⁰⁸ Fortunately, King's attitude was not shared by either his top blue-seas' admirals like Nimitz and Halsey or his fellow-members on the JCS, particularly its Chairman, General Marshal. King had apparently bought Low's scheme only because it solved a knotty technical problem and not because it promised surprise much less its fringe element of deception.

CASE 68:
Adm. Nimitz, Midway Island, Pacific 1942
The U.S. Pacific Fleet Commander sets a counter-trap.

The Commander-in-Chief of the Japanese Combined Fleet, Admiral Isoroku Yamamoto, planned his Operation MI as a trap to lure the remaining U.S. Navy carriers to Midway Island and destroy them there. As described elsewhere,³⁰⁹ it became a case of the trapper trapped.

By their solution of Yamamoto's detailed and comprehensive operations order of May 20ᵗʰ, Nimitz knew with complete confidence the Japanese fleet's strength, deployment, strategy, timetable, and place of attack. Moreover, he even knew of the Japanese Naval General Staff's Aleutian diversion.³¹⁰ Although the American cryptanalysts had gotten no advance indications of the submarine diversions, the news on D-minus-3 of the actual sub attacks at Madagascar and Sydney were correctly interpreted as inconsequential sideshows.³¹¹

To turn the tables, Admiral Chester W. Nimitz, the Commander in Chief, Pacific Fleet, used two deception operations. The first tricked the enemy into disclosing his main target. The second lured him into Nimitz' counter-trap.

That preliminary deception is an example of a very rare and extraordinarily cunning type of ruse, those designed to get the enemy to inadvertently reveal his intentions by reacting in a specific way that can be secretly monitored. The idea began with Lieutenant Commander W. Jasper Holmes.

Holmes was a regular Navy officer with a master's degree in engineering from Columbia University. While temporarily retired on physical disability from

---
307 Burke Wilkinson, *By Sea and By Stealth* (New York: Coward-McCann, 1956), 204.
308 Wilkinson (1956), 205-212.
309 Whaley, *When Deception Fails: The Theory of Outs* (FDDC, Aug 2010), Case 2.2.8.
310 Rear Admiral Edwin T. Layton, "And I Was There": Pearl Harbor and Midway—Breaking the Secrets (New York: Morrow, 1985), 406-448; David Kahn, *The Codebreakers* (New York: Macmillan, 1967), 561-573, 603-604, 606; Walter Lord, *Incredible Victory* (New York: Harper & Row, 1967), 7, 9, 15-28, 76.
311 Layton (1985), 436.

1936 to 1940, he had worked at the University of Hawaii as chief of its Materials Testing Laboratory. One of the lab's contracts was to study certain engineering problems at Pan Am's trans-Pacific airport on Midway. Then, five months before the Japanese attack, Holmes rejoined the Navy and was assigned as the combat intelligence officer in Commander Joseph J. Rochefort's Combat Intelligence Unit (CIU). That name disguised the group at Pearl Harbor busy reading the Japanese diplomatic ciphers (called MAGIC) and doing traffic analyses of their Navy radio traffic. From February 1942 on, the U.S. codebreakers were reading most of the enemy's naval operations cipher (the JN-25).

Since April 27th, Rochefort's cryptanalysts had been piecing together Japanese signals that indicated Yamamoto was brewing up a major action whose main target was designated by the two code-letters "AF". In Hawaii it was agreed that "AF" probably meant Midway, and Nimitz began planning accordingly. Unfortunately, his rival codebreakers (Op-20-G) at Navy headquarters in Washington concluded that "AF" designated the Aleutians. Then, on May 20th, Yamamoto radioed his operation order giving the detailed plan and order of battle for the assault on the Aleutians and on "AF". The Americans intercepted the entire message and five days later Rochefort presented Nimitz a 90% decryption. It revealed the Aleutians were the diversion and "AF" the main target. While Nimitz was still confident that "AF" was Midway, Washington now decided it was Oahu or even some spot on the U.S. Pacific coast.[312]

As Holmes recalled:[313]

> One morning he [Joseph Finnegan, a cryptanalyst-translator], Dyer [chief cryptanalyst], and I chanced to be at Rochefort's desk when the subject came up again. I had never been to Midway, but ... was familiar with some of Midway's problems. I suggested to Rochefort that fresh-water supply was a constant problem at Midway, and a breakdown of its new fresh-water distilling plant would be a serious problem. Since there was a cable connecting Oahu and Midway, communications could be carried on in strict secrecy without committing anything to the air waves. Finnegan grinned and remarked that if the Japanese discovered that Midway was short of fresh water, the Wake radio intelligence unit would surely report it to Tokyo. Rochefort looked at him thoughtfully and said "That's all right, Joe." From Rochefort, that was high praise.

Rochefort checked out Holmes's suggestion with Admiral Claude C. Bloch who, as Commander, Hawaiian Sea Frontier, had jurisdiction over Midway.

---

312 Layton (1985), 405-417; W. J. Holmes, *Double-Edged Secrets: U.S. Naval Intelligence Operations in the Pacific during World War II* (Annapolis: Naval Institute Press, 1979), 88-89.
313 Holmes (1979), 90-91.

Bloch gave preliminary approval and the two officers worked out the detailed plan. On May 19th, Rochefort had Layton take the proposal directly to Nimitz who authorized it. Later that same day Bloch launched the deception operation by sending a coded order over the secure underwater cable to the Navy commander on Midway directing him to radio two messages back. Midway complied. The first message, sent immediately to Bloch in plain language, was an emergency request for water. The second, sent in a strip-cipher that Rochefort knew the Japanese had captured on Wake, was a follow-up report of an explosion at the water distillery.[314]

Both communications were picked up by the Japanese listening post on Kwajalein and immediately passed to the Special Duty Radio Intelligence Group at Owada. The Japanese Navy was electrified; and, by the end of the day, Rochefort and Bloch were delighted to read an intercept from the aviation commander of the Japanese "AF" task force requesting that headquarters supply his force with a two weeks' supply of distilled water. Here was the final proof that "AF" was Midway. To sustain their deception, Bloch now replied in plain-text to Midway that a barge load of fresh water would be sent immediately from Pearl.

The final act in this deception operation was bureaucratic, letting the Australian cryptanalytic team in Melbourne take credit by breaking the news to Washington, which it did the next day, May 20th, D-minus-14. Nimitz and Rochefort were pleased to have confirmed the AF = Midway equation, particularly because it got King and his team of faulty cryptanalysts back in Washington off their backs at the crucial moment.[315]

While King and his staff contributed nothing to Nimitz' own deception efforts, they were now concerned that his cryptanalysts were the victims of Japanese radio deception designed to sucker Nimitz into a trap of their own.[316] Prodded by Washington about this possibility and understandably concerned with his own bailiwick, the Hawaiian Army Commander, Lt. Gen. Delos C. Emmons, cautioned Nimitz on May 25th that:[317]

> Japs may be practicing deception with radio orders intercepted by us. Estimates should be directed at capabilities rather than probable intentions. Forces reported in Cominch dispatch 21st have sufficient strength to make damaging raid on Oahu with view to wrecking facilities Pearl Harbor and Honolulu.

---

314 Holmes (1979), 90-91.
315 Layton (1985), 422.
316 Layton (1985). 421, 426; Holmes (1979). 89; Gordon W. Prange, *Miracle at Midway* (New York: Mc-Graw-Hill, 1982), 73.
317 Quoted in Layton (1985), 426.

The next day Nimitz called in Layton and told him of Emmons' warning. Layton recalls that: "Nimitz was too much of a realist not to take very serious account that the Japanese might be deceiving us. He questioned me closely about the possibility ...."[318] Fortunately Nimitz had learned to trust his own Intelligence staff over that in Washington.

Nimitz' second deception was to permit Yamamoto to continue to believe he would both gain surprise in his attack on Midway and meet no reinforcements there. To do this the American admiral mounted a radio deception operation. As Layton recalled:[319]

> Even if we could no longer eavesdrop directly on the Japanese moves, we could fool Admiral Yamamoto into believing that our carriers were still in the South Pacific. So as Task Force 16 [carriers *Enterprise* and *Hornet*] slipped out of Pearl Harbor on 28 May, and Spruance set course for the aptly named Point Luck some 350 miles northeast of Midway, we began an elaborate radio deception to disguise our own movements. At Efate. 1,500 miles to the southwest in the New Hebrides, seaplane tender *Tangier* pretended to be a full-fledged carrier making transmissions in a pattern similar to that of a task force flying routine air operations. The same ploy was used by heavy cruiser *Salt Lake City* on patrol in the Coral Sea. The idea was to persuade Japanese traffic analysts at the Owada intelligence center outside Tokyo that Halsey's two carriers were more than 1,000 miles away from Midway.

These ruses succeeded, thereby contributing significant to the subsequent decisive American victory at Midway.

CASE 69:
Col. Evans F. Carlson, Tinian Island, Pacific 1944
A US Marine planning officer sells his deception to the CO.

In mid-1944 the Planning Officer of the US 4th Marine Division was Col. Evans F. Carlson. In designing the amphibious assault on Japanese-held Tinian Island, he had two handicaps: 1) the enemy was fully alert and even knew the day of attack; 2) the triangular island had only three beaches, one per side and only two of which were approachable by existing amphibious craft, a point also recognized by the enemy.[320]

---

318 Layton (1985), 427.
319 Layton (1985), 433, 436.
320 Whaley (1969), A394-A396; Michael Blankfort, *The Big Yankee: The Life of Carlson of the Raiders* (Boston: Little, Brown, 1947). 337.

Carlson came rather well prepared for this task. A career Marine assigned to US Naval Intelligence, Capt. Carlson had marched with and closely observed Mao Tse-tung's Eighth Route Army in combat against the Japanese in North China in 1937 and again in 1938. He published two perceptive books about their slippery guerrilla tactics, tactics to which he had quickly become converted.[321] The fact that this experience also converted him to the Chinese Communist philosophy made him a controversial figure for the rest of his career, supported by powerful political figures, admired by his troops, and an embarrassment to his superiors. Given his own command in 1942, the Second Marine Raider Battalion (the famed "Carlson's Raiders"), he applied the training methods and leadership principles he had learned from Mao Tse-tung's Eighth Route Army. And he had tested these tactics with his Raiders in their hit-andrun operation against Makin Atoll later that year. On that occasion he had deliberately selected as his point of landing the beach that had the most difficult approach. He did this on the correct assumption that it would be least guarded.[322]

Now, with Tinian offering not merely a "difficult" approach but an "impossible" one, Carlson opted for the "impossible" beach. He presented his plan to Maj. Gen. Harry Schmidt, CO of the 4th Marine Division, and the latter's Chief of Staff, Col. Walter Rogers. Carlson proposed that to ensure surprise the division must land on the small and inaccessible beach section that could only hold perhaps 250 men. Summing up, Carlson argued that "We can shoulder our way in through the enemy's back door. It's the only way to surprise him."[323] General Schmidt and Colonel Rogers enthusiastically approved Carlson's plan.

The impossible was made possible by an improvised carpet spread from the front of the smaller landing craft to enable them to cross the razor-sharp coral shallows. When Carlson was wounded on Saipan on June 22nd, the final Tinian planning was handled by others.

The landing on July 24th was opposed by a single machine-gun nest, the 6,000 defenders being deployed uselessly at the other two beaches. Soon after the war the then Lt. Gen. Schmidt gave full and proper credit: "Carlson made a good-sized contribution to the winning of the Pacific war."[324] Both the official US Navy and Marine histories of this operation (published, respectively, in 1953 and 1960) omit mention of Carlson's key planning role. By then his Communist sympathies had made him a "nonperson" in Washington.

---

321 Evans Fordyce Carlson, *The Chinese Army* (New York: Institute of Pacific Relations, 1940); Evans Fordyce Carlson, *Twin Stars of China* (New York: Dodd, Mead, 1940).
322 For the Makin raid see Whaley (1969/2007), Example B25; and Blankfort (1947). 42-43.
323 Blankfort (1947), 337.
324 Blankfort (1947), 338.

CASE 70:
Lt. Col. Leonard Durham, The Pentagon 1970s
Selling deception planning to US generals.

Admittedly, many Americans—constrained by moral or religious teachings or driven by the Goliath belief in sheer force—resist dabbling in deception. During the early 1970s such involvement was resisted even at the Pentagon.

At that time Lt. Col. (USAF) Leonard E. "Len" Durham had the largely thankless task of heading the tiny Special Plans office for the Joint Staff of the Joint Chiefs of Staff (JCS). "Special Plans" was the U.S. Government's naively assumed "cover" designation for the deception planning groups scattered throughout the services. At first I thought how clever of them to have phony titles and phony personnel playing the con man's "big store" in the Government phone books and on Pentagon office door plaques as a lure for foreign spies. But no, our deceivers innocently believed that phrase concealed their mission. Few knew their own history, and none knew this small part. The phrase had been coined thirty years earlier in WW2 by British deception planners as the official cover title for their work. German Intelligence never penetrated this simple euphemism; but, as some historians of Intelligence already knew from the public record, Soviet Intelligence had—through their premier "mole", Kim Philby.[325] The Americans got this already "compromised" term from their British teachers in WW2 and, none the wiser, some even unknowingly revived it in this new millennium.

In any case, Colonel Durham had the hard job of trying to sell deception to American generals who seemed to find it all too complicated, virtually incomprehensible, a "tangled web". His most effective pitch was to take the skeptical West Point, Annapolis, or USAF academy-graduate general to a football game. There, as one deceptive play after another unfolded before their eyes, he would repeatedly shout, above the roar of the crowd, "THAT'S WHAT I MEAN!"[326]

Interestingly, Durham had been taught this ploy in 1971 by none other than Major General (USA, Ret.) William A. Harris, who had so successfully led General Bradley's deception unit in WWII. Harris had told Durham:[327]

> Yeah, Vince Lombardi. I used to use that expression all the time during the war with some intransigent American general who would say, "Well, I don't want anything to do with that sort of garbage—deception." I would say, "Well, what about the Notre

---
325 What I did not know in the early 1970s was that the Soviets had made multiple penetrations of the WW2 British deception system.
326 Author's recollection of a conversation with Col. Durham at that time.
327 *Verbatim Transcript* (1971), 120.

Dame football team? They don't use all straight power. They use deception."

CASE 71:
General MacArthur, Inchon, Korea 1950
Selling the idea to the JCS.

> Like Montcalm, the North Koreans would regard an Inchon landing as impossible. Like Wolfe, I could take them by surprise.
>
> — MacArthur, 23 August 1950

In 1950 the United Nations Command under General Douglas MacArthur was bogged down in the early stages of the Korean War. His remaining troops in Korea had been driven back into a tightly compressed perimeter defense of the port of Pusan. MacArthur recognized the need to seize the initiative. And the only way he could conceive doing so was by restoring the mobility of his army.

Being a peninsula, Korea is an attractive target for outflanking amphibious surprise attacks. MacArthur grasped this simple but then doctrinally unpopular point within a fortnight of the outbreak of the war. Accordingly, he had his staff scout a suitable beach to try an amphibious end-run. Among several candidates, Inchon had all the "don'ts" on the current amphibious doctrine list—poorly sited for naval support fire, little shelter from weather, beaches inadequate to receive a large force, unsatisfactory offshore configuration, mined approaches, etc., etc. If not strictly "impossible", Inchon was, as MacArthur's Chief of Staff mused, "the worst possible place we could bring in an amphibious assault." And this was precisely why MacArthur chose it—the "worst" place was the "best" gamble.[328] Detailed planning was in the hands of Maj. Gen. Edwin "Pinky" Wright, chief of both MacArthur's G-3 and the Joint Strategic Plans and Operations Group (JSPOG).

To implement his bold plan, MacArthur needed approval from the JCS; but the JCS was less than enthusiastic and sent a delegation to Tokyo. The JCS-MacArthur conference took place during the late afternoon on August 23rd in MacArthur's magnificent headquarters in the Dai Ichi Building across the moat from the Imperial Palace. Representing the JCS were General J. Lawton Collins, Chief of Naval Operations Admiral Forrest Sherman, and Lt. Gen. Idwal H. Edwards (representing the Air Force's Gen. Hoyt Vandenberg). From Pearl Harbor came Admiral Arthur W. Radford (CINCPAC) and Lt. Gen. Lemuel

---
328 Whaley (1969/2007), Case A59.

C. Shephard Jr (head of Fleet Marine Force, Pacific). The meeting opened with a one-hour briefing by Wright and nine other members of MacArthur's staff. Then Sherman and Collins gave their argument for the JCS. MacArthur later recalled that:[329]

> I waited a moment or so to collect my thoughts. I could feel the tension rising in the room. Almond shifted uneasily in his chair. If ever a silence was pregnant, this one was. I could almost hear my father's voice telling me as he had so many years ago, "Doug, councils of war breed timidity and defeatism."

MacArthur now opened his 45-minute rebuttal, delivered without notes:[330]

> The bulk of the Reds are committed around Walker's defense perimeter. The enemy, I am convinced, has failed to prepare Inchon properly for defense.
>
> The very arguments you have made as to the impracticabilities involved will tend to ensure for me the element of surprise. For the enemy commander will reason that no one would be so brash as to make such an attempt. Surprise is the most vital element for success in war. As an example, the Marquis de Montcalm believed in 1759 that it was impossible for an armed force to scale the precipitous river banks south of the then walled city of Quebec, and therefore concentrated his formidable defenses along the more vulnerable banks north of the city. But General James Wolfe and a small force did indeed come up the St. Lawrence River and scale those heights. On the Plains of Abraham, Wolfe won a stunning victory that was made possible almost entirely by surprise. Thus he captured Quebec and in effect ended the French and Indian War. Like Montcalm, the North Koreans would regard an Inchon landing as impossible. Like Wolfe, I could take them by surprise.

If imitation is the highest form of flattery, MacArthur showed uncharacteristic humility by acknowledging that Wolfe's "impossible" exploit at Quebec in 1759 inspired his replication at Inchon nearly two hundred years later, particularly as everyone present at this meeting knew that MacArthur himself was a master of amphibious operations. But his humility was politic. No doubt he thought it prudent to cite a classic case study known in outline to all present rather than appear to beat his own drum. However, during the concluding discussion, MacArthur reverted to his usual tactless style when, in answer to a question

---

329 MacArthur (1964), 349.
330 Nor with either stenographer or tape recorder. Consequently the text quoted here is its author's own later reconstruction (See MacArthur [1964], 349-350) but supported in essence if not detail by the recollections of others present. See James (1985). 469, 470.

about the difficulties entailed in amphibious operations, he dismissed the point with a sharp reminder of his own expertise in that subject.

MacArthur portrays this meeting in typical fashion—the lone hero winning over weak and indecisive mortals by the sheer power of his charismatic words at the crucial moment. Certainly MacArthur was a stubborn salesman; but he was not entirely alone at the beginning of the conference. Two days before, Admiral Sherman had privately remarked to the Seventh Fleet commander that: "I'm going to back the Inchon operation completely. I think it's sound." Marine Lt. Gen. Shepherd and Admiral Radford were already predisposed to an amphibious operation although not at Inchon because they thought it made for a too difficult landing. Even Army Chief of Staff Collins only opposed Inchon as the landing site because he thought it too far north and was prepared to back another site further south.[331]

Seven days later, the Joint Chiefs wired their decision: "We concur after reviewing the information brought back by General Collins and Admiral Sherman, in making preparations and executing a turning movement by amphibious forces on the west coast of Korea—at Inchon."[332] But the JCS nervously insisted on receiving reports of MacArthur's further plans, urged reconsideration of some more southern beach for the operation, and clearly wanted to retain the right of a last minute veto contingent on any unfavorable development at the Pusan perimeter. On D-minus-8 the JCS ordered an immediate detailed report.[333] MacArthur resented this intrusion and circumvented it by a ruse. The next day he sent off a general reply and promised details would follow by courier by D-minus-4. In fact, while the courier, Lt. Col. Lynn

D. Smith, was leaving Tokyo on D-minus-5, MacArthur personally ordered him not to arrive in Washington "too soon". Smith reached Washington on D-minus-1 and was scheduled to brief the JCS next day. So, on Inchon D-day he gave a long presentation followed by many questions. By the end, it was too late to abort the operation even had the JCS chosen to do so. The first wave of Marines were already ashore.[334]

It is hardly necessary to remind the reader that MacArthur achieved his goal. Moreover, although this initial brilliant amphibious stroke was to prove the last in the three-year long war, it served to make the enemy conscious—perhaps even hyperconscious—of the need to divert at least some portion of his troop strength and planning effort to guard against a repetition. The situation thus was comparable to that during General Alexander's campaign up the Italian peninsula in WW2. There, by maintaining a continuous amphibious threat

---

331 James (1985), 467-468, 471.
332 Quoted in MacArthur (1964), 351.
333 James (1985), 471-474.
334 Brig. Gen. Lynn D. Smith, "A Nickel After a Dollar," *Army*, Vol.20 (Sep 1970), 25, 32-34.

following the early landings at Salerno and Anzio, Alexander had tricked the Germans into keeping two or more precious divisions in continual reserve awaiting a never-to-materialize event.

CASE 72:
Castro and His Invasion of Cuba, 1956
Wherein Fidel wisely rejects the advice of both his teacher and his principle field commander.

Fidel Castro and Che Guevara had the same training in guerrilla warfare and the same field experience, yet Castro was a master of deception and Guevara was not. In Mexico during 1956, Cuban lawyer Castro arranged for himself, Argentine physician Guevara, and their small band to take classes in guerrilla warfare from Spanish Civil War veteran Colonel Alberto Bayo. When on November 15th Castro publicly announced he would invade Cuba before the year's end. Colonel Bayo was appalled, remonstrating, "Don't you know that a cardinal military principle is to keep your intentions secret from your enemy?" Castro casually answered:[335]

> "You taught me that, but in this case I want everyone in Cuba to know I am coming. I want them to have faith in the 26th of July Movement. It is a peculiarity all my own although I know that militarily it might be harmful. It is psychological warfare."

This remarkable statement—as well as later reflections and actions by Castro—show an intuitive rather than theoretical grasp of the means of his victory. It also typifies the barriers of preconception that balk understanding of deception operations. Thus Bayo and Guevara, both conventionally-minded experts on unconventional operations, failed to grasp the psychological and highly deceptive nature of the operations Castro would actually use in taking Cuba. They sincerely believed guerrilla warfare would work in 1954 Cuba and never understood Castro's strategy: the psychological undermining of the Batista dictatorship by pretending to have an invincible guerrilla army. Castro had independently reinvented "token" or "simulated insurgency" (see Case 58), a most advanced form of deception.

For Castro, Che Guevara and his other guerrilla captains were more useful as photogenic character actors than as combat soldiers. It was a simulated army, deployed for easy victories over the visiting foreign correspondents whose enthusiastic stories carried weight with Batista's increasingly disaffected supporters. Moreover, being little more than phantom-like "token insurgents", they suffered few casualties. Fortunately for the Cuban Revolution, Castro

---

335 Jules Dubois, *Fidel Castro* (Indianapolis: Bobbs-Merrill, 1959), 138, from author's interview with Bayo.

heeded his psycho-political intuition and threw away the rule books while Guevara was writing them. Unhappily for Guevara, his absurd filibusterings around Latin America led to his miserable death in Bolivia in 1967—a small fish who never learned how to swim in the sea of the people.[336]

It is not surprising that Guevara passed Bayo's 3-month course in 1956 with the colonel's rating of "No. 1 in the class", while Castro was unrated—an indifferent student who took little part in the lectures and field exercises.[337]

CASE 73:
Richard Bissell and the Bay of Pigs, Cuba 1961
A failure to communicate the CIA deception plan.
On 17 April 1961 U.S. President Kennedy sent 1,443 brave men off on a filibustering expedition to the Bay of Pigs to accomplish some never agreed upon task of grand strategy. That quick disaster has been analyzed ad nauseam and the richly deserved blame laid at various doorsteps ranging from the CIA and the JCS up to the young and inexperienced Commander-in-Chief. But all these studies have, I believe, overlooked one instructive element in the story—the original deception plan and how it got muddled along the way.

Richard M. "Dick" Bissell Jr was a Yale PhD in economics, ex-professor, and successful wartime administrator when in 1954 at age 45 he joined the CIA as Special Assistant to the Director. One of his early tasks was to write up the history of the recently concluded Operation SUCCESS, the CIA planned and directed deception operation that had tumbled the Arbenz regime in Guatemala (Case 58).

Four years later Bissell moved up to succeed Frank Wisner as Deputy Director heading the Plans Division (i.e., covert operations). Now it was his turn to try his own hand at deception planning.

President Eisenhower had decided it was time to remove Fidel Castro. As Bissell later freely acknowledged, his scenario was simply a more elaborate and sophisticated replication of the Haney-Wisner plan that had worked to

---

336 I owe this distinction between Castro and Guevara to Dr. Ernst Halperin during conversations in January and February 1969. At my urging Halperin coined the term "token insurgency" on February 18th to characterize this new and distinctive type of psychological guerrilla warfare, one which Halperin had already discovered had been invented and used by the CIA'S Frank Wisner for the successful takeover of Guatemala in 1954 and replicated by Richard M. Bissell, Jr., in his *original* 1960-61 CIA plan for the Bay of Pigs. See also Whaley (1969), 107-115 and Case A65; Ernst Halperin, *The National Liberation Movements in Latin America* (Cambridge, MA: Center for International Studies, MIT, June 1969, Center Paper No.A/69-6), 13-14, 18-45, 53-67; and J. Bowyer Bell, *The Myth of the Guerrilla; Revolutionary Theory and Malpractice* (New York: Knopf, 1971), 210-243.

337 Dubois (1959), 127, interview with Bayo; Tad Szulc, *Fidel: A Critical Portrait* (New York: William Morrow, 1986), 350, 358, citing Bayo's 1960 memoir.

perfection in Guatemala (Case 58). Haney's scheme was in the forefront of Bissell's mind when he got this new assignment.

Bissell's new deception plan for Cuba was intended to convince Castro, his senior chiefs, and the Cuban public that a strong U.S.-supported force of Cuban insurgents had landed to trigger an irresistible insurrection. In other words, this original plan was meant to be nothing more than a "token" (simulated) insurgency. A rag-tag band of Cuban exile patriots would be landed at a remote and easily defended beachhead where they would sit in relative safety, going nowhere. Meanwhile the carefully orchestrated international press and radio media would trumpeted this pseudo "invasion", thereby provoking a mass uprising of the Cuban people. The American policy makers generally presumed the Cuban people to be ripe for rebellion. This crucial assumption was false. Unfortunately, these officials remained unaware of strong evidence that the great majority of the populace were still basically too neutral to support an uprising and the one semi-organized opposition group was too small and too weak to revolt.[338]

Consequently, as Bissell's plan moved up from Langley to the White House for approval and then over to the Pentagon and back to Langley for implementation, its original intent of deception by psychological warfare was misunderstood. The plan was now being handled by senior military and intelligence officers who did not understand deception. Bissell's plan became quickly translated into a plan that they could understand, namely a conventional military invasion and insurrection.

Does this mean that the original deception plan might have succeeded? Almost certainly not. Both plans shared the assumption that a public perception of an invasion—whether simulated or real—would provoke the desired popular uprising and consequent regime change in regime. Bissell himself later admitted that he'd come to believe that even his version of the plan would probably have failed.[339]

---

338 As reported to me at the time by my four friends at the U.S. Information Agency (USIA) who ran its small research (intelligence) department. They had known of this weak anti-Casto sentiment from a recent public opinion survey research study inside Cuba that they had covertly commissioned through Lloyd Free and issued 13 Apr 1970. Free's 7-page report wasn't read by President Kennedy's advisers until after the Bay of Pigs fiasco despite JFK's specific enquiries about the state of public opinion on Castro in Cuba. See Hanley Cantril, *The Human Dimension: Experiences in Policy Research* (New Brunswick: Rutgers University Press, 1967), 1-5.

339 My recollection of a private conversation with Bissell in 1969 at the Harvard Faculty Club.

CASE 74:
Capt. Liddell Hart, 1927-1954
The historian as teacher.

Captain Sir Basil Henry Liddell Hart has been called "the Captain who taught Generals." His admirers (if not exactly "students")[340] included Churchill, Wavell, Dorman-Smith, T. E. Lawrence, Rommel, Mellenthin, Bayerlein, Guderian, Yadin, and Beaufre.

General Wavell raised an interesting criticism of his friend Liddell Hart's main theory in early 1942 while desperately embroiled trying to stave off the Japanese advance in Southeast Asia. One day in late January or February at his ABDA headquarters on Java, shortly before its fall, Wavell took time to read a draft of Liddell Hart's *The Strategy of Indirect Approach* and write his old friend: "My main conclusion was that with your knowledge and brains and command of the pen, you could have written just as convincing a book called The Strategy of Direct Approach."[341] In effect, Wavell recognized that Liddell Hart had got it wrong—not all wrong but rather simply missed the key implication of his own evidence and line of argument. Liddell Hart was really writing about deception in general and not just about the "direct" versus "indirect" geographical approaches. Even he applauded direct, straight-ahead attacks when they were well-covered by deception, if not of place, then of timing, strength, style, and so forth.

■ ■ ■ ■ ■

I choose to end this section on salesmanship with the biggest, most important, most geographically widespread, and most complexly coordinated of all deception plans, BODYGUARD. Placed here it also serves as a bridge to the next chapter, on deception planning in its institutional setting. An entire book could be written on this one example of planning; and, in a sense, already has—in Anthony Cave Brown's *Bodyguard of Lies*, although that early effort only skimmed the surface of the planning process itself. I will merely sketch an outline of that process. But BODYGUARD was preceded by a lesser known plan that was cancelled—itself an important example of the learning process in deception planning. We will first look at this cancelled plan, Plan JAEL, and the excellent reasons why.

---

340 Jay Luvaas, "Liddell Hart and the Mearsheimer Critique: A "Pupil's Retrospective," *Parameters*, Vol.20 (Mar 1990), 9-19.

341 Quoted in Lewin (1980), 222.

CASE 75:
Plan JAEL, London 1943

Col. Clarke convinces the Supreme Command to drop the previously failed plan.

Plan JAEL followed the fiasco of COCKADE[342] and was its obvious attempt at a successful replication. However, beginning in early fall of 1943, Col. Bevan and his LCS deception planners in London initially repeated COCKADE's error of trying to simulate threats against Hitler's Fortress Europa at too many places, from too many directions.

Fortunately Col. Dudley Clarke intervened from Cairo. He convinced London of this flaw but London's fiddling adjustments gradually led to JAEL simply vanishing to become replaced in January 1944 by BODYGUARD, the comprehensive new plan that, together with its superb cross-Channel FORTITUDE, would produce an enormous and decisive success for deception.[343]

CASE 76: Plans BODYGUARD & FORTITUDE, London 1943-44

OVERLORD was the code name for the Anglo-American effort to recapture Hitler's "Fortress Europe". BODYGUARD was the overall strategic deception plan to disguise the general place, time, and strength of that great war-winning enterprise. FORTITUDE was the subordinate operational (grand tactical) deception plan to disguise the specific place, time, and strength of the main amphibious assault across the English Channel onto the beaches of northern France. The real target was the Normandy Peninsula; the notional (dummy) target was set 170 miles (280 kilometers) eastward on the coast at Calais.

Consider the following paragraph:[344]

"German intelligence was quite unable to determine the time, place, or strength of the OVERLORD beachhead. Their faulty appreciation read July rather than 6 June 1944, the Pas-de-Calais rather than Normandy, and credited the Allies with 42 quite mythical divisions. Of over 200 relevant agent reports received by German intelligence before D-Day, only one disclosed the correct time and place. And it had been audaciously planted by Allied intelligence on a thoroughly *discredited* former Abwehr collaborator. The closest the Germans came to penetrating the secret of D-Day was having learned the code-name

---

342 Whaley, *When Deception Fails* (FDDC, Mar 2010), Case 2.2.6.
343 Holt (2004), 496-498, 506, 507, 825; Mure (1980), 237.
344 Verbatim, as I published it in 1969 in *Stratagem* as Case A45. That was an accurate appraisal based on my analysis of unclassified documents available long before the semi-official accounts of the Double-Cross System (Masterman's revelations in 1972 about the role of Allied double agents and Bevan's LCS), ULTRA (Winterbotham's revelations in 1974 about the Allies reading of the German codes), the elaborate build-up of the notional order-of-battle that credited the Allies with a much larger combat force (Clarke's work leaked in 1977), and finally the full details of FORTITUDE (Hesketh's study leaked in scraps in 1982 & 1987).

OVERLORD itself and correctly inferring that this referred to a cross-channel assault into France. This was the achievement of "Cicero", the Turkish [Albanian] valet-spy who was passing on the secret papers of the British Ambassador in Ankara. However, the Germans failed to make use of {German Ambassador to Turkey} Von Papen's suggestion for a counter-deception propaganda campaign: publicizing the code-name OVERLORD and implying the Germans knew its detailed content, thereby forcing the Allies to adopt a new plan."

Allied security (an important part of the negative, dissimulative, or "hiding" half of deception) had been adequate to keep the German intelligence snoopers *puzzled* about the nature of the Allies' big secrets. However, it was the simulative or "showing" half of deception that made them *certain but wrong*.[345]

---

345 The rich details of the successful Allied BODYGUARD & FORTITUDE deceptions is best told in Holt (2004).

CHAPTER 7:
Institutional Deception Planning

> An Intelligence organization resembles a human head. It has its sources, run by various collecting agencies, which correspond to the sense organs; these feed their information into the collating centre, which corresponds to the brain.
>
> — R. V. Jones, "Scientific Intelligence,"
> *Research*, Vol.9 (Sep 1956), 347

Deception planners do not work in a vacuum any more than do Jones' Intelligencers. Both work within a more-or-less dense network of military or political-military organization and bureaucracy. This section examines deception in this institutional context. The main purpose here is to collect evidence that may reveal different "styles" of planning imposed by different organizational structures and traditions.

We also see a learning process in the growth of each of these organizations. Each grew in direct response to lessons learned. In this section that driving force is largely only implicit—time alone preventing an explicit account of the step-by-step changes in these organizations to meet the growing perceptions of need. For those details, the reader is directed to the footnoted source references.

CASE 77:
The Barcelona Defense Committee, Spain 1936
A committee of Anarchists plans an ambush that wins the Battle of Barcelona.

The notion of a committee of several hundred civilian men and women planning a major military deception operation is absurd. That they were Anarchists makes it ludicrous. But here is an interesting case because it was both unique and brilliantly successful.

On 17 July 1936, four senior Spanish generals including Francisco Franco attempted a *pronunciamiento*, the traditional Spanish/Latin American-style military coup d'état. The generals intended and expected a quick stroke to seize the centers of civil administration culminating in the rebels unchallenged pronouncement of a new government. They blundered and instead created a civil war that would bleed Spain for the next 31 months.

The lines were quickly drawn between virtually all the Army officers and most of the regular troops in the Nationalist ("Rebel") zone and the hastily improvised militias in the dwindling Republican Government ("Loyalist") zone. It was professionals versus amateurs.

The Loyalist militia columns were a patchwork of Socialist miners, Anarchist trade-unionists, and Communist students, in a harlequinade of uniforms, accompanied by their women-in-arms. At first they were widely, spontaneously, and romantically dubbed "guerrillas". Although a Spanish word with a rather precise meaning, it was misapplied to these militia, who were merely irregular scratch forces foolishly trying to fight a conventional modern war. Real guerrilla resistance did develop behind the Rebel lines; but that came later.[346]

For the Insurgent generals, their coup's success hinged on the swift seizure of the main administrative centers, particularly the national capital city of Madrid and the great provincial capital of Catalonia, Barcelona. Both cities successfully resisted the rebel columns. The famous Battle of Madrid is of no interest here, having been fought along entirely conventional lines and without guile. The relevant case is the Battle of Barcelona.

At the coup's outbreak on 17 July 1936, the senior local officer at Barcelona who sided with the Rebels was Cavalry Brigadier-General Alvaro Fernández Burriel. Two days later he led local Rebel regulars in an effort to take over the city. Meeting unexpectedly strong resistance from hastily formed local militias, his effort had failed by that evening, with some final hold-outs surrendering the following morning. Burriel retreated to the city outskirts where he awaited reinforcement by Infantry General Mañuel Goded, one of Generalissimo Franco's favorites.[347]

The reinforced Rebel column entering Barcelona was led by General Goded with Burriel as his second-in-command. It was a large well-armed force of regulars, locally garrisoned, familiar with the terrain and the layout of the metropolis. The column's officers expected a disorganized resistance either at the outskirts or among the city streets. They welcomed either. Their target was the central square with its key administrative buildings.

The civilian defenders correctly assumed that this would be the Rebel strategy and planned their resistance accordingly. The defenders of Barcelona were the large community of Anarchists there. Organized as the locally powerful trade

---

346 Barton Whaley, *Guerrillas in the Spanish Civil War* (Cambridge, MA: Center for International Studies, M.I.T., 1969, multilithed).
347 A capsule biography of Goded is *Wikipedia*, "Manuel Goded Llopis" (accessed 9 Feb 2010).

union syndicate (CNT), they drew some support from the non-Soviet Marxist POUM, and some Loyalist assault guard and civil guard units.

To understand the Anarchist-led defense, we must discard the popular notion of bomb-throwing terrorist chaos, which is correctly called Nihilism. Spanish Anarchism stemmed instead from the tradition of Bakhuninism. Brought to Spain in the late 1800s, it preached that governance, organization was not only useful but inevitable. What it opposed was all forms of hierarchical organization, which it believed was the cause of tyranny. The Spanish Anarchists were mainly educated urban craftsmen and technicians.

The Anarchist committee correctly identified the Rebel's intention, strategy, and capability to carry it out against relatively untrained riflemen. The consensus was that the only feasible resistance would have to be an ambush.

The Anarchist Telephone Workers Union agreed to handle communications. The American IT&T under Colonel Sosthenes Behn had just installed a state-of-the-art telephone system in Barcelona and the union workers agreed to coordinate the whole show by telephone without the knowledge of the company's capitalist managers.

All went according to plan. The Rebel column, meeting only harassing rifle fire at the city outskirts, moved confidently into the broad avenues. One street barricade after another was abandoned in face of the advancing regulars, which pressed rapidly and eagerly toward the central square. On reaching their goal they were surprised to see themselves ringed by rifles from every building. The previously abandoned barricades leading out of the square had also been quickly manned. The nearly bloodless Battle of Barcelona ended on August 11th when the entire Rebel column laid down arms.[348]

Generals Goded and Burriel surrendered, were court martialed, and sentenced to death. The following day they were taken to the Montjuich Castle in Barcelona where they were executed by firing squad. When three bitterly fought years later, Franco's rebels finally won the war, their historians rewrote this battle to attribute Goded's defeat to having been "outnumbered" when, in fact, he'd been out-thought.

CASE 78:
The German General Staff in WW2

As we have seen, the German military had dabbled in deception planning during the Great War (Cases 6 & 37) and had developed it to a fine art in their post-war evasions of the disarmament provisions of the Versailles Treaty

---

348 I owe this account of the planning and execution of this decisive conclusion to Insurgent's effort to take Barcelona to a 1970s Lecture by MIT Associate Professor of History William Braach Watson.

(Cases 8, 37, 39). And we have seen how Hitler exploited deception to the hilt in his grand strategy of bluff from 1935 to the outbreak of WW2 in 1939 (Case 40). During this period, the principle of surprise began to take an increasingly major place in German military doctrine, and deception was accepted as its handmaiden. However, deception planning was not institutionalized, remaining the practice of individual commanders and staff officers.

Tactical level deception was first institutionalized in the German Army by the mid-1930s when its intelligence branch, the so-called Abwehr, created the organizational machinery. This was the D Group (Gruppe Ill-D), one of the half dozen main divisions in Col. Franz von Bentivegni's military security section (Abteilung Ill). Group D (subdivided into two geographic desks) was responsible for developing deception operations in coordination with the Army, Navy, and Air Force general staffs and for providing disinformation suitable for dissemination by the Abwehr's counterespionage (Ill-F) and other services.[349]

Strategic level deception was first institutionalized in early 1940.[350] The occasion was the planning of the spring offensive on the Western Front. The initiative was taken at the highest level of command, in Hitler's own military staff, the Supreme Command of the Military Forces (OKW, *Oberkommando der Wehrmacht*). The simple instrument that accomplished this revolution was a document called the *Timetable*. This was the OKW's master schedule governing the operation. Moreover it coordinated the entire plan by specifying for each step the military operations, time-schedules, and deceptions. Because it was a standard form, it served as a constant reminder to all staff officers, from the Führer on down, that each stage of the operation should be accompanied by and coordinated with appropriate deceptive measures. The first of these Timetables was issued on February 22nd in conjunction with the more general directive titled *Guidelines for Deception of the Enemy* (see Appendix A).

Henceforward every German strategic campaign plan was closely coordinated with its cover plan through a *Timetable*. I do not know the administrative genius who first proposed this primitive PERT-type chart, but it was someone in the OKW and it was approved by Hitler. In any case, both the *Timetable* and various "Guidelines" for deception originated in Maj.-Gen. Walter Warlimont's plans section (Abteilung L), which was under Lt.-Gen. Jodl's operations staff (WFSt).[351]

It was Hitler's style to devise the broad outline of his real plan and then even specify the main themes and ruses of its deception plan, leaving it to his

---

349 Whaley (1973), 171.
350 I suspect this may have happened as early as the invasion of Poland in 1939 or even Austria in 1938, but I have yet to find confirming documents.
351 Whaley (1969), A192, A194; Whaley (1973), 171-172.

personal staff (usually Keitel as head of the OKW or Jodl as chief of its WFSt) to coordinate the detailed real and cover planning with the appropriate segments of the military, intelligence, propaganda, and foreign affairs bureaucracies. Thus, from 1940 on, the Germans had a completely centralized deception planning team embedded within Ops at the very top of the administrative ladder.

CASE 79:
The British "global deception" System in WW2

Earlier cases have traced the tradition of British military deception from Henderson and Swinton in the Boer War (Cases 2 and 3), through Allenby and Meinertzhagen in WW1 (Cases 33, 34, 35), to Wavell (Case 10) and Dudley Clarke (Cases 11, 46, 47, 50) in early WW2. To that point British deception was an informal art, taught only by word-of-mouth or by personal example and passed along for four decades in a chain from Henderson to Clarke. There were no specialized deception planning staffs, only single devious officers in Intelligence or Ops or, specifically, plans with a flair for deception. Wavell and Clarke were about to change all this.

Admittedly important groundwork was already laid in London. The Secret Intelligence Service (S.I.S., the so-called M.I.6) had been running a small and primitive double-agent system against the Germans from the outbreak of the war in 1939 until 1941 with support from the Security Service (the so-called M.I.5).[352] This was evidently the notion of M.I.5's able Assistant Director of B Division, Dick White. As one of his officers later recalled:[353]

> He wrote a memorandum in the early days in which he pointed out that spies captured in England could be used, if they could be "turned round", to send false information to Germany and that this was altogether a better plan than that of their summary execution. Probably he did not realize at the time the extent to which his plan could be developed and how triumphantly successful it would turn out to be.

Thus M.I.5's main contribution was from its newly created special B.1a section, which provided the case officers for the turned agents. This section was headed by Major (Seaforth Highlanders) T.A. "Tar" Robertson.[354] Robertson was highly experienced in counter-espionage, having been recruited into M.I.5 back in 1933 (he was a friend of the then Director's son) and trained from the beginning in C-E by Guy Liddell.[355]

---

352 Masterman (1972), 36-59.
353 Masterman (1975), 221.
354 Masterman (1975), 219, 220.
355 West (1982), 43.

Moreover, the Government Code and Cipher School at Bletchley Park, which was under M.I.6, had since 1940 been slowly improving its ULTRA readings of German radio commandand-control nets that would soon prove so crucial in getting feed-back from the enemy on the British deception efforts.[356]

Also, camouflage, which had become dormant between the wars, had been quickly reestablished in the British armed services. First, in response to the imminent threat of German bombings on the eve of war in 1939 the Air Ministry created "Colonel Turner's Department" (which was, for cover, its official name) to spoof the Luftwaffe's aerial reconnaissance and bombers. This proved quite effective.[357] Second, the fine British tradition for field military camouflage created in WW1 by, among others Solomon J. Solomon, was revived on 14 October 1940 by Major Richard Buckley (who'd served in WW1 as a camouflage officer under Solomon), who now directed the first course of the Royal Engineer's Camouflage Training and Development Centre at Farnam Castle.[358]

The Inter-Service Security Board (ISSB) had come into being on an ad hoc basis to handle the security and deception aspects of the planned British operations in Finland during the Russo-Finnish War. In March 1940 the ISSB, sponsored by the Joint Intelligence Committee (JIC) was made a permanent organization, supported and staffed by the War Office, policy directed by the JIC, and chaired by the head of M.l.11.[359]

In July 1940 M.I.5 created the low-echelon W. Branch (the "W" standing for wireless) to coordinate the double-agent system with M.I.6. Then, on September 30th, at the instigation of the Director of Military Intelligence, this body was moved further up the chain of command, renamed W. Board, and given the specific mission of disseminating false information. Membership was initially confined to the Directors of Intelligence for the three service agencies and the Chief of the Security Service (M.I.5) with Lieut.-Commander Ewen Montagu (RNVR) as Secretary. W. Board was an informal committee that held no regularly scheduled meetings and met a total of only 15 times during the war.[360]

As this was too austere a level to handle the day-to-day needs of the double-agent system, the Twenty Committee was created as a sub-committee on 2 January 1941. Its initial membership, appointed by W. Board, comprised junior officers representing M.I.5, which provided the chairman (Maj. J. C. Masterman, an Oxford history don and famous detective fiction novelist who now served

---
356 Lewin (1978), 42-72.
357 Cruickshank (1979), 4-11.
358 Fisher (1983), 16; Barkas (1952), 24-31, 43.
359 F. H. Hinsley and others, *British Intelligence in the Second World War*, Vol.1 (Cambridge: Cambridge University Press, 1979), 93, 94.
360 Masterman(1972), 61-62; Montagu (1978), 40-41, 53-54.

in B-1a, the section responsible for running all double agents in Britain), the secretary (John H. Marriott, a young Cantabridgian and solicitor now with B.1a as its deputy head under Robertson), and a member from Iberian Section (Tomàs 'Tommy" Harris, a wealthy art dealer who had transferred from SOE to M.I.5's B.1a as a case officer for double agents); the War Office; GHQ Home Forces; Home Defence Executive (Sir Findlater Stewart or, as his alternate, John Drew); Air Ministry Intelligence (F/Lt. Archibald Cholmondeley); Naval Intelligence Division (Lieut.-Commander Ewen Montagu, RNVR, the up-and-coming barrister who also served as Secretary on W Board); M.I.6 (Martin Lloyd, a former schoolmaster at Rugby now with Section V), and Colonel Turner's Department at the Air Ministry. At any one time, the Committee totaled between 12 and 14 members.[361]

In early 1943 Twenty Committee got its American OSS/X2 liaison member. Norman Holmes Pearson, a Yale professor of English. When Pearson could not attend, his alternate was his X-2 deputy, Edward J. Lawler. Lawler, a former IRS investigator, also successfully deceived his Committee colleagues—in this case into believing he was a prominent journalist in America.[362]

Examination of the membership of Sir John Masterman's Double-Cross Committee reveals a common factor, most were military amateurs. To continue with only British examples, this was also true of J.H. Bevan's London Controlling Section, Dr. R.V. Jones's Air Ministry Scientific Intelligence department, the several Camouflage units, and Peter Fleming's "D" Force. Does this mean that "amateurishness" is a desirable quality in seeking recruits for deception? Not necessarily, given the brilliantly successful counterexample of Brigadier Dudley Clarke's "A" Force. But this question calls for further research.

For the duration of the war, Twenty Committee met once a week—a total of 226 times—initially at M.I.5 headquarters in temporarily evacuated Wormwood Scrubs Prison and later in fashionable St. James's Street. Given the complexity of bureaucratic interplay that the Committee represented, it is remarkable that "only on one occasion was a vote taken; all other decisions were arrived at after discussion and without a vote."[363]

After over a year substantial progress had been made in building up a sizeable cadre of double agents. But a key problem became clear: the many missed opportunities for using the doubles as part of more sophisticated deception plans to support specific current military operations such as the failed raids

---

361 Masterman (1972), 62-70; West (1982), index entries under Masterman, Marriott, and Harris; Nigel West, *MI6: British Secret Intelligence Service Operations. 1909-45* (New York: Randon House, 1983), 133.
362 Winks (1987), 285. Lawler's impersonation has misled some subsequent historians to assume the "New York newspaper publisher" was Ralph Ingersoll.
363 Masterman (1975), 223.

on Dakar and Dieppe. The cause was that the present deception organization lacked access to and coordination with the higher levels of command.

General Wavell, back in Cairo, was quite aware of London's missed opportunities and recommended his own solution. This was that a controlling body be set up in London to coordinate deception operations in all theaters of war whose local commands should each have its own deception unit. Preoccupied with battles in North Africa and the Balkans, he sent Dudley Clarke to represent him in London at the meeting in March 1941. During that meeting, when asked by Admiral of the Fleet Dudley Pound if he would accept the job of controller of all deception, Clarke declined, explaining:[364]

> Sir, I am a staff officer of Archie Wavell's who alone is conducting active operations at this time. You can't pinch a man's butler when he has only been lent you for the night.

Accordingly, in October 1941, the Chiefs of Staff created the office of Controlling Officer of Deception and appointed Colonel Oliver Stanley, a former Secretary of State for War, to this post, which carried with it a tiny Deception Staff comprising a single staff officer.[365]

Although this reorganization improved matters somewhat, the new setup was still limited to tactical deception planning and ops. Worse, Stanley was wedded to the narrow view that opportunities for deception must be awaited, not created. Consequently little was accomplished in his first four months. Then, in early 1942. Wavell began complaining that LCS wasn't doing its job, urging boldness and more imagination in deception, particularly in long range and intensive planning and organization. Wavell's pressure was decisive with the War Cabinet Office, which replaced Stanley in June.[366]

The new Controller of Deception was Colonel John Henry "Johnny" Bevan, a City of London stockbroker who had served with distinction in WW1 and had spent the previous month as Stanley's staff officer before finding himself in his boss's shoes. Bevan's organization was renamed (for security reasons) the London Controlling Section (L.C.S.) and enlarged.[367] Its extraordinary cast of characters is worth a quick look for what it can tell us about the size, composition, competence, and eccentricity of this, the world's first team of strategic deception planners:[368]

---

364 Mure (1980), 83.
365 Masterman (1972), 101-109; Cruickshank (1979), 34. See Appendix D-1 for the 1942 directive established the LCS.
366 Cruickshank (1979), 34-35; Masterman (1972), 107.
367 Holt (2004), index; Brown (1975), 269-271; Masterman (1972), 107; Cruickshank (1979), 35.
368 The most detailed account of the LCS is in Holt (2004), 166-214 and index.

- Major Ronald Wingate as Executive Director, a former Indian Civil Service officer with great experience of intelligence and devious politics in both India and the Middle East.[369]
- Wing-Commander Dennis Wheatley, first aboard, was a best-selling author of trashy detective, espionage, and occult novels. Indeed he was a convinced occultist. His stepdaughter, Diana Younger, an SOE operative with 6 paradrops into Nazi-occupied France, was dating Major H. Wentworth Eldredge, a member of the SHAEF Special Plans Branch, a family connection that significantly enhanced liaison among the Anglo-American deceptionists.[370]
- Major Harold Petavel, a soap factory manager in peacetime who became a leading intelligence officer at the outset of the war.
- Major Derrick Morley, a peacetime financier and ship-owner.
- Commander (RN) Alec Finter. Rated by Eldredge as ineffective, the only "lemon" in the group.[371]
- Commander (RNVR) James Arbuthnot, a big noise in the tea trade.
- Lieutenant Lady Jane Pleydell-Bouverie, a 20-year-old Auxiliary Territorial Service officer.
- Professor Edward Neville da Costa Andrade, a distinguished scientist whose hobby was, he said, "collecting old scientific books and useless knowledge". He had invented the little "crickets" that Allied paratroops used at night for mutual recognition and his specialty was in applying science to the deception of the enemy.
- Sir Reginald Hoare served as LCS's liaison with the Foreign Office. A senior partner in Bevan's stockbrokerage firm, Hoare was a banker and a diplomat (and brother of the Ambassador to Spain) with much experience of the devious politics of central and eastern Europe.
- Lieutenant Colonel William H. Baumer, the American representative of the U.S. War Department who in early 1944 was sent to Moscow with Bevan to coordinate the D-Day BODYGUARD deceptions with the Russians.[372]

---

369 His memoirs are Wingate (1959).
370 BW 's conversations in early 1973 with Wentworth and Diana Eldredge; *Verbatim Report* (1971), 14; Dennis Wheatley, *The Deception Planners* (London: Hutchinson, 1980).
371 *Verbatim Transcript* (1971), 71.
372 For Baumer's own account of his wartime and post-WW2 role in deception see *Verbatim Transcript of Stratagem Conference, Pentagon, 21 June 1971.*

This is an interesting list. Three observations: First, excepting the Americans, all were solid "establishment" types. That is not surprising given the way the English ran their wars. Second, it was a rather incestuous group, recruitment having been mainly (perhaps even entirely) through personal acquaintanceship or, in the case of the Americans, personal recommendation. However, the third observation is somewhat unusual in that all members were more-or-less what the English themselves always tolerantly and often rather affectionately characterize as "eccentrics". Does this mean that eccentricity, that is unorthodoxy, is a necessary qualification for a top quality deception planner? This quite serious question will be examined in the conclusions. The quick answer is "yes ... but". However further research is called for.

■ ■ ■ ■ ■

General Sir Archibald Wavell arrived in India on 11 July 1941 to take over as Commander-in-Chief. He brought with him only Lieut.-Col. Bernard Ferguson as his ADC. He began working up plans for the invasion of Iran, which took place in August. Japan's entry into WW2 in December and her rapid expansion into Southeast Asia revived Wavell's need for a deception planner on his staff. As seen (Case 13), he specifically requested and got Lieut.-Col. Peter Fleming for this role.

Fleming reached Delhi in late March 1942 where he set about recreating the Cairo "A Force structure in India. This was known initially as G.S.l.(d), that is the deception section of the General Staff's Intelligence Division.[373] The somewhat slipshod details in Fleming's second deception operation, PURPLE WHALES[374] in June, made Fleming realize that his staff would have to be enlarged to properly handle both the complex details of planning and the sheer bulk of intelligence input. GHQ agreed and G.S.l.(d) was given a larger 'staff and larger and more efficient offices on the first floor of headquarters building.[375] October saw him in London to consult with Bevan and the LSC with a stopover in Cairo to see Gen. Alexander and no doubt touch based with "A Force. In March 1943 Peter Thorne, an old family friend, came on board as deputy, his "quick, incisive brain and ready sense of humour" making him Fleming's "ideal anchor-man".[376] And Wavell contributed his youngest offspring, the sprightly 19-year old Joan, as a secretary on Fleming's staff.

At this point, except for its attachment to Intelligence rather than Plans, Fleming's organization and its capabilities had become a close imitation of Clarke's "A" Force. Henceforth its deceptions would involve a close interweaving

---

373 Hart-Davis (1974); Fergusson (1961), 74.
374 See Whaley, *When Deception Fails: The Theory of Outs* (FDDC, Aug 2010), Case 2.2.2.
375 Hart-Davis (1974), 275.
376 Hart-Davis (1974), 278-279.

of disinformation from several agents and double-agents with the visual, sonic, and wireless illusions created by specially trained deception companies lent to combat units as needed. As with his counterparts in Cairo and London, Fleming placed great stress on creating notional units and selling these to the enemy and with similarly sensational results. Thus, from Japanese documents captured at the end of 1943 it was learned that they had an extraordinarily exaggerated notion of Allied strength in South-East Asia, which they credited with more than 50 divisions.[377] Even at peak strength in May 1945, the South-East Asia Command had only 17 divisions.

Wavell was kicked upstairs as Viceroy of India on 20 October 1943. This ended his career as a soldier and, except for his youngest daughter and his friendship with Fleming, all connection to the deception apparatus he had created in India.

Fleming's unit continued under the newly created post of Supreme Allied Commander, South-East Asia, ably filled by Admiral Lord Louis Mountbatten who appreciated Fleming as much personally as he did his work in deception. After all, Mountbatten was a skilled amateur magician and had cheerfully played his part the previous year in "The Man Who Never Was Ruse".

In March 1944 the deception unit was once more expanded and renamed D Division. Then, in 1945, when Mountbatten moved his headquarters to Ceylon, D Division was made a Command Unit so it could remain behind in Delhi where it was renamed officially Force 456. However, it continued to be called D Division with the odd result that:[378]

> Peter ... was in a pleasant position to exploit the independence and slight ambiguity of nomenclature that his unit enjoyed: with one hand, as head of D Division, he would write an order for the commander of Force 456; and with the other hand, as commander of Force 456, he would accept the order and go quietly off to do whatever he wanted.

And what he wanted most was to inspect and join in the fighting, visiting the front ostensibly and indeed in part on business but sticking around virtually AWOL to join various patrols and raids with Orde Wingate's Chindit units. On one occasion in early April 1944 he accompanied a Chindit diversionary raid.[379] Brigadier Bernard Fergusson, his old friend from Wavell's HQ who now commanded a Chindit brigade, noted that Fleming's "knack of getting into uncomfortable places is only equaled by his skill in getting out of them."[380]

---

377 Hart-Davis (1974), 284.
378 Hart-Davis (1974), 278.
379 Michael Calvert, *Prisoners of Hope* (London: Cape, 1952), 102-103.
380 Bernard Fergusson, *The Wild Green Earth* (London: Collins, 1952 edition), 94.

By early 1945 "D" Division deployed at least three deception companies, the 51ˢᵗ Indian, 53ʳᵈ, and 57ᵗʰ, in direct support of combat units.[381]

After VE-Day, the Executive Officer of LCS, Colonel Ronald Wingate came out to India to play a last-minute role in deception planning.[382] And Major Jasper Maskelyne turned up to take over camouflage duties and escape-and evasion lectures.[383]

Following the war Peter Fleming would precede his brother Ian in writing a tongue-incheek thriller novel and then literally drop dead of a massive heart attack during a grouse shoot, elegant to the end.

■ ■ ■ ■ ■

Meanwhile Wavell's flowers had taken strong roots in London where it was soon decided by General Sir Hastings Ismay, Chief of Staff to Churchill in the latter's post as Minister of Defense, that the Americans should be sold as well.[384] Accordingly in late 1942, Ismay ordered Dudley Clarke in Cairo and John Bevan in London to fly to Washington to brief the JCS. This key meeting, which took place in late September, inspired the special British-American liaison on deception that paid such generous dividends through the rest of the war.[385]

In early May 1943 Fleming flew with Wavell's Director of Military Intelligence, Brigadier Walter "Bill" Cawthorn, to Quebec to attend the Anglo-American Quadrant Conference. There, with Cawthorn's support, he pressed to be given control of strategic deception throughout the Pacific. The Americans, however, did not yield.[386]

Next month, June, the office of the Chief of Staff to the Supreme Allied Commander (COSSAC) was created to work up preliminary plans for the Allied invasion of Europe. General Sir Frederick Morgan, COSSAC personified, soon expressed a strong desire for a special Anglo-American deception unit at COSSAC headquarters to handle the tactical deception. Colonel Bevan, the Controller of Deception, agreed and wrote his friend in Cairo, Dudley Clarke, asking if he could spare one of his more widely experienced "A" Force deceptionists. Clarke sent his own Deputy (and closest friend), Noël Wild,

---

381 Kirby, Vol.4 (1965), 362n4, 477, 502, 503.
382 Sir Ronald Wingate, *Not in the Limelight* (London: Hutchinson, 1959), 183ff.
383 Fisher (1983), 314.
384 From November 1941 to February 1942 Lieut.-Commander Ewen Montagu of the Twenty Committee had been in Washington, D.C., liaising on deception (presumably double-agent aspects) with the British Security Coordination (BSC) and briefing the Americans. Winks (1987), 282.
385 Delmer (1971), 31; Mure (1980), 131.
386 Hart-Davis (1974), 285.

who flew to London that Christmas—a surprise present indeed, as Clarke had misled Wild to believe it was only a briefing trip. By that time COSSAC had expanded into SHAEF so Wild was promoted full colonel and assigned to SHAEF's G-3 Plans Division. There he created the small SHAEF deception unit, known officially as the Committee of Special Means (CSM) or Ops.B SHAEF. His deputy was an American, Lt. Col. "Freddy" Barnes who had been recommended by Baumer; and the two other American members were Major (USMC) "Al" Moody and Major Jack Deane.[387] The British members included Lieut.-Col. J. V. B. Jervis-Reid as Executive Officer, Lieut.-Col. Roger Fleetwood Hesketh as Intelligence Officer, and Major Stephen Watts seconded from M.I.5.

Wild's CSM directly supervised the Special Plans Sections attached to U.S. 12th Army Group (Col. William A. Harris), U.S. 6th Army Group (Brig. Gen. John R. Deane, father of Jack Deane and one of those select few who had made it into George Marshall's "little black book" in their Fort Benning days), and British 21st Army Group (Col. David Strangeways). Each of these sections was assigned battalion-sized deception operation units such as the 23rd Hq Special Troops that serviced the U.S. 12th Army Group.

When General Montgomery returned from Italy to England to take command of the British forces for the invasion (21st Army Group) he brought along Colonel David Strangeways who had been his 8th Army deception officer at Alamein. Strangeways now headed "R" Force, the deception team with Monty's 21st Army Group. The only slightly sour notes produced by Wild's otherwise fine orchestra came from "R" Force, which of course had to conform to Montgomery's aversion to both ULTRA and deception.[388] Indeed, after the war when Monty was Chief of the Imperial General Staff, he and Strangeways finally had a falling out with Strangeways demoted to Major and shipped out.[389]

CASE 80:
The U.S. Army creates its first deception units, 1943-45

As we have seen, the Americans have produced their share of stratagematic commanders before WW2, notably Washington, Jackson, Sherman, Funston, and Marshall. But all these commanders operated without benefit of specialized deception planning staffs or operational units. If the commander ordered deception, individual staff members and scratch units were temporarily coopted to get the specific job done.

---

387 Delmer (1971), 36, based evidently on Delmer's extensive interviews with Wild; Masterman (1972). 131.
388 Mure (1980), 236.
389 According to Eldredge and Harris in *Verbatim Transcript* (1971), 36, 90.

The art of military camouflage had been practiced by the US. Army since its inception under Lt. Gen. Washington. However this was the responsibility of each unit—and with no camouflage field manuals to guide them. Consequently deception was practiced on a hit-or miss basis, dependent on the individual commander's grasp of its possibilities and techniques. Mostly this was a primitive matter, exemplified as long ago as 1054 by Scottish King Duncan in his order to his troops before the Battle of Dunsinane to "Let every soldier hew him down a bough, and bear't before him; thereby shall we shadow the numbers of our host, and make discovery err in report of us."[390]

The first specialized camouflage units were created in 1915 on the Western Front, almost simultaneously in the French (who coined the word in 1917). British, and German armies. The American Expeditionary Force simply copied the T/O&E of its allies. These first

U.S. Army camouflage units were drawn from the Corps of Engineers, an appropriate choice because of the Engineers' skill with carpentry and painting and the other crafts needed for camouflage. Indeed this was undertaken entirely on the initiative of the Corps, which simply undertook this task without any such mission having been formally assigned.[391]

The U.S. Army camouflage service vanished entirely in the inter-war period. All that remained was a handful of enthusiasts who, on their own, kept the art alive. The complete absence of camouflage in the 1940 maneuvers prompted G-2 and the Engineers to slowly press ahead on their own—with some help from the British—and during WW2 camouflage again became a regular service of the Corps of Engineers, providing both research and field Camouflage Companies and Battalions.[392] From at least as early as 1942 the T/O&E of each U.S. Army carried an Engineer Camouflage Battalion.

In late summer 1943, the British partly convinced, partly induced General Devers, commander of all U.S. Army forces in the European Theater of Operations (ETOUSA), to form a small deception planning staff known as the Special Plans Section within his G-3 (Plans) Division. This group learned and practiced this art under the close tutelage of its British counterparts.

Toward the end of the year ETOUSA, at the urging of its Special Plans Section (and probably prodded by their Anglo-American directing body, Wild's CSM), asked the War Department in Washington to create a self-contained unit specially and solely designed for tactical deception. ETOUSA's cabled

---

390 Shakespeare, *Macbeth* (c.1605), Act 5, Scene 4.
391 For camouflage in WW1 see Roy R. Behrens, *False Colors: Art, Design and Modern Camouflage* (Dysart, Iowa: Bobolink Books, 2002), 58-107; and Major E. Alexander Powell, *The Army Behind the Army* (New York: Scribner's, 1919), 82-97.
392 Blanch D. Coll, Jean E. Keith, and Herbert H. Rosenthal, *The Corps of Engineers: Troops and Equipment* (Washington, DC: Office of the Chief of Military History, 1958), 81-87.

request, written by Ralph Ingersoll, included specific recommendations for the new unit's T/O&E. This request and recommendation was approved by the War Department. Accordingly, on 20 January 1944, the 23rd Headquarters Special Troops was activated at Camp Forrest, Tennessee. Thus was created, for the first time in American military history, such a unit. Capt. Ingersoll flew back to the States to personally get this unit underway, "despite of all hell and opposition", as his boss, Col. Harris, put it.[393]

The 23rd was a reinforced battalion-sized unit, commanded throughout its 21-months existence by a bird colonel. At full strength the 23rd mustered 1,106 troops (80 officers, 3 warrant officers, and 1,023 enlisted men). It was structured as follows: Headquarters Company whose 108 officers and men exercised overall direction. The 603 Engineer Camouflage Battalion Special (with 379 officers and men), which handled conventional camouflage and the inflatable rubber dummy tanks, trucks, and guns, was composed mainly of New York and Philadelphia artists with an average IQ of 119. The Signal Company Special (296 officers and men, of whom 196 were radio operators), which handled the radio deceptions. The 3132 Signal Service Company Special (147 officers and men), which handled sonic deception, was indeed the first such unit in the U.S. Army. And the 406 Engineer Combat Company Special (168 officers and men), which handled security and rough jobs in general.

What was the 23rd's learning curve and what was its final score? First the learning process:

Table 80a: Plans and Operations of the 23rd, France & Germany, 1944-45

	OPERATION/ PLAN	DATE	RESULT
1.	no name	6 Jun 1944	abort/situation unsuitable
2.	TROUTFLY	7 Jun 1944	abort/change of battle plan
3.	ELEPHANT	1-4 Jul 1944	part success
4.	BRITTANY	9-12 Aug 1944	success
5.	BREST	20-27 Aug 1944	part success (part backfire)
6.	no name	1 Sep 1944	abort/too late
7.	BETTEMBOURG	15-22 Sep 1944	part success
8.	WILTZ	4-10 Oct 1944	unknown
9.	VASELINE	10 Oct 1944	abort/change of battle plan
10.	DALLAS	2-10 Nov 1944	probable success
11.	ELSENBORN	3-12 Nov 1944	part success

---

393 *Official History of the 23rd Headquarters Special Troops* (1945), 1; *Verbatim Transcript of Stratagem Conference* (1971), 22, 27.

	OPERATION/PLAN	DATE	RESULT
12.	CASANOVA	4-9 Nov 1944	success
13.	KOBLENZ	6-14 Dec 1944	part success
14.	KOBLENZ II	21 Dec 1944	abort/theft of equipment
15.	KODAK	22-23 Dec 1944	success exceeding expectations
16.	METZ I	28-31 Dec 1944	unknown
17.	METZ II	6-9 Jan 1945	unknown
18.	L'EGLISE	10-13 Jan 1945	unknown
19.	FLAXWEILER	17-18 Jan 1945	probable success
20.	STEINSEL	27-29 Jan 1945	probable success
21.	LANDONVILLER	28 Jan - 9 Feb 1945	unknown
22.	WHIPSAW	1-4 Feb 1945	part success
23.	MERZIG	13-14 Feb 1945	failed
24.	LOCHINVAR	1-11 Mar 1945	part success
25.	BOUZONVILLE	11-13 Mar 1945	part success
26.	VIERSEN	18-24 Mar 1945	success

Scanning this list we see a pattern of ups-and-downs but gradual overall improvement in performance. Aborts became less common due to closer liaison and coordination with the combat units being supported. And simulation of the various portrayed divisions grew more realistic as measured by the number and quality of their different signatures.

What was the final score? The 23rd generated a total of 26 tactical deception plans in support of General Omar Bradley's 29 U.S. divisions during their ten months from Normandy in June 1944 until March 1945. Of these 26 plans, we see from the table below, 5 aborted and 21 became actual operations. Of these latter, 4 were entirely successful, 11 were at least partly successful, and only 1 failed completely. Of the 5 operations whose results are unknown, the very lack of evidence suggests possible failure or only negligible success. On that most pessimistic assumption we get 15 "successes" as against 6 "failures" plus 5 aborts—a cost-effective record given the small size of the unit (1,106 officers and men, mainly non-combat engineers and signals personnel) and the nature of the German reaction to its deceptions.

Table 80b: Results of the 23rd's Deception Plans. 1944-45[394]

RESULT.	No.	%
Success	4	15.5
Part or Probable Success	11	42.5
Failure	1	4.0
Unknown (likely failure)	5	19.0
Aborts	5	19.0
TOTALS:	**26**	**100.0**

It is the unanimous judgement Bradley's deception staff (Gen. Harris, Col. Ingersoll, and Maj. Eldredge) that the biggest flaw with the 23rd was its CO. Colonel Harry L. Reeder commanded the unit throughout its existence. He was a regular officer since before WW1 with considerable tank experience. On the face of it, this does not seem an inappropriate background for a CO of a field deception unit. However, Ingersoll had requested "A young man, with great imagination." And got the opposite. According to Harris, Reeder came in under a cloud. He had just been relieved of command of the 46th Armored Infantry Regiment and, with his career in jeopardy, had called in a debt from an old friend in Chicago. Luckily this friend happened to be Commanding General of the Second Army, in which the 23rd was being formed; and he promptly assigned Reeder to fill the 23rd's vacant bird-colonel CO slot. Gen. Harris summed him up: "They put this old fud in command and he spent the entire time that he was in Europe trying to get my job and trying to frustrate us in anything we did." Maj. Eldredge called him "such a let up—mentally." The official history was more tactful: "The assignment in 'DECEPTION' must have looked highly irregular to an old soldier. Nothing that he had learned on the Mexican Border with the Maryland National Guard or while occupying Germany ... or in Panama, Benning, Leavenworth or the Desert Training Center seemed to apply."[395]

Fortunately, Reeder's top priority—bureaucratic politics—was not shared by the other officers in the unit. Most wanted to contribute to winning the war and worked actively to that end.[396]

After VE-Day the 23rd was shipped back to the States preparatory to transfer to Pacific 'Theater. The Japanese surrender in August ended this requirement and the 23rd was deactivated on 15 September 1945.

---

394 This generated from *Official History 23rd* (1945), Enclosure I; modified by details in pp.8-31; and corrected by upgrading two cases from more recently available data.
395 *Verbatim Transcript of Stratagem Conference. Pentagon. 21 June 1971*, 27, 32.
396 Verbatim Transcript, 31-33.

CASE 81:
Admiral Halsey's "Dirty Trick Department" in WW2

Admiral William F. "Bull" Halsey, Commander of the Third Fleet and (until 15 June 1944) the South Pacific Area, was involved in strategic deception at least as early as October-November 1943 in the Bougainville campaign.[397] But, as that operation was conducted jointly with MacArthur, it is difficult to separate out Halsey's contribution, if any, to the deception planning.

In reminiscing about a later period (November 1944), Halsey passed the following intriguing remark:[398]

> After the movie, I sat in on the nightly meeting of my Dirty Trick Department—Mick Carney, Ham Dow, Doug Moulton, Harold Stassen, and Johnny Lawrence—and listened to them concoct new methods of bedeviling our gullible enemy. (The Navy prefers me to drop this topic right here.)

When Halsey published this vignette in 1947, it is surprising that the Navy censor passed even that brief but provocative mention of deception. At any event, this 5-man "Dirty Trick Department" comprised:

- Rear Adm. Robert B. "Mick" Carney, C.of S., SOPAC and Third Fleet
- Lt. Comdr. Leonard J. "Ham" Dow, Halsey's Communications Officer
- Capt. H. Douglas "Doug" Moulton, Halsey's Air Operations Officer
- Lt. Comdr. Harold E. Stassen, Halsey's Flag Secretary
- Lt. Comdr. John E. "Johnny" Lawrence, an Air Combat Information Officer

Here we glimpse a Commander working intimately (and apparently effectively) with his deception planners. If naval deception was new to Halsey, intrigue was not. In setting the scene for the victory at Midway on 2-3 June 1942, Halsey had connived with Nimitz to circumvent the direct orders of Admiral King in Washington (Case 68).[399]

CASE 82:
Admiral Yamamoto and His Staff in WW2

Pearl Harbor teaches an important lesson about how and where to look for the deception planners in various military and political-military organizations. It answers the mystery of why all early historians of that event have missed the

---
397 For deception in the Bougainville operation see Whaley (1969), A338-A339.
398 Fleet Admiral William F. Halsey and Lieutenant Commander J. Bryan III, *Admiral Halsey's Story* (New York: Whittlesey House, 1947), 235.
399 Layton (1985), 415.

crucial fact that the Japanese had a major and well-coordinated deception plan to insure their surprise attack—they simply didn't know where to look.

On 17 October 1945, as part of the famous *Strategic Bombing Survey (Japan)*, a questionnaire was issued to the Liaison Committee to guide its post-war interrogations of Japanese officials about their planning and conduct of the war.[400] Recognizing that deception may have played a role, the designers of this questionnaire wisely included a question to draw out the respondents:[401]

> [Question] 21.9: Give complete details of how the [Pearl Harbor] attack plan developed. Discuss: What deceptive measures to draw U.S. attention elsewhere were employed?

A good question but unfortunately wasted by the interrogators who consistently asked it of the wrong respondents. The questionnaire was very long, covering the war in great detail. There was no intention that all respondents would have all the questions put to them. Carefully designed "filter questions" (of the "if 'no', skip the next block of subquestions" type) eliminated many irrelevant ones. However, the interviewers, faced with this question on deception, asked it only of those Japanese who filled slots in their organization chart that corresponded to those in the American organization chart of who would deal with deception. Consequently this key question was put only to Captain S. Tomioka, Chief of the Operations Section of the Naval General Staff; Commodore T. Miyo, a member of that section; Combined Fleet Staff members Captain K. Kuroshima and Commander Y. Watanabe; and Commander M. Fuchida, CO of the Air Unit on carrier *Akagi*. These were not the officers involved in the deceptions. Even so they gave one partial answer:[402]

> The Main Force in the Inland Sea Area and the land-based air units in the Kyushu Area carried on deceptive communications, and deceptive measures were taken to indicate that the Task Force was still in training in the Kyushu Area.

Curiously the only historian or intelligence analyst who picked up on this published answer—and from a secondary source at that—managed a badly garbled paraphrase, neglected to give her source, and missed its significance.[403] This fact points up the old problem of recognizing deception even in those few cases where it is explicitly disclosed by one's sources. It is a matter of the salience or relevance of a particular type of data to one's chosen research

---

[400] The complete questionnaire, list of interrogatees, their answers, and the researchers' analyses are published in *U.S. Strategic Bombing Survey/Pacific): Interrogations of Japanese Officials* (2 vols., Washington, DC: 1946).

[401] As quoted in *Hearings before the Joint Committee on the Investigation of the Pearl Harbor Attack*, 79th Congress. Washington, DC: U.S. GPO, Vo1.13 (1946), 397.

[402] Hearings, Vol.13 (1946), 397. *Curiously, Wohlstetter* (1962). 379, manages a badly garbled paraphrase of this answer, neglects to give her source, and misses its significance.

[403] Wohlstetter (1962), 379.

question. In this case Roberta Wohlstetter, a brilliant historian and skilled intelligence analyst, was so preoccupied with the question of surprise that she overlooked the 14 bits of evidence of deception that passed before her sharp eyes. Each of these 14 bits was dismissed in turn as just so much "noise"; they did not suggest to her the new category of deception that they were. But here I am drifting off into the fascinating problem of how to detect deception rather than how to plan it.

How then was the Pearl Harbor deception planned? The Japanese had not institutionalized deception planning the way the British or, later, the Americans had. Indeed they did not have specialized deception planners. Sometimes it was a subsidiary function of Plans, other times of Intelligence, and occasionally of the Commander himself. In the Pearl Harbor case, the persons involved were limited to the Commander and a few key members of his planning staff.

As Commander-in-Chief of the Combined Fleet, Admiral Isoroku Yamamoto kept the naval part of the deception planning entirely to himself and key members of his staff. Yamamoto was a power unto himself, more so than in an other navy. The Pearl Harbor attack plan had been his idea and he virtually forced it upon the rest of the Japanese naval bureaucracy. And, having done so, he kept the others in the dark as much as possible and for as long as possible about the specifics of his attack plan. It is clear from Professor Prange's detailed reconstruction of Yamamoto's Pearl Harbor planning conferences that he was throughout preoccupied with the need for surprise and impressed this on all his staff. Specific deception plans he left to his devoted staff.[404]

Although Yamamoto did not immerse himself in the deception planning, he was acutely aware of its value as the best guarantee of his paramount dependence on surprise. And not just dependence on the "principle" of surprise, but his belief that surprise could be created from deception. His biography virtually guaranteed this.[405]

CASE 83:
MacArthur's Deception Planners, 1942-51

General Douglas MacArthur encouraged deception planning in his commands in WW2 and the Korean War. However he accomplished this without a specialized deception planning team. Instead, this function was imbedded as an integral part of his personal staff, particularly his G-3.

---

404 Gordon W. Prange, *At Dawn We Slept: The Untold Story of Pearl Harbor* (New York: McGraw-Hill, 1981).
405 Ken Kotani, *Japanese Intelligence in World War II* (Oxford: Osprey, 2009), index under "Yamamoto".

Most of his senior staff praise the "Old Man" for working closely with his planners and his tact in dealing with them. His airforce chief, General George C. Kenney, summed this up:[406]

> In a big staff conference, or in conversation with a single individual, MacArthur has a wonderful knack of leading a discussion up to the point of a decision that each member present believes he himself originated. I have heard officers say many times, "The Old Man bought my idea," when it was something that weeks before I had heard MacArthur decide to do. ... As a salesman, MacArthur has no superior and few equals.

He relished this role. Indeed he created it by encouraging the petty personal jealousies and bureaucratic infighting that marked his staff to a degree not found at other WW2 Allied GHQs. He played the Machiavellian divide-and-rule game as well as his President.[407]

MacArthur had a remarkable talent for considering his and his enemy's available options as a conscious and rational planning process. His physician and aide, Col. Roger O. Egeberg, M.D., describes this staff planning process precisely.[408]

> When they and MacArthur had agreed on a near-term objective they would gather to discuss the ways in which it might be attained. MacArthur would hear these planners out, ask questions usually broad, and at the end of the conference which might last hours or all day or lop over onto the next day, he would say "Thank you very much, gentlemen," and then for a day or two he would ponder the problem himself. While we were in the jeep together he might in a way ask me questions and then answer them. From some of these interchanges I got a clear picture of the connection between chess and war. He might say, "Now if we do this which Steve [Chamberlin] suggested that they might do this we should answer in one of three ways" and he would outline what they might be, and the same for the other alternatives and then he would go to the Japanese answer to the 6 or 7 possibilities. By the time he had done this for a day or a week, he would call his staff in, established the strategy which was amazingly frequently the

---

406 General George C. Kenney, *The MacArthur I Know* (New York: Duell, Sloan and Pearce,1951), 64-65, 69.

407 D. Clayton James, *The Years of MacArthur*, Vol.2 (Boston: Houghton Mifflin Company, 1975), 593-598.

408 Roger Olaf Egeberg, "General Douglas MacArthur," *Transactions of the American Clinical and Climatological Association*, Vol.78 (1966), 165.

opposite from the feeling of the majority and which would seem always to have been right.

MacArthur used a similarly rather informal setup—even some of the same personnel—five years later during the Korean War when he again brought deception into play at Inchon (Case 71). Again deception planning was centered on his G-3, now Major General Edwin K. "Pinky" Wright. However, in addition to being G-3, Wright also chaired the Joint Strategic Plans and Operations Group (JSPOG), which had been created two years before the new war and comprised 8 general officers drawn from the three services.[409]

CASE 84:
The Soviet General Staff in WW2

Throughout the Great Patriotic War, as the Soviets call their role in WW2 on the so-called Eastern Front, the Soviet General Staff was headed by General (later Marshal) Zhukov. As seen in his earlier battle against the Japanese (Case 9), he brought to this position a successful experience with surprise-through-deception. Unfortunately he now had to deal with a Supreme Commander, Stalin, for whom surprise had on 22 June 1941 suddenly become an embarrassing word.[410]

To get around Stalin's inhibiting effect on surprise-through-deception mindset, Zhukov and his pragmatic staff quietly introduced deception on a trial-and-error basis. This story was first sketched in a post-Stalin history written by a key member of Marshal Zhukov's staff, Gen. Shtemenko. His account describes each major operation in chronological sequence together with a summary of each operation's deception plan. This exemplary format gives us our best single source for tracing the evolution of Soviet deception planning on the Eastern Front from the primitive plans of 1941 through the increasingly sophisticated ones until VE-Day in May 1945.[411]

And it set the stage for the Soviet campaign against Japan later that year. This was Operation AUTUMN STORM. Here, the Soviets applied all of the separate deception techniques that had worked against the Germans. It was the most sophisticated deception plan and operation they would carry out. And it had proven so successful that it became the ideal model for all the senior Soviet of that generation—a generation that would call The Manchurians.[412]

This generation would last nearly a quarter of a century, not ending until 1968 with the sophisticated deception operation that led to the Soviet's surprise

---
409 James (1985), 75.
410 Whaley, *Codeword BARBAROSSA* (1973).
411 Shtemenko (1968).
412 Despres, Dzirkals, & Whaley (1976); David M. Glantz, *The Soviet Strategic Offensive in Manchuria, 1945: "August Storm"* (London: Frank Cass, 2003).

invasion of Czechoslovakia. Thereafter the old lessons of Manchuria were largely forgotten in the Soviet and Russian military. Ironically, as we'll see below (Case 87), they would inspire the American planners of Operation DESERT STORM, in the first Gulf War of 1991.

CASE 85:
The Israeli Deception Planners, 1948-1986

Since 1948 (see Case 57) the Israeli Army (Zahal) has been in the forefront of those few armies that make systematic and effective use of deception. It draws from four traditions. First, the Old Testament with its many examples of covert intelligence and battlefield ruses such as Gideon's lights and trumpets (Case 23). Second, the agent network in Palestine in 1915-1917 with 15 Jews of the Zionist intelligence service, "Nili", led by the remarkable Aaron Aaronsshon, a major inspiration for the modern Israeli intelligence services.[413] Third, the Special Night Squads authorized in 1938 by Wavell and recruited by Orde Wingate, which mark the beginning of the Israeli Army (Case 14). Fourth, the indigenous self-defense groups set up, first in Poland, and brought to Palestine by the likes of Menachim Begin.

The Israeli General Staff ran war games and counter-terrorist games on a regular basis since 1974.[414] For example, the 1976 Entebbe Raid was gamed out beforehand, even though that elaborate rescue operation in far-off Uganda was planned on only 5 days notice. Although the job is deemed important, working directly under the Chief of Staff, the permanent gaming staff was (at least until 1980) small: 1 colonel, 4 majors, and 1 secretary. In its first five years it designed and ran over 90 games. These ranged from simple "pencil-and-paper" games, through command-post exercises (CPX), up to large scale field training exercises (FTX) and typically lasted one or two days.[415]

In summer 1979, the General Staff gamers assisted in the design and administration of the senior-level two-day KINGFISHER game at Tel-Aviv University held in conjunction with the International Seminar on Problems in Political Terrorism and Combatting Terrorism jointly sponsored by the Office of the Prime Minister's Adviser on Combatting Terrorism and Tel Aviv University's Center for Strategic Studies. Later interviews with three participants as well as a reading of the official report show that deception planning was a significant part of the game, whose scenario was focused on

---

413 Whaley, *Stratagem* (1969), 81-82; Anita Engle, *The Nili Spies* (London: Hogarth, 1959); Efraim Dekel, *Shai: The Exploits of Hagana Intelligence* (New York: Yoseloff, 1959); Meinertzhagen (1959/1960), 5; *Wikipedia*, "Nili" (accessed 13 Oct 2010).

414 Interview in 1980 with an Israeli General Staff Officer. I do not know the post-1980 status of Israeli gaming.

415 Information in 1979 from one of the Israeli General Staff gamers.

a hypothetical skyjacking in the Middle East. The KINGFISHER scenario is reproduced below as Appendix D-6.[416]

In addition, until at least the mid 1980s, every strategic political-military plan was also gamed out by the Prime Minister's own special gaming staff, which was created and directed by the recently retired colonel (Yaakov Heichal) who had pioneered the General Staff games. This has been the case since shortly before the air strike on the Iraqi nuclear reactor in 1981. The players (who comprised all the planners and senior officers and officials selected to direct the real operation) found that, without exception, every one of these games revealed at least one major planning flaw that led to either redesign or, in cases where that was not feasible, simply aborting the operation.[417] Certainly many and I presume every political-military operation involves gaming the deception plan along with the real plan. Apparently this is considered good training for Israeli soldiers, diplomats, and statesmen, significantly expanding their understanding of deception planning and operations beyond the direct experience of a few actual operations, whether failed or successful.

While the Israeli Army and Government games were used primarily for refining Israeli plans, including the deceptive parts of each, such games can also be used to detect potential deceptions of enemies. Perhaps the Israelis do this now, but I know that this was not the case at the time of Egypt's almost total surprise attack that began the 1973 Yom Kippur War.[418]

CASE 86:
The KGB's Role in Political-Military Deception Planning, 1960s

This story was first and best told in detail in the memoir of the then deputy head of deception operations for the Czechoslovakian intelligence service, which was then a closely controlled tool of the Soviet KGB. I refer the reader to that admirable insider's account.[419]

CASE 87:
Gen. Schwarzkopf's Deception Planners, Iraq 1991
The American planning team for Desert Storm emulates the Russian Autumn Storm.

We saw (Case 84) how the Soviet General Staff evolved increasingly sophisticated deception plans and operations during the course of WW2 on

---
416 Interviews in fall 1979. *KINGFISHER Game: Summary of Procedures and Analysis* (Tel Aviv: July 1979).
417 Conversation in 1985 with an official of the Israeli Prime Minister's Office.
418 See Whaley, *The Maverick Detective: The Whole Art of Detection* (draft in progress), Chapter "Selecting,Teaching, and Training", section on "Gaming".
419 Ladislav Bittman, *The Deception Game: Czechoslovak Intelligence in Soviet Political Warfare*. (Syracuse: Syracuse University Research Corporation, 1972).

the Eastern Front against German Army and how, in Operation AUTUMN STORM, it peaked with the final Manchurian Campaign against the Japanese in Autumn 1945.[420]

It is ironic that the American "Desert Storm" operation against Iraq in 1991 took both its name (rather than the originally intended "Desert Sword") and "inspiration, concrete guidance, and a virtual model" as a result of the planning team that went to the Gulf from Fort Leavenworth's School of Advanced Military Studies where they had previously studied the Manchurian case in detail.[421]

It is a credit to Gen. Schwartzkopf, as commander, that he fully accepted the recommendations on deception from this planning team. That he did so was presumably aided at least in part by the fact that his hobby—conjuring tricks—would have conditioned him to understand how deception worked. Moreover, he shared this art with at least two of his planners.[422]

CASE 88:
Dudley Clarke's Ideal Strategic Deception Planning System

EDITOR'S COMMENT: Brigadier Dudley Clarke was General Wavell's chosen agent for reintroducing in WW2 the lost art of deception to the British Army's organizational charts. In the following memorandum, Clarke gives his American allies his recommendations on how best to set up a military deception planning organization. Because of its importance, I give this rare paper here complete and word for word.

"Some Notes on the Organization of Deception in the United States Forces"

Deception of the enemy on a systematic, continuous and theater-wide basis was first started, so far as I am aware, by General Wavell in the Middle East at the end of 1940. The instrument that was devised to effect it was "A" Force; and if I personally were to start all over again with the experience of the four succeeding years before me I would still build up a machine on the same lines as the "A" Force of 1944. At the same time I am fully conscious that "A" Force was first shaped to meet the special needs of particular personalities and conditions and then developed to keep pace with a vastly changing strategy, so that, however well it may have fitted into the British Mediterranean War Machine, it provides by no means a set pattern for other nations and other theaters. We have in fact, both here and in N.W. Europe, seen failure in attempts to build up an American "A" Force. It seems clear, therefore, that the United States will

---
420 Despres, Dzirkals, & Whaley (1976).
421 David M. Glantz, *The Soviet Strategic Offensive in Manchuria, 1945: "August Storm"* (London: Frank Cass, 2003), xix, xx.
422 Interview around 1986 with a member of that team, himself an amateur magician.

need to design a special deception organization to fit their own characteristics and the peculiarities of their own theaters of operations. Nevertheless I am venturing to suggest that any such organization will only succeed if it is firmly based on certain principles, which I have become convinced from my own experience are sure foundations for this very specialized work. The aim of this paper is to present those principles in an objective and impersonal manner, so that the authorities concerned may avoid the very real danger of blunting this sensitive weapon by forcing it into place in a rigid military machine. Rather, I suggest, should the machine adapt itself to turn this new weapon to the best advantage against the enemy as it has successfully done with so many other innovations. I have stressed this point at the beginning because I myself have had to meet a certain American intolerance of the apparently illogical situation of "A" Force in fitting neither into a square nor a round pigeon-hole. This comes, I know, from an understandable dislike of "private armies", and a neatness of mind which ranges each component of the war machine in its appropriate staff section. I am sure that a more sympathetic view would prevail if there were a clearer understanding of the conditions under which "A" Force came into the world and grew up, and I will therefore preface any thesis on principles with an attempt to describe in brief the background from which they have emerged.

"A" Force started under two handicaps of which any similar American organisation is happily free. The first handicap was a lack of precedent: Deception on a big scale had never been practiced before and it had to prove its worth at the same time as it was trying to find its feet. As a result the early "A" Force could only operate freely in the zones of operation of the more imaginative commanders who, amid the successive adversities of 1941, were prepared to give a trial to anything which offered them a prospect of help. This led to the organization extending in an unbalanced way, dependent upon "selling" itself, and inevitably shaped to suit the personalities concerned. Chief among the latter was of course General Wavell, who numbered amongst his characteristics a sense of security-mindedness far beyond anything we know at the present time. It may well be that we no longer need it to that degree; but in 1941 he was striving, with pitifully inadequate forces, simultaneously to recover a shattered army from Greece and Crete, to conquer the vast territory of Italian East Africa, to invade Vichy-French Syria, defeat the rebel forces of Iraq, and to launch a counter-offensive against the German-Italian Desert Armies on the Egyptian border. Small wonder, perhaps, that he placed security in the forefront of his policy, but to the budding "A" Force it represented the second major handicap and one which made the "selling" process all the more difficult. At that time we thought, rightly I believe; that deception would only succeed so long as the enemy was kept in ignorance of the fact that it was being practiced at all. From this it followed that only the smallest possible inner circle of our own people was initiated into it, and every effort was made to hide from all the rest the fact that any Deception Organisation even existed. Hence "A" Force started on the basis of a "Secret Service"—and in fact remained so until well on in 1943—a circumstance which had the greatest influence on its growth and on the shape it finally assumed. In the early days the Commander of "A" Force received his instructions in every case direct from the Commander-in-Chief himself, either verbally or in the C-in-C's own handwriting, and dealt with nobody except his Chief of Staff and the two Directors of Operations and Intelligence. He held, as cover, an appointment on the C-in-C's personal staff, and no deception document was ever handled in GHQ outside the C-in-C's personal secretariat. When instructions had to be issued by GHQ to implement a deception scheme the C-in-C personally addressed them to the Army Commander concerned with the request that no one but his Chief of Staff should be informed of their real purpose. In consequence of this very elaborate protection "A" Force was able to preserve an almost complete incognito, and it was probably not until 1943 that the enemy began to detect the existence of a far-reaching deception machinery in the Allied ranks. On our side the incognito was dispelled to a certain extent during the operations against Sicily, when certain details of the cover plan for the landings had necessarily to be disseminated amongst a large force of British, American and Canadian troops to whom it was probably something of a novelty. Since then the Germans cannot fail to have realized a good deal of the deceptions that have been practiced upon them and, although the need for stringent secrecy regarding deception is still as great as ever, the organizations employed upon it no longer have to be hampered by the conditions which affected "A" Force so greatly at the start.

I have tried to picture this background in some detail in order to explain the fact that "A" force never started as a logical blueprint conception, but developed by trial and error to fit every kind of condition extending from defeat to victory. For all its rigidity the British Army is not a very logically minded institution, and often has succeeded by this process of trial and error in producing something which "works" no matter how illogical it may appear. The peculiar British system of brevet promotion is a good example which works extremely well, though it must seem strangely puzzling to an American. I will not, therefore, defend the logic of "A" force, but will claim that in shaping itself into something workable it has discovered a few basic facts which must be inseparable, from any other organization of the same type.

The first concerns the scope of the organization's activities and, in particular, the directions in which they should be focused. Until this is properly understood there will be a tendency to muddle deception with psychological warfare and even to suggest that the same instrument can serve both purposes. A moment's examination of the aims of the two will show this to be fundamentally unsound, and any attempt to mix both in practice will be highly dangerous. Nevertheless the danger is often present and is sometimes curiously difficult to dispel. The essential difference lies of course in the audience for whom the two organisations cater. Psychological warfare starts at the apex of a triangle and endeavors to spread its arms as wide as it can to embrace the broadest possibly base. It matters little if many of its audience can detect the origin of their messages nor if a privileged few can recognize distortion of the truth; its appeal is to the masses and it is unlikely to influence the thought or actions of the enlightened inner circles of the General Staff. Deception, on the other hand works in exactly the opposite way. It starts at the base of the triangle and concentrates its influence towards a single point at the apex; its essential aim is to conceal the origin of its messages by directing them upon this single point from as many different directions as possible. It cares little for the thoughts and actions of the masses, but it *must* penetrate directly into the innermost circles of all. Its audience is narrowed down to a small handful of individuals, as represented by the senior members of the enemy's Intelligence Staff, and sometimes even to a single individual in the person of the Head of that Intelligence Staff. If they can influence him to accept as true the evidence they have manufactured for his benefit, then they have accomplished their entire aim, since it is only through the Head of the Intelligence that any enemy commander receives the impression of his opponent upon which he has to base his plan of operation. It is necessary, therefore, that the single-purposeness of any deception machine should be recognized from the start and its shape dictated by the overriding need to concentrate every ounce of its diverse efforts upon that one ultimate target. As a corollary it follows that those who direct the deception machine must have an adequate knowledge of the small group of men on whom all their activities are focused, of their national characteristics, their language, thoughts and professional methods with all their strengths and their weaknesses.

It is this note on personalities which leads me to the next principle, which I firmly believe to be a foundation stone in the successful application of deception. Deception is essentially an art and not a science, and those who practice it must be recognized as falling into the category of artists and not of artisans. This is, I know, difficult to accept in professional military circles where it is widely believed that the art of war can be taught to the average educated man, even though he may have little aptitude for it. But, nevertheless, I am convinced it is true; and twice in "A" Force I have seen highly qualified and highly intelligence staff officers of the British Regular Army fail completely to cope with the work, although both did brilliantly afterwards on the Operations Staff. What they lacked was Just the sheer ability to create, to make something out of nothing, to conceive their own original notion and then to clothe it with realities until eventually it would appear as a living fact. And, since that is precisely what the Deception Staff must do all the time, it follows that the art of creation is an essential attribute in all who are charged with such work. To expect those who have not this art to produce the required results will lead to risks beyond that of mere failure.

If this thesis is accepted it is easy to see why one brain—and why one alone—must be left unhampered to direct any one deception plan. It is after all little more than a drama played upon a vast stage, and the author and producer should be given as free a hand in the theater of war as in the other theater. (Also, of course, in both they must have the necessary qualifications to justify that confidence). It is not a bad parallel to compare a Commander in the Field with the impresario who wants to mount a successful play at his theater. He decided on the type of play he wants—drama, comedy, musical, etc. and instructs an author to produce a script. Having accepted the script, he appoints a producer to mount the play. From that point onwards he may well leave everything else to those two, and look only to the results obtained. Provided these are satisfactory, the impresario who is not himself an author or producer, wisely leaves them to rule the cast, scenery, costumes and all else that goes to make the play. The wise Commander-in-Chief will follow the same example. In his case the matter is simplified by the fact that the head of his Deception Staff doubles the roles of author and producer. The Commander therefore tells him what sort of deception he needs, examines the plans produced for him with the required aim in view and, once the final version is approved, watches only the results and leaves all else to his specialist. In both peace and war, however, the Chief is the best judge of the results; in both cases he assesses them by the reactions of the audience (or the enemy), and should interfere in proportion to the degree in which they fail or succeed to achieve the object he himself has set.

And it is this mention of the "object" which brings me to the last of the principles I have tried to enunciate. For the theatrical impresario this presents no difficulty—all he wants is to see the audience moved to tears, laughter or rhythm in concert with the plan—but to the General it is a problem which merits most careful thought. His audience is the enemy and he alone must decide what he wants them to do—to advance? to withdraw? to thin out or to reinforce? Whatever he chooses, the main point is that his "object" [objective] must be to make the enemy DO something. It matters nothing what the enemy THINKS, it is only what he DOES that can affect the battle. It is therefore wrong, and always wrong, for any Commander to tell his Deception Staff to work out a plan "to make the enemy think we are going to do soand-so." It may be that the plan will succeed but that the enemy will react to it in a totally unexpected way, upon which the Commander will probably blame the Deception Staff who have in fact produced exactly the results they set out for. It is this boomerang effect which has made many people apprehensive of using the deception weapon, and it cannot be stressed too strongly that, if used in the wrong way, it can prove a real danger. But there is one sure way to avoid any possible risk, and that is to get the OBJECT right. Given a correct "object", the deception plan may fail but it cannot in any way do harm. Give it a wrong "object" and it will invariably give wrong results. Our theatrical impresario after all will not attempt to dictate to the author the plot of the play, but that is precisely what the General does who tells his Deception Staff that he wants the enemy to be made to "think" something. It assumes a knowledge of the enemy's likely reactions which the Deception Staff should know from experience very much better than the General. It is for the latter to say what he wants then to do, and for the specialists to decide what the enemy must be made to think in order to induce then to act in the manner required. Perhaps an illustration will explain this best. In the early part of 1941 General Wavell wanted the Italian reserves drawn to the south in order to ease his entry into Northern Abyssinia. He considered this might be done by inducing them to reinforce the captured province of British Somaliland, and he gave instructions for a Deception Plan to be worked to persuade the Italians that we were about to invade Somaliland. Deception was new then and on the surface that appeared to all concerned to be a perfectly laudable object. The plan, innocently ignoring the real object of influencing the location of the enemy's reserves, was entirely successful; but the results were totally unexpected. In face of the threatened Invasion, the Italians evacuated British Somaliland. Not only had General Wavell to draw upon his own meager forces to re-occupy the country, but the Italian garrison was freed to swell the forces in the north which were to block our advance at Keren. Had a different object been chosen, quite a different deception plan would have emerged and perhaps a quite different effect produced upon the actions of the enemy.

That concludes this brief review; and I will end by summarizing that to be successful any deception organisation needs:

    a. To be so organized that it directs the whole of its efforts to influence the enemy's intelligence staff—and that alone.

    b. To be composed of senior officers with a real knowledge of the intelligence staff that is to become their audience.

    c. To be directed, as specialists in an art, by a Commander and Staff who tell them what results they require and who leave them unhampered to arrange the best means of obtaining those results.

    d. To be given an object in terms of the manner in which the enemy is required to ACT in order to further the operational plans of their own Commander.

Provided these four principles are faithfully observed, it matters little how the organization is shaped and it can best take the form most suited to the nationality concerned and the theater of war affected.

Rear H.Q. "A" Force
c/o G.H.Q. M.E.F.
30 October 1944

/s/ D. W. Clarke
D. W. CLARKE
Brigadier
Commander "A" Force

PART THREE:
Analysis & Conclusions

> Yes, the game is all over and there is really nothing more to be done about it. We've had some gay and some grim moments, haven't we?
>
> — Col. John Bevan, letter to Col. Noël Wild, 24 Sep 1945

We have surveyed 88 cases of deception planners and planning. As these represent merely an "opportunity sample", no statistical analyses are warranted. Consequently any generalizations drawn from such a presumably rag-tag sample should be taken only as hypotheses—all subject to verification or falsification.

The analysis and tentative conclusions are given in the following five chapters, titled, successively: The Planning Process, Social/Institutional Factors, Cultural Factors, Personality Factors, and Selection/Teaching/Training.

CHAPTER 8:
The Planning Process

> The most effective way to conceal a simple mystery is behind another mystery. This is literary legerdemain. You do not fool the reader by hiding clues or faking character à la [Agatha] Christie but by making him solve the wrong problem.
>
> — Raymond Chandler, "Twelve Notes on the Detective Story, Addenda" (1948)[423]

The planning process has two dimensions, that is, it can be analyzed from two viewpoints—one objective, the other subjective. First, we can ask and analyze what the planner does. Second, we can ask and try to analyze how the planner thinks. The first question will be discussed here. It gives us the stuff from which field manuals and text books can be written and training courses developed. The second question, which was explored throughout Part Two, has implications for efficient selection of candidate planners.

8.1. The Basic Process

All deception planning can be described by a single set of ten steps:[424]

Note that, unlike many planning processes which are circular, deception planning is usually linear, although ideally with feedback for fine tuning. Deception planning becomes a circular process only during those very rare

---

[423] Raymond Chandler, "Twelve Notes on the Detective Story, Addenda" (revised 18 Apr 1948), as published in Frank McShane (*editor*), *The Notebooks of Raymond Chandler* (NY: The Ecco Press, 1976), 38. Chandler paraphrased himself the following year in his manuscript notes: "[T]he only reasonably honest and effective method of fooling the reader ... is to make the reader exercise his mind about the wrong problem ... which will land him in a bypath because it is tangential to the central problem. And even this takes a bit of cheating here and there." See D. Gardiner & K. S. Walker, *Raymond Chandler Speaking* (Boston: Houghton Mifflin, 1962), particularly pp.68-69.

[424] As condensed from Whaley (1982), 188-189; and reprinted in Whaley, *Readings in Political-Military Counterdeception* (FDDC, Dec 2007), 38-40. If this list strikes some readers as obvious or simplistic, it didn't to two former mid-level Soviet intelligence officers when they read it recently. They are KGB Colonel Oleg Gordievsky who ran deep cover ("Illegals") and Boris Volodarski a GRU Spetznaz officer. Both, according to a mutual colleague, judged it the most useful check-list they had seen for its concise yet comprehensive statement of the deception planning process.

extended campaigns of "serial" deceptions where each successive deception builds upon its predecessor.

1) **Understanding the GOAL of the operation, military or otherwise.**

   This is usually (and ideally) defined by the Commander.

2) **Deciding how we want the target to REACT.**

   This is also set by the Commander, but usually only implicitly.

3) **Deciding what we want the target to PERCEIVE.**

   Not what we want the target to THINK. (Case 11)

4) **Deciding specifically which facts or objects are to be HIDDEN and which SHOWN.**

5) **Analyzing the PATTERN of the REAL thing to be hidden to discover the specific characteristics ("signatures") that must be deleted or added to create another pattern that will suitably dissimulate it.**

6) **Doing the same for the FALSE thing to be shown to create a pattern that will suitably simulate it.**

7) **At this point, having designed a desired EFFECT together with its concealed METHOD, the planner must now explore the means available for presenting this effect to the target.**

   If the deception assets available for the job are inadequate, the planner must either get them or abort the plan and go back to step 4 or 5. If no plan seems feasible, it is desirable to so inform the Commander and recommend that he select an alternative goal.

8) **Having designed the effect and the method, the planning phase has ended and the OPERATIONAL PHASE begins.**

   At this point, the deception planner normally hands over to operational units to present ("sell") the effect. However, the planner should keep a watching brief over the operational phase, steps 8-to-10, in order to be able to effect modifications or take advantage of unexpected developments.

9) **Selecting the CHANNELS through which the various false characteristics are to be communicated.**

   These must, of course, be ones open (directly or indirectly) to the target's sensors. Thus an Intelligence officer should not plant disinformation in a newspaper unless he has reason to believe the enemy monitors that paper. Channel selection is sometimes the responsibility of the planning staff but, more often, that of the operational staff.

10) For the deception to succeed, the target must accept ("buy") the EFFECT, perceiving the projected illusion.

Deception will fail at this point only if the target takes no notice of the presented effect, notices but judges it irrelevant, misconstrues its intended meaning, or detects its METHOD. Conversely, the target will:

- take notice, if the effect is designed to attract his ATTENTION;
- find it relevant, if the effect can hold his INTEREST;
- form the intended hypothesis about its meaning, if the projected pattern of characteristics is CONGRUENT with patterns already part of his experience and memory; and
- fail to detect the deception, if none of the ever-present characteristics that are INCONGRUENT are accessible to his sensors.

Effective deception planning must take into account all four of these contingencies. And a wise deceiver will seek feedback, monitoring the target's responses, to assure that these four contingencies are being met.

8.2. The Things Manipulated

Between 1969 and 1982 I developed a 9-item checklist of the distinctly different types of objects, facts, or things that persons can misperceive.[425] These are the 9 categories of subjects a deception planner can try to manipulate through simultaneously hiding (dissimulating) or showing (simulating). In other words, those false elements of reality a deception target can be led to perceive as real. These nine items are:

    PATTERN

    PLAYERS

    INTENTION

    PAYOFF

    PLACE

    TIME

    STRENGTH

    STYLE

    CHANNEL

A deception planner chooses from this menu as many or as few categories as the situation calls for and his resources and inventiveness permit.

---

425 Whaley, *Textbook of Political-Military Counterdeception* (FDDC, Aug 2007), 116.

There are pronounced differences in the frequency with which these categories have occurred in military operations. Examining 108 modern battles at the strategic and large-scale tactical levels, I found the following:

Table: Frequency of the Nine Ways to be Deceived in Military Operations, 1914-1968

TYPE OF SURPRISE.	No.	PERCENT
Place	78	72.2
Time	71	65.7
Strength	62	57.4
Intention	36	33.3
Style	28	25.9
Payoff	3	2.8
Players	2	1.8
Pattern	1	0.9
Channel	1	0.9
N =	(108)	

Here we see that surprise of PLACE, TIME, and STRENGTH have occurred most frequently. Those are the three most frequently mentioned categories in the standard military literature.

However, my study was not only the first to give a more nearly comprehensive list but the first to estimate the relative levels of frequency for the other categories. Thus the categories of INTENTION and STYLE are also common enough to deserve the planner's close attention. And, as deeper analysis showed, all five categories are found about as often in "tactical" operations as in "strategic" ones. And the remaining categories of PAYOFF, PLAYERS, PATTERN, and CHANNEL are both rare and limited to strategic operations, although they surely could be applied to tactical ops under certain conditions.

Finally, the thought processes of deception planners are also independent of their level of operation, ranging from the grand strategic down through the strategic and operational (grand tactical) to the tactical.

CHAPTER 9:

Social/Institutional Factors: Networks, Institutions, & Traditions

Although deception plans obviously take place inside a human head, they are rejected or accepted, constrained, encouraged, modified, or implemented through group activity. Ingersoll's colleagues in Bradley's Special Plans Section rejected one weird plan after another until they agreed that an occasional one made sense. Similarly with both the Twenty Committee and Col. Fleming's "D" Division in India in WW2. And, on the other side of the Iron Curtain, with the plans put forward to Maj. Bittman's Department for Disinformation in Prague.

Because of the unique features in the example of the Anarchist committee planners for their stunningly successful defense of Barcelona at the beginning of the Spanish Civil War (Case 77), it is almost presumptuous to draw a general conclusions. I can only suggest that committee deception planning of this type can work only under special circumstances, specifically when the members 1) share a common goal; and 2) decide by consensus. It is a style of military planning similar to that found in several guerrilla resistance movements and among certain tribes that have practiced "primitive warfare" directed by "councils of war" such as the Greeks at Troy (Case 65). Yet, if we reflect a moment, this was precisely the style of deception planning and coordination that would be adopted (by Churchill's insistence) and successfully practiced by the British only four years later in WW2—the executive committee system. The only differences between the committees of the Spanish Anarchists and the British gentlemen was in committee size large versus small) and manner of recruitment (open enrollment versus "old school tie"). It even proved a congenial style of planning for a few Americans: Gen. Harris' Special Plans Branch (Cases 18, 70, 80) and Adm. Halsey and his "Dirty Trick Department" (Case 81).

9.1. Policy Constraints and the Supreme Command

Even the best laid deception plans of subordinate commands can be aborted by the Supreme Command when it chooses to redefine the rules of the game. These rule changes can be either in the political constraints or in the priorities assigned among the various subordinate commands. We saw consideration of higher politics intervene to veto military deception SOP in several cases: Castro-versus-Bayo and Guevara (Case 72), London versus Alexander in Italy[426] and in the Iranian hostage rescue attempt (Case 64). It did so again in cancelling the forged message from the Italian King on the eve of the Allied invasion of Sicily[427] and in aborting the "A Force plan to use the U.S. military attaché in Cairo as a deception channel.[428]

Another frequent type of intervention by the Supreme Command is the reshuffling of priorities among lower commands. In WW2 this kind of intervention occasionally interfered with Alexander's ability to plan his campaign in Italy, his theater being number two in the scales of grand strategy.[429] And such tinkering constantly plagued Wavell and Mountbatten in their China-Burma-India theater, which had the lowest priority of all. As their chief deception planner, Peter Fleming, said to one of his team, it's impossible to tell a convincing lie unless you knew what's the truth.[430]

9.2. Commanders and Their Staffs

Before the 1800s. most deception planners were the commanders themselves: Hannibal, Caesar, Belisarius, Chinggis Khan, Subotai, Bayan, Saxe, Frederick the Great, Marlborough, Bonaparte, Washington, Mao, among others. We seldom need look behind these commanders for clever illusionists whispering strategies and suggesting stratagems, because these "notable Captaines stratagematique" performed virtually unsupported by the advice of specialized military staffs.[431]

During the 1800s, the growth and international diffusion of the Prussian general staff system gradually shifted planning and decision-making from individuals to committees. Even then it seems that the outstanding military innovators—generals Washington, Wellington, Jackson, and Sherman—pretty much kept their own counsel in matters of grand tactics and broad strategy, which they deemed to include deception.

It is only when we enter the 1900s that we find military deception planning routinely delegated to staff. Even then, some modern commanders did continue

---

426 Whaley, *When Deception Fails: The Theory of Outs* (FDDC, Aug 2010), Case 3.2.3.
427 Whaley, *When Deception Fails* (FDDC, Aug 2010), Case 2.8.6.
428 Whaley, *When Deception Fails* (FDDC, Aug 2010), Cases 2.5.1.
429 Whaley, *When Deception Fails* (FDDC, Aug 2010), again Case 3.2.3.
430 As paraphrased in Hart-Davis (1974), 284.
431 Some early commanders such as Chingghis Khan did have primitive general staff systems. The early Renaissance Italian city state of Florence had its Council of Ten for War, on which Machiavelli served as Secretary beginning in 1498. And these and still others commonly had courtly political advisers who sometimes contributed military advice. Thus the difference between that period and the 1800s and 1900s was more quantitative than strictly qualitative.

to involve themselves directly in the deception planning process. Thus, Funston, Monro, Allenby, Wavell, Rommel, Manstein, Zhukov, Yamamoto, MacArthur, Mao, Yadin, and Dayan sometimes acted as their own deception planners as well as encouraging its practice by their staffs. Others like Pershing, Marshall, Alexander, Slim, Mountbatten, Bradley, Nimitz, Halsey, and Schwarzkopf—believing deception to be of significant value—actively encouraged its use. Patton, while trusting the details of camouflage and deception to his staff, was an enthusiastic advocate and practitioner of "surprise" and the "end run", which reflect a high sense of guilefulness. Although this is a short list, it is suggestive that all those named enjoyed more-or-less great success in battle at relatively low cost. Patton's troops, for example, consistently achieved the highest Allied-versus-German kill-ratios of any other regular combat divisions and corps in Europe.

Conversely, we find that many—and I suspect most—commanders still harbor the view of the majority of WW1 generals that deception is either irrelevant or, at best, "comic opera" or mere "witty hors d'oeuvres before battle". Mark Clark, Montgomery, Westmorland are prime examples. Such commanders have a distressing record of handing in big butcher's bills even in victory.

The more successful Commanders have been those who recognize that their real plan and the deception plan go hand-in-hand, each supporting the other. Such Commanders actively participate in the planning process.

Even Commanders who have little or no understanding of deception can be induced by their deception officers to give the necessary minimal input. Thus General Montgomery had no difficulty answering Colonel Clarke's key question, "What do you want the enemy to do?"[432] Moreover, Monty worked mainly through his Chief of Staff, Brigadier De Guingand who had, as we have seen, a flair for deception himself.[433] At worst, faced with a Commander who ignores deception, the planner should have the active cooperation of the Chief of Staff. Thus first Col. Clarke in Algiers and then Col. Wild in London worked their plans smoothly through General Eisenhower's cooperative Chief of Staff, General Walter Bedell Smith.[434]

9.3. Intelligence or Operations?

Where does deception planning best fit within the Commander's staff structure? Our cases show it arising at three main places: Intelligence, Operations, or (within the latter) Plans. However, the cases also reveal that

---

432 Mure(1980), 274, for Clarke's view.
433 De Guingand (1947), 189.
434 Mure (1980), 10-11, 273, for the views of both Wild and Clarke.

its specific location has been until recently an historical accident—a matter of whom the Commander selects or which staff officer takes the initiative.

This arbitrary selection and self-selection is effective only in a small, tight-knit staff that works as a team in closest collaboration with the Commander. Prime examples are Col. Henderson, Brig. Shearer, and Col. Fleming who as Intelligence officers, served their Commanders well as deception planners and operators. Or General Allenby, Admiral Yamamoto, and Admiral Halsey who worked closely with staff teams of deception planners and operators.

However, in more diffused organizational structures, which necessarily includes all large bureaucracies as well as some smaller ones, the best fit seems to lie within Ops. Let's consider some expert opinions:

Colonel Noël Wild served in deception for two years with Dudley Clarke's "A" Force as deputy director and then for another two years as head of Eisenhower's deception unit, SHAEF "Ops B.1". He found that Clarke's approach worked best, arguing for Clarke that:[435]

> His object was not merely to induce the enemy to "think" but to "act" so that deception was an operational matter as opposed to an intelligence one. He held that Intelligence was only as useful as the operational use to which it could be put. In this respect, deception should be kept apart from Counter-Intelligence.

Brigadier Dudley Clarke had a perspective of five years experience heading British deception planning in the Near East and Mediterranean and helping its world-wide diffusion. He offers us his own conclusions and recommendations on this problem:[436]

> 1) Deception is essentially a matter for the "Operations" Branch of the Staff, and not the "Intelligence". There was a popular misconception that because Deception involved some "cloak-and-dagger" business, it must be under the control of "I". I found this a grievous handicap, first in the early days, and later when I had to argue fiercely with the Americans when we came under Eisenhower's command at A.F.H.Q. in Algiers.
>
> 2) The "I" Branch, of course, provides Deception with two of its most valuable weapons—a means of direct communication with the enemy's Intelligence, and an evaluation of his reaction to our own deceptive efforts. But first of all there has to be a Deception Plan, and this is just as much a function of "Ops" as the real plan. Secondly, Deception has to be implemented by many more sources than those under the control

---

435 Noël Wild, "Foreword" in Mure (1980), 9.
436 Clarke (1972) in Mure (1980), 273.

of "I"—movements of troops and ships, targets for the [Air Force] and many others which are under the exclusive control of "Ops".

3) It follows, therefore, that the officer in charge of Deception should be a trained "Ops" officer able to meet the Planning Staff on equal terms. His place must be under the Director of Operations and, as he has to deal with all three Services, it is a great advantage if he can have direct access to the Commander-in-Chief.

Wild elaborates, "We had fought in the Middle East and vanquished the erroneous concept that deception was essentially an Intelligence matter." But in London it was viewed differently:[437]

> Secret Intelligence (spies) seems to have a boyish attraction for the uninitiated. Except in the actual running of agents and countering espionage and specialized techniques such as ULTRA, Intelligence, per se, is merely the handmaiden of operations. It is in the main concerned with the mundane functions of any military staff. Unfortunately even the initiated came to regard themselves as unique specialists. ... It was in such a cosmopolitan jungle that I had to establish the deception organization within SHAEF.

My own bias since 1951 has been that of an intelligencer. In studying deception since 1968, I was initially flattered to see many outstanding intelligencers like Henderson, Shearer, De Guingand, Eldredge, and Jones performing brilliantly at deception. While I never proposed in writing that deception should be an Intelligence function recruited mainly from among intelligencers, I did vaguely harbor this belief. Since the 1970s I have been persuaded otherwise. I now think that, while intelligence officers often make good deception planners, that task is best planned and executed as an integral part of operations. **Rule: Assign deception planning and operations to Plans and Operations—but don't hesitate to coopt intelligence analysts.**

9.4. Level of Operations: The Tactical-Strategic Continuum

Deception planning and operations occur throughout all military levels, from grand strategy, through strategy, and grand tactics, down to the tactical. Or, to use the terms of Soviet military doctrine, from strategy, through operational art, to tactics. The only significant differences for planners as they move upward from smaller to larger units are:

---

437 Wild in Mure (1980), 10.

1) Access to more deception assets.

2) A greater variety of such assets.

3) A more bureaucratized planning environment.

4) The availability of more and different types of options.

5) Usually longer lead times.

Otherwise, the individual planners all face the same set of basic options—what things to hide (dissimulate) and which to show (simulate).[438] Moreover, the planning process is also the same for all planners, as will now be discussed.

9.5. Enemy Capabilities & SOP

The deception planner must always try to match his deception assets to the enemy's intelligence collection capabilities and standard procedures.

One example: In WW1 the Germans systematically monitored and analyzed the enemy public media for tidbits of military, economic, and political intelligence. In WW2 they did not. Nor did the Japanese. But the British and Americans did.

Another example: Fleming's "D" Division in South-East Asia in WW II could never play the elaborate radio games of creating and shuffling large numbers of notional divisions, corps, and even an occasional army group around the map that London and Cairo could. Japanese Intelligence in that area simple lacked enough suitable radio equipment and trained operators to intercept such a large volume of radio traffic.[439] Nor did the Japanese have the analytical procedures to effectively interpret those few messages they did manage to intercept and read. Fleming was able to triple the number of Allied divisions on the Japanese enemy-order-of-battle maps at Japanese headquarters; but he had to do this almost entirely with planted documents, agent, and double-agent reports.

---

438 Whaley (1982), 182-188.
439 Hart-Davis (1974), 284.

CHAPTER 10:
Cultural Factors

Whenever the target of your deception belongs to a different culture than yours, problems of cross-cultural communication of the intended deception will arise. These communication problems can range from the trivial to the decisive, that is, from minor glitches to complete failure. But wise deceivers will appreciate this problem, try to discover how it is apt to work in specific situations, and plan accordingly. Similarly, the opposing deception analysts will benefit from doing the same.

10.1. Ethical Constraints

Each culture and sub-culture shares a more-or-less distinctive set of ethical values. These will include attitudes about surprise and deception. A clear statement of the ethical dilemma and its cause was well put by a late 19th Century British officer, wiser than most:[440]

> As a nation we [British] are bred up to feel it a disgrace even to succeed by falsehood; the word spy conveys something as repulsive as slave; we will keep hammering along with the conviction that 'honesty is the best policy,' and that truth always wins in the long run. These pretty little sentences do well for a child's copy-book, but the man who acts on them in war had better sheathe his sword for ever.

These words were written by the then Colonel (later Field-Marshal Lord) Garnet Wolseley, who along with General Lord Roberts was one of the two most successful senior British soldiers of his time. Despite his high authority, this particular part of his advice was overlooked even by his protégés, thereby proving his point. Wolseley's words were not given their full weight until WW2 when Col. Bevan's London Controlling Section (LCS) hung them prominently in its conference room at Storey's Gate.[441]

Wavell saw the matter similarly, complaining early in WW2 that:[442]

> Possibly because the British character is normally simple and straightforward, more probably because our military training is stereotyped and unimaginative, deception of an enemy does

---

440 Colonel Garnet Wolseley, *The Soldier's Pocket-Book for Field Service* (1869), 169.
441 Brown (1975), 9.
442 Wavell (1942), as reprinted in Wavell, *Speaking Generally* (London: Macmillan, 1946), 80.

not seem to come naturally to us. Hence we are apt to suffer in the field through lack of guile and to fall too easily into the enemy's traps and to miss opportunities of setting traps of our own.

But there are both changes and differences in ethical standards. Thus, the ethics of one culture can change from generation to generation—as seen from the Medieval to the Renaissance periods *within* Western civilization. Or these standards can differ *between* any two cultures at any one time.[443] Moreover, it can be important in knowing one's enemy to recognize when ethical standards differ within one of its cultural sub-groups and another might permit driving a wedge between them—as say between the extreme interpretations of Islamic law by Taliban or al-Qaida and more conventional or even secular Moslem groups.

10.2. Deception and National Character

Knowing one's enemy works at two levels: the cultural and the personal. Let's begin here with a brief look at the cultural level.

Some types of deception that worked well against the Germans did not necessarily work as well against the Italians or the Japanese. For example, in WW2, the rather sophisticated British deceptions that usually fully succeeded against the German Intelligence services did not do quite as well against the Italians or the Japanese services. The Italian services were themselves a bit too devious to be readily taken in. Japanese Army and Navy Intelligence services were generally weak at the strategic level and when accurate tended to be disbelieved by senior commanders.[444] And even the separate German services varied considerably in their levels of gullibility. Thus the military Abwehr tended to be quite gullible, the civilian Sicherheitsdienst somewhat less so, while the Army's Foreign Armies West was generally more skeptical.[445]

10.3. National Military Doctrines

The military doctrine of any given nation at any given time is a consequence of three main factors: previous experience, emulation of another nation's doctrine, and cultural bias.

For example, MacArthur recognized that the Japanese military code of *bushido* with which all officers and men were indoctrinated made the Japanese soldier

---
443 Whaley, *The Prevalence of Guile* (FDDC, 2007), 64-70.
444 Ken Kotani, *Japanese Intelligence in World War II* (Oxford: Osprey, 2009).
445 David Kahn, *Hitler's Spies: German Military Intelligence in World War II* (New York: Macmillan, 1978), 363-367.

feel his nation was invincible yet, as an individual, was willing to die, suicidally if necessary, for his emperor-god. He concluded that this made the Japanese a tough enemy in the attack, but "When he is attacked—when he doesn't know what is coming—it isn't the same." Unwilling to even contemplate defeat, they were unable to either plan or execute withdrawals. As MacArthur said in 1942, before he began his own offensive that would prove his point about Japanese inflexibility, "The hand that closes, never to open again, is useless when the fighting turns to catch-as-catch-can wrestling."[446]

During the early stages of the war in the Pacific, the Japanese naval commanders were indeed obsessed by offensive doctrine. So much so that they deliberately avoided diverting time, thought, training, or aircraft to reconnaissance, which they deemed a defensive concept. Only after their catastrophic defeat at Midway in May 1942 did the Japanese recognize this need for more and better reconnaissance.[447] Moreover, this abhorance of defensive thinking even extended to such seemingly obvious details as having their aircraft carriers fitted with bomb-resistant armored flight decks, fire-fighting equipment, and training for the deck crews. Again Midway proved them wrong when easily spread fires contributed to the crippling loss of 4 of their 10 carriers.

The Japanese Army in Burma was no better. Indeed it was so inefficient that Peter Fleming's "D" Division found it difficult to sell their deceptions. As Fleming's biographer sums up:[448]

> D Division's greatest problem was the incompetence of the Japanese intelligence staff. Although amazingly credulous, and willing to swallow (as Peter put it) the "most outrageous and implausible fabrications", they were often so slow-witted that they failed to make even the most obvious deductions from the information which they had been fed. Nor were D Division's designs furthered by the fact that many local Japanese commanders apparently held their intelligence staff in the utmost contempt and paid little or no attention to their advice and warnings. ... [This] inefficiency of the Japanese themselves ensured that the deception practised in South-East Asia could never be anything like as sophisticated as that carried out from London or from Cairo. In the Middle East and even more so in Europe, the efficiency and skill of the Axis intelligence staff meant that far more complicated and subtle ruses could be employed, with a very good chance that the enemy would make the deductions which the Allies wanted.

---

446 William Manchester, *American Caesar* (Boston: Little, Brown, 1978), 281.
447 Gordon W. Prange, *Miracle at Midway* (New York: McGraw-Hill, 1982), 181.
448 Hart-Davis (1974), 283, 284.

10.4. The "Not Invented Here" Syndrome & Its Alternatives

Three syndromes overlap the social (particularly institutional), cultural, and personality factors. They are the familiar syndromes or states of mind of "Not Invented Here", "Proudly Found Elsewhere", and "Best Practice". The first is a sure formula for disaster. The second is often dysfunctional. Only the third offers at least an effective temporary patch for problems.

The infamous "Not Invented Here (NIH)" syndrome vividly describes that pernicious tendency of parochial, nationalistic bigots to be so proud of themselves and their tribe and so disdainful of all outsiders that they routinely fail to appreciate that they might sometimes profit by borrowing or at least adapting weapon systems, procedures, tactics, or strategies from foreigners. Not Invented Here seems to be a particularly powerful slogan among post-WW2 American military commanders, service schools, and manuals. So powerful that even such a relatively mild accommodation to foreign experience (particularly Chinese Communist, Vietcong, and British) as the current American counterinsurgency manual, *FM 3-24* (co-written by Gen. Petraeus), seems almost revolutionary.

The "Proudly Found Elsewhere" (PFE) syndrome at least demonstrates a willingness to replace failed weapons, doctrines, strategies, or tactics with those of their more cost-effective enemies. Although this sounds logical, it often proved a poor choice. For example, the Japanese and Chinese governments became so impressed by the apparent prowess of French military doctrine in the mid-1800s that they slavishly imposed that model on their own army.

However, the most cost-beneficial strategy is to seek "Best Practice". That is, do comparative research on the range of each desired product (such as a weapon system) or method (such as a doctrines or tactic) to discover the one that consistently gives the most appropriate and effective outcome.

CHAPTER 11:
Personality Factors

> The real way to get value out of the study of military history is to take particular situations, and as far as possible get inside the skin of the man who made a decision, realise the conditions in which the decision was made and then see in what way you could have improved on it.
>
> — A. P. Wavell, lectures, 1935[449]

What makes a "deception-minded" planner? If we can draw up some kind of "psychological profile" of these persons and it turns out to contain only a few characteristics, all easily identified in others, we have a basis for efficiently selecting deception planning candidates.

There are only three ways to pick a candidate for deception planning—or, for that matter any other specialized task.

1) At random—just assign 'em, hope for the best, evaluate their performance, and weed out the worst.

2) Have a "little black book" either literally like Gen. Marshall (Case 7) or in the back of your mind like Wavell, Clarke, and MacArthur.

3) By profile. Screening by profile can be either by a records check of past performance or by some testing or interview procedure.

Fine so far, but what do we look for in picking people for deception work?

I met Eliahu "Eli" Zeira in 1974 when we were consulting on separate projects for The RAND Corporation in Santa Monica, California. Major-General Zeira had recently been retired from the Israeli Army as Director of Military Intelligence and had many years experience in the design and conduct of counter-espionage, counter-terrorist, and deception operations. As an amateur magician, he expressed particular pride in & enjoyment of his deception work. I asked him my favorite question, "If you took an assignment to set up a deception-planning team in an unfamiliar country and could not bring along your own people, what *types* of local recruits for your new staff would you ask to interview?" This question is, of course, worded to rule out "networking" and force the subject to generalize. Zeira thought a while and then answered that

---
449 Quoted in Connell (1964), 161.

he would interview only three types of people: anyone with a reputation for success because they threw away the rule books, persons with an unusual sense of humor, and magicians. Then, by interviewing he would seek to weed out the merely lucky insubordinates, the insane comedians, and the bad magicians.

Bits and scraps of evidence to support Zeira's hunch has been met several times throughout the preceding pages (and throughout my other studies). This evidence will now be arrayed and discussed. And, I believe, a common factor can be identified.

11.1. The Maria Theresa Syndrome: Break the Rules to Make Your Own

The highest decoration of the Austrian-Hungarian Empire was the Theresaordnung, the Order of Empress Maria Theresa. It was even rarer than the British Victoria Cross, the American Medal of Honor, or the German Pour le Mérite ("The Blue Max"). Legend has it that to earn it one had to have risked death by firing squad for deliberately disobeying orders and to win despite those orders—a delicate balancing act indeed.

A similar ethic was encouraged in the Israeli army but with neither such extreme rewards nor punishments. Insubordination is a touchy subject in any organization, particularly military ones where lives as well as treasure are at stake. Outright refusal to carry out orders is clearly disruptive of discipline and may threaten the common cause; but what of the officer who takes more devious—even deceptive—ways to go against orders?

Rommel was a master practitioner of the art of insubordination—in both attack and defense. For exceeding orders and winning in the first World War he received the Pour le Mérite, the Kaiser's highest decoration; and for deliberately disobeying and winning in the next he got his field-marshal's baton. Among other things, he simply ignored Hitler's orders, even burning the one that ordered all uniformed British behind-the-lines Commandos to be shot.

Wavell never *technically* disobeyed; but he did deliberately keep his masters so much in the dark about his own devious plans that he was often able to forestall their expected vetoes.

General Grant also used this ploy. As Halleck complained about Ulysses Grant to the War Department in 1862, "It is hard to censure a successful general immediately after a victory, but I think he richly deserves it."[450] Instead Lincoln promoted Grant to command of all Union armies.

---

450 Quoted in William S. McFeely, *Grant: A Biography* (New York: Norton, 1981), 105.

Like T.E. Lawrence before him, Orde Wingate did not hesitate to lie and cheat his military and political superiors to gain his ends. Col. Ingersoll was formed in a similarly ruthless mold. And the OSS X-2 delegates with LCS, Pearson and Lawler, freely lied about their personal background to win undeserved credit with their British colleagues.

Peter Fleming risked court martial by his frequent and protracted vanishing acts. These jaunts into and behind the front lines put him at risk of capture and interrogation that might have revealed his secrets of strategic plans, ULTRA, and Deception. Sir John Masterman flaunted the British Official Secrets Acts and deftly employed blackmail to publish his *The Double-Cross System*.

Dr. R. V. Jones disobeyed a Cabinet decision that vetoed one of his plans, which his superiors considered immoral. Jones disobeyed on the thin pretext that he had not been officially notified, thereby continuing the double-agent game that cut civilian casualties in London.

Admirals Nimitz and Halsey conspired twice to deceive CNO King on the eve of their decisive victory at Midway. Colonel Haney let his American guerrilla leader, "Rip" Robertson, accompany his force behind Korean-Chinese lines in direct disobedience to higher orders.

Col. Bevan could and did break the rules. As one of his American colleagues recalled:[451]

> At one time he had made the decision and started implementing before ... the Combined Chiefs of Staff had actually made a decision to do a certain operation. I remember asking him about this, and to whom he [felt he] was responsible. And I will never forget his answer. It was, "To God and history."

And, when General MacArthur conspired to get his brilliantly successful Inchon operation (Case 61) underway before the JCS could have vetoed it, he also followed this same route of insubordination—until even he finally got caught out by his rash decision to go a river too far.

Bonaparte, Monro, Lawrence, Marshall, Rommel, Wavell, Clarke, Bevan, Ingersoll, Patton, MacArthur, Haney, and Dayan. They all tossed out the rule books—and wrote their own. Wavell urged his fellow commanders to be "bold" and never allow themselves "to be bound and hampered by regulations", citing with approval the execution by firing squad of Admiral Viscount Byng in 1733 for giving a helpless enemy fleet time to escape while he fussed about trying to get his ships into the precise battle order required by the "very long-winded and complicated instructions lately laid down by the Lords of the Admiralty."[452]

---

451 Major Gen. William A. Harris in *Verbatim Transcript of Stratagem Conference* (1971), 29.
452 "The Good General", a 1939 lecture published in Field-Marshal Earl Wavell, *Soldiers and Soldiering* (London: Jonathan Cape, 1953). 20-21.

In sum, a kind of oblique insubordination seems a characteristic of our deceivers. More precisely, what all of these men engaged in was that kind of calculated manipulation of others that is now euphemistically called "information management" but is in fact deception. It should not be surprising that, having discovered the value of deception of an enemy, our deceivers might apply it to their own bureaucracy.

11.2. The Pleasures of Deceiving: An Odd Sense of Humor

> His appreciation of the gravity of affairs and his vindictive feelings were struggling against his strong sense of humour.
>
> — Colonel E. D. Swinton, "The Second Degree," *Blackwood's Magazine* (1908)

World-class military deception expert Amrom Katz, when asked which was his favorite practical joke, replied "My next". His new acquaintance then asked—somewhat nervously—what that next one would be. She drew the unreassuring reply, "How do you know I'm not already doing it?"[453]

Deceiving can be pleasurable. So say all deception planners who address this issue. Brig. Dudley Clarke judged his wartime service with "A" Force the second happiest experience of his life, second only to his earlier quiet days as Adjutant of the Surrey and Sussex Yeomanry.[454] Commenting on their closely shared wartime deceptions, Col. Bevan wrote his friend and colleague, Col. Wild, to ask rhetorically "We've had some gay and some grim moments, haven't we?"[455] Dr. R. V. Jones is as explicit as he is concise in summing up his wartime work as "exhilarating."[456] One of Jones' favorite maxims is the sentence from Francis Bacon, himself a practiced deceiver, that ends, "the deceiving of the senses is one of the pleasures of the senses."[457] The sheer delight in his deception planning infuses all of Jones' lectures, writings, and interviews. Colonel Meinertzhagen's diaries and memoirs describe his deceptions—both real & fictitious—with mischievous glee. T.E. Lawrence summing "Meiner" up as a man "who took as blithe a pleasure in deceiving his enemy (or his friend) by some unscrupulous jest, as in spattering the brains of a cornered mob of Germans one by one with

---

453 Fly-on-the-wall recollections of the author.
454 Mure (1980), 105.
455 John Bevan, letter to Noël Wild, 24 Sep 1945, as reproduced in Mure (1980), opposite 113.
456 Jones (1978), 532.
457 Francis Bacon, "The Advancement of Learning" (1605), Book 2, Chapter 10, Paragraph 13.

his African knobkerri."[458] And I noticed when interviewing Richard M. Bissell Jr, Major Eldredge, Colonel Ingersoll, General Zeira, O/C Eamon Timoney, Lieutenant (USNR) Douglas E. Webster, and Col. Hy Rothstein that all recalled their devious plans and ops with open pleasure.[459]

This atmosphere is readily communicated to the entire planning team. Cholmondeley's "corkscrew mind" prodded his colleagues on the Double Cross Committee to ever higher flights of fancy in deceiving the Germans.[460] Peter Fleming's "D" Division colleagues found that "one of the main pleasures of working in his office was the constant boiling-up of ideas. Many were absurd, and the air was constantly full of jokes, but beneath the high spirits the purpose was deadly serious, and even the most abstruse projects were seriously intended."[461] Similarly Colonel Billy Harris' Special Plans Branch was suffused with the infectious high-jinks of Ralph Ingersoll.

Deception is a game. When their WW 2 deceptions ended. Colonel Bevan wrote wistfully to Colonel Wild, saying 'Yes, the game is all over and there is really nothing more to be done about it."[462] Norman Holmes Pearson of OSS/X-2 and the LCS called it "the spy game".[463] Masterman likened "running a team of double agents" to "running a club cricket side";[464] and Yamamoto compared all war including deception to a game of chess.[465] Wavell saw an analogy between war and contract bridge.[466] German WW2 intelligencers called their double-cross wireless operations against the British and Russians a "radio game" (Funkspiel). Indeed, many deception planners and operators borrow Kipling's phrase in calling deception "The Great Game". All this is, of course, a small and clearly non-random "opportunity" sample; but I have found no exceptions to the rule. And it is the same response I get from all other types of deceivers I have interviewed—magicians, card sharps, con artists, spies, and terrorists.

Deceivers have a heightened sense of humor. Dudley Clarke's was "puckish with a "boundless sense of the ridiculous". We find these same qualities in Suvorov, Swinton, Bols, Meinertzhagen, Churchill, Jones, Fleming, Cholmondeley,

---

458 Lawrence (1935), 384. Meinertzhagen was unhappy with this passage, "a quite untrue account of me, almost amounting to libel." Meinterzhagen (1960), 38. In fact, Meiner often overtly lied; and, although he sometimes did carry a knobkerrie, he did his killing with pistol, rifle, and—or so he claimed—bayonet.
459 During author's interviews and conversations in, respectively, 1969, 1973, 1973, 1974, 1979, and 1987.
460 Macintyre (2009), 11ff.
461 Hart-Davis (1974), 281-282.
462 John Bevan, letter to Noël Wild, 24 Sep 1945, reproduced in Mure (1980), opposite 113.
463 Winks (1987), 249.
464 Masterman (1972), 90.
465 Layton(1985), 446, Yamamoto's reference being specifically to the Sino-Japanese version of chess called shogi.
466 "Military Genius", an article in The Times, 23 Oct 1942, as republished in Field-Marshal Earl Wavell, Soldiers and Soldiering (London: Jonathn Cape, 1953), 47.

Montagu, Watts, Barkas, Crichton, Wintle, Eldredge, Katz, Agayants, Bittman, and Zeira. T.E. Lawrence, usually brooding and introspective when writing, displayed an "impish sense of humor" with intimates and even in occasional passages of his *The Seven Pillars of Wisdom*. At least nine of these men even carried their humor to the point of practical jokes: Meinertzhagen, Bols, Lawrence, Swinton, Jones, Clarke, Montagu, Wintle, and Katz. Indeed, as Jones was first to point out,[467] practical joking and military deception are identical psychological processes with the same psychological consequences to both deceiver and deceived. Katz and Dr. William R. Harris agreed.

Wry wit—carefully limited to private moments—marked the style of Wellington, Allenby, Marshall, and Dayan. Although usually humorless in conversation, Wavell (because he was shy), Fergusson (because he was slow), and Masterman (because he was imperious) wrote with flashes of wit. Others like Ingersoll and, even more so, Liddell Hart and Rommel took life (and themselves) a bit too seriously to become noted for their humor, but they shared with the others an acute sense of the incongruous.

Orde Wingate, wrapped up in his religious vision, was quite without humor; but he viewed life as a ridiculous process with himself as its most absurd actor. This quality repelled many of Wingate's commanders but attracted both Wavell and Churchill, both of whom made good use of this odd man. And Wingate inspired those who served under or worked with him, including such notably deceptive generals as Dayan and Fergusson.

What of the other world-class deception planners? No one ever accused Rommel or MacArthur of being amusing fellows. Rommel, however, was credited with "intuition". Montgomery claimed to have "intuition" but this was a lie designed to conceal from subordinates his detested dependence on ULTRA intelligence.[468] Moreover, "Monty" was among the least stratagemic of senior commanders. He was no Allenby, Wavell, Rommel, or Patton. His rare successes of stratagem (such as at Alamein) must be credited to his staff.[469]

A sense of humor, particularly of the more off-beat types, seems to be closely associated with an ability to plan military deceptions, detect them, or both. Why? R. V. Jones gave us part of the answer in his essay on "The Theory of Practical Joking" (1957). There he proposed the startling hypothesis that the design of military deception operations is not just analogous to the design of jokes but is, in fact, identical. I believe Dr. Jones was right—and certainly so on the anecdotal level. Any systematic proof would have to be based on a survey of past cases but that would be limited to the small proportion of commanders, planners, or intelligencers on whom we have data on their sense of humor.

---

467 Jones (1957).
468 Winterbotham(1974), 74.
469 See Cases 18 (fn 122), 45 (Alam Halfa), and 46 (Alamein).

Why is an offbeat sense of humor such a pronounced characteristic among the more effective deceptionists? As I have long argued,[470] humor requires precisely the same manipulation of congruities and incongruities that defines deception. Consequently, it is not surprising that the more clever military deception planners tend to have highly developed senses of humor.

Of course, military deception planning "is not", to lift a quote slightly out of context, "just fun, games, and nonsense, but downright dangerous precisely to the degree that it is skillfully employed by its practitioners."[471] For every Flight-Lieutenant Cholmondeley there should be a Major Masterman riding herd: for every Colonel Wintle a Brigadier Clarke; for every Colonel Ingersoll a General Harris—the bright realists to harness and, when necessary, veto the brilliant dreamers. But let there be no mistake—all effective deception planning teams have been led by officers of intelligence, youthful enthusiasm for their work, and considerable humor. It is the Colonel Reeders who are unfit for deception at any level, not the Clarkes and Bevans and Baumers and Harrises. It is the latter who should command deception teams.

11.3. The Empathic Mind: Know Your Enemy

> Know your enemy and know yourself; then, in a hundred battles, savor a hundred victories.
> If you are ignorant of the enemy but know yourself, your chances of wining or losing are equal.
> If you are ignorant of both your enemy and yourself, you will lose every battle.
>
> — Sun Tzu, *Ping Fa* [The Principles of War] (c.350 BC), Chapter 3, Whaley translation.

The ability to keep one eye always on the other side of the hill, to put oneself into the mind of the enemy, seeing things as he sees them, is what psychologists call empathy. It marks most consistently successful commanders. The most influential Chinese military theorist, Sun Tzu, advised the Commander that to

---

470 Whaley, *Humor as a Deception Operation* (manuscript in progress since 1978).
471 Irving Louis Horowitz, *The Rise and Fall of Project Camelot: Studies in the Relationship Between Social Science and Practical Politics* (Revised Edition, Cambridge, Mass.: The MIT Press, 1974). "Postscript", 398. If we substitute "social science" for "deception planning", we restore Horowitz's context.

"Know your enemy and know yourself" was the best prescription for victory. And the Greek military historian Polybius warned that:[472]

> It is to be ignorant and blind in the science of commanding armies to think that a general has anything more important to do than to apply himself to learn the inclinations and character of his adversary.
> —Polybius, *Histories* (c.145 BC), Book 3

Swinton quoted this line from Polybius to his students[473] and applied it to his own work in deception (Case 3).

The great Japanese swordmaster, Musashi, remarked that:

> The way to win in a battle according to military science is to know the rhythms of the specific opponents, and use rhythms that your opponents do not expect, producing formless rhythms from rhythms of wisdom.
> — Miyamoto Musashi, *The Book of Five Rings* (1643/1993 Cleary translation), 15

American Confederate General Robert E. Lee on learning that his opposing number, the U.S. Army General George McClellan, had been relieved by President Lincoln for incompetence, wittily remarked: "I am sorry to part with General McClellan. We have come to understand each other so well." After the war, Lee explained to a Yankee general, " You people changed your commander in front of me so frequently that it was no small labor to study them and it was a work constantly to be renewed."[474]

The third of Masterman's seven objectives in working the double-cross system was specifically "To gain knowledge of the personalities and methods of the German Secret Service."[475] Montague agreed, writing that "when one is working a deception …, one has to put oneself into the mind of the enemy and try to assume his degree of general knowledge.[476]

German General Rommel German, being a highly innovative commander himself, was always looking "over the hill" to try to understand his opponent's thinking. In 1944 he wrote that:[477]

---

472 [Note missing]
473 Swinton (1909), 37.
474 Lee as quoted in Gamaliel Bradford, Jr., *Lee the American* (Boston: Houghton Mifflin, 1912), 194.
475 Masterman (1972), xii.
476 Montagu (1954), 131.
477 Rommel (1953), 519.

> When two armies meet on the battlefield, each of the opposing commanders has his own particular plan according to which he intends to engage his enemy, and the battle develops out of the two opposing plans. ... In these circumstances, it is extremely important for the commander to know his opponent and be capable of assessing his psychological reactions. Senior officers should be closely informed on the psychological stresses to which [the enemy] commander is exposed during battle and should be provided with the necessary psychological equipment to enable them to turn this knowledge to advantage.

Rommel even took his own advice. For example, when in early 1941 he arrived in North Africa to create and lead the Afrika Corps, Rommel carried with him and closely annotated a translation of a booklet titled *Generals and Generalship* by British General Wavell, his first opponent there.[478] Conversely, when British General Montgomery, a quite conventionally-minded commander faced Rommel, the best be could do by way of understanding his new enemy was to place a *photograph* of Rommel in his office.[479]

Rommel's own 1937 military memoirs, *Infantry Grieft An* [The Infantry Attacks], was translated into English by the U.S. Army in 1943. General Patton was reportedly "electrified" by this edition, reading it again and again until he knew it almost by heart.[480]

Others among our deceivers who were highly empathic include Wavell, Allenby, Marshall, Jones, Shearer, Crichton, and Clarke. Clarke was quite specific, his favorite maxim being "Put yourself in the enemy's place."[481] He added that: "It is a tremendous advantage if the officer in charge of Deception has a good personal knowledge of the enemy."[482] And Wellington coined a popular but too often disregarded soldiers' phrase when he urged his officers to always look "at the other side of the hill."

Field-Marshal Lord Wavell advised students of war to read fewer books on strategy and principles and read more biographies, memoirs, even historical novels. These latter, he wrote, let one "Get at the flesh and blood of it, not the skeleton."[483]

Wavell's favorite maxim was the lines from a Kipling poem: "Man cannot tell, but Allah knows/How much the other side was hurt."[484] And in a paper issued

---

[478] Richard Mead, *Churchill's Lions* (2006), 480.
[479] Macksey (1976), 244.
[480] Rommel (1937/1979 tr), publisher's note, v.
[481] Quoted in Mure (1980), 267.
[482] Clarke (1972) in Mure (1980), 273-274.
[483] "Generals and Generalship", a 1939 lecture published in Field-Marshal Earl Wavell, *Soldiers and Soldiering* (London: Jonathan Cape, 1953), 33-34.
[484] Bernard Fergusson, *The Wild Green Earth* (London: Collins, 1952 edition), 269-270.

to his commanders at a time when the fortunes of war were against them, he ended by urging "Finally, when things look bad and one's difficulties appear great, the best tonic is to consider those of the enemy."[485] The same was true of Maj.-Gen. Orde Wingate, as one of his brigade commanders recalled:[486]

> Wingate always reminded us, when we felt that specter of Japanese omniscience creeping up on us, to think not of "The Japanese," but of one specific Japanese of the same rank as ourselves. He counseled us to picture the headache that we were giving to Major Watanabe, our opposite number, who was getting hell from his superiors for being outwitted by our antics. This was wise indeed. Poor Watanabe! I grew quite sorry for him. The sweat was streaming down his spectacles in the miserable hut to which he had been driven by the allied bombing as he sought to sift the good intelligence from the bad. Then he would hurry on his equipment, march twenty miles to intercept us, and find us once more vanished, into the boundless and silent forest.

Empathy can even extend to one's individual opponent. For example, the American Civil War often pitted Yank against Reb commanders who had personally known each other from military academies or pre-war service; and some took these occasions as an opportunity to assess their opponent's likely intentions. Similarly during the Allied invasion of Syria in 1941 when Vichy French officers fought their Free French ex-colleagues. As a British participant observed of the opposing French commanders at Damascus:[487]

> By all accounts [General] de Verdilhac was a charming and dedicated man; and to illustrate the tragedy of this appalling war between Frenchmen, he was [General] Legentilhomme's camarade de promotion both at St Cyr and at the Staff College; they were close friends, and Legentilhomme used to scratch his head and try to guess, from his long personal knowledge of de Verdilhac, what his next move might be, just like the two leading characters in General Swinton's [short story in] *The Green Curve.*

Dr. R. V. Jones, as head of British WW2 Scientific Intelligence with its "Wizard War" deception games feared that his peacetime colleague, Carl Bosch Jr, might be his opposite number on the wartime German side. "If so, he would know

---

485 "A Note on Command", originally issued in March 1942 and republished in Field-Marshal Earl Wavell, *Soldiers and Soldiering* (London: Jonathan Cape, 1953), 130.
486 Fergusson (1952), 270.
487 Bernard Fergusson, *The Trumpet in the Hall. 1930-1958* (London: Collins, 1970), 105-106.

all my weak points; and he was such an expert hoaxer that he might easily have misled us." (Case 19)

Among non-deceptive commanders, Field-Marshal Montgomery is an instructive example. From 1941 through 1944, a photograph of his arch enemy, Rommel, hung on the wall above his desk. Typical of Monty, this was pure show, mere symbolism, at most a bravado act of exorcism. It was a gesture without psychological insight, for he never took any interest in the personalities of his opponents, leaving that to his Deception and Intelligence staffs.

Empathic ability cuts to the core of the old and unending "capabilities" versus "intentions" controversy. Conventional intelligence methods can give solid or at least adequate estimates of an opponent's material capabilities but they tend to give unreliable estimates of how that opponent hopes to use or not use those capabilities. Consequently, intelligence services and the commanders they serve tend to hedge their bets by assuming the worst-case based only on the capabilities. But that is the alternative which always costs more, often proves unnecessary, and occasionally even backfires. To the degree intelligence can add enemy intentions to its analyses, the equation tilts toward the better outcome. Empathy is one powerful way to reveal intentions.

Let us agree that empathy is a valuable, sometimes perhaps a necessary quality for a deception planner. But then how do we acquire it? One obvious way is to have a secret channel to enemy headquarters, one that is always accurate in what it reports and more-or-less complete in detail. In WW2 MAGIC served this purpose for Nimitz and MacArthur in the Pacific against the Japanese and ULTRA did so for the British and Americans in Europe versus the Germans. One historian of ULTRA summed up its service to Churchill:[488]

> Down the line from Bletchley came this extraordinary facility to place himself inside his enemy's mind—to read his operation orders, to study his manoeuvres in battle almost as they took place or even before they happened, to learn in advance about his weapon development, to observe the rise and fall in the status of his commanders.

But such near omniscience is all too rare. And the enemy may discover such secret channels at any time and cut them off—or even begin to play a counterdeception game. Moreover, even complete omniscience is no guarantor of victory. Thus we may know everything about the enemies location, strength, and D-day/H-hour as of D-minus-1 yet still be taken by surprise when the enemy commander suddenly decides to launch his attack now, on D-minus-1. This never happened—perhaps *couldn't* happen—with meticulous commanders like Montgomery (footnote 122) but regularly

---

488 Lewin (1978), 184.

happened with hyper-impatient ones like Rommel (Cases 6, 42, 43 or Patton (Case 54, footnote 122).

11.4. The Prepared Mind: Know Your Subject

I suggest that all persons who consistently and successfully plan deceptions have precisely one thing in common. Jones calls this both the "alert mind" and, quoting Louis Pasteur, "the prepared mind".[489]

What makes a deceiver? Some of us are better at it than others. This quality is a mix of personality and experience. We could say that some deceivers are born, others made; but that would be a simplistic view, slighting the fact that personality is itself a combination of genetics and learning. It is better to say that some persons choose to engage in deception for the sheer pleasure of it, others because they must—either their jobs or their survival require it. In either case, to be a deceiver it helps to have a "prepared mind".

The prepared mind is one open to unusual events. It is not tied to written rules and someone else's SOP. It tolerates the absurd, the ridiculous. It notices the anomalies, the discrepancies, the incongruous happenings that crop up from time to time and seizes eagerly upon them as food for thought. It is the humor factory without which we cannot create, repeat, or even appreciate a joke, seeing the difference between what is funny and what isn't. It is also, as I have argued elsewhere, the mental quality essential for detecting deception directed against us.[490] My hypothesis is that this characteristic is the single strongest correlate with deception planning ability.

---

[489] R. V. Jones, "Chance Observation and the Alert Mind", *Advancement of Science* (March 1965), 531-544.
[490] Bart Whaley, *Detecting Deception* (draft, 1987).

CHAPTER 12:
Selection of Deception Personnel

> "I did send for thee to tutor thee in stratagems of war."
> — Shakespeare, *Henry VI*, Pt.1 (1623)

Is it possible to effectively and efficiently select, teach, and train persons for deception work? And, if so, how? The case studies have given us strong evidence about the type of persons one would want to select as candidates for deception work. However, these same cases offer only weak clues about how their selection and subsequent teaching and training can be best achieved.

12.1. Prior Experience

Experience is clearly a major factor in making a skilled deceiver; but the sheer frequency of an experience is never a guarantee that lessons will be learned. Montgomery had as much battle experience as Rommel, Mark Clark had even more than Patton, Che Guevara had the same guerrilla training and experience as Castro yet neither "Monty" nor Clark nor "Che" learned to understand military deception. Some gamblers never learn and blame their losses on bad luck rather than marked cards or stacked decks. Some persons are simply better at learning certain things than others, and deception is no exception. Thus skill at deception is, among other factors, a matter of psychology, of personality.

Many, perhaps most, of the skills brought into play at the cutting edge of battle are unique to the soldier's profession. Few civilians enter military service already skilled even with firearms much less the other hardware of combat: artillery, rocket launchers, radar, lasers, etc. Even fewer come prepared with combat doctrine and the principles of war. An exception is a talent for deceiving. Most, perhaps all, military deception planners, put on uniform with a mind already tuned to thinking deceptively. It is a skill that cuts across professions.

While I was the first to argue explicitly in print that deception is a general phenomenon and therefore susceptible to a general theory,[491] the notion is hardly original. Several military experts have implied this generalization by asserting analogies among ostensibly separate fields where deception plays a significant part:

---
491 Whaley & Bell (1982), throughout; and Whaley (1983), p.1.

Magician-camoufleur Major Jasper Maskelyne (1949) saw a close analogy between magic and both camouflage in particular and military deception in general; British physicist, practical joker, and military deception planner Dr. R. V. Jones (1957) argued for a common theory linking the scientific method, practical joking, and military deception. Gen. Patton used the analogy between the "end-run" in football and surprise attack in war; British military theorist Captain Sir Basil Liddell Hart (1929) recognized an analogy between military deception and deception in sports. Later (1954) Liddell Hart added deception in international politics at the level of 'grand strategy' as well as in business and sex. But, of course, Machiavelli had long since made the general connections among deception in war, politics, and (implicitly in his one work of fiction) everyday life. Finally, bringing these separate links full circle, both Field-Marshal Wavell (1942) and former Director of Israeli Military Intelligence Major-General Eliahu Zeira (1974) understood that the fundamental methods of military deception planners and magicians are the same.

12.2. Selection

> The best soldier has in him, I think, a seasoning of devilry. Some years ago [1932] a friend of mine in a discussion on training defined the ideal infantryman as an "athlete, marksman, stalker". I retorted that a better ideal would be a "cat-burglar, gunman, poacher". My point was that the athlete, marksman, or stalker, whatever his skill, risks nothing; the cat-burglar, gunman, and poacher risk life, liberty, and limb, as the soldier has to do in war.
>
> — Field-Marshal Earl Wavell, "The Soldier as Individual" (1945) as reprinted in Wavell, *The Good Soldier* (1948), 47

What qualities do we want in our deceptive soldiers? Wavell hammered out his strong views in repeated lectures and publications. He attacked the conventional view that the desirable candidate was an "athlete, marksman, stalker" and said the characteristics he sought were those of a "successful poacher, cat-burglar, gunman, and poacher." He admitted that the first set of qualities were fine in peacetime, but insisted that only the latter were of value in war.

The strong knack for deceptivity is evidently a special talent. Those who delight in detecting deceptions are likely to be persons who enjoy solving mysteries.

Conversely, those who enjoy practicing deception are apt to be found among practical jokers and machiavellians. On the principle of, "It takes one to know one," good detectives are often—but hardly always—good deceivers. But how best to select such persons?

Perhaps the simplest way to find either type is to put them to "The Gossip Test." During and immediately after WW2 young Francis Crick worked as a physicist for the British Admiralty. Although he'd been quite successful at designing improved model non-contact naval mines, he didn't relish maritime weaponry R&D as his lifetime career. One day he became aware that he was always chatting to friends and colleagues about the latest science news about R&D in antibiotics—penicillin was the current rage. He didn't have expert knowledge, but enough enthusiasm to share this bit of medical gossip. As he would recall:[492]

> This was a revelation to me. I had discovered the gossip test—
> what you are really interested in is what you gossip about.

Crick decided to combine his academic & on-the-job training in applied physics with courses in molecular biology. The conquence was pre-doctoral research in collaboration with American zoologist James Watson that produced their double-helix model of DNA and a shared Nobel Prize.

So, clearly, one interviewing technique is to get your candidate to talk about their hobbies and other extracurricular passions. Do they enjoy *solving* mysteries—puzzles of nature and humankind? Do they enjoy creating mysteries—practical jokes, deceptions? If neither, terminate the interview. If both, recruit them immediately, at least as your sorceror's apprentices.

The psychologist's Mach[iavellian] Scale could be one of a few potentially useful tools for selecting candidates for training in deception or for practicing it.[493] It is a simple paper-andpencil test. Other plausibly useful screening tests are the Miller Analogies Test (MAT), Wason's 2-4-6 Task, the Social Inference Test (TASIT), and the Ickes Empathy Test.

---

492 Francis Crick, *What Mad Pursuit: A Personal View of Scientific Discovery* (New York: Basic Books, 1988), 17.

493 Richard Christie and Florence L. Geis, *Studies in Machiavellianism* (New York: Academic Press, 1970).

12.3. Teaching & Training

> I was practicing in a bunker down in Texas and this good old boy with a big hat stopped to watch. The first shot he saw me hit went in the hole. He said, "You got 50 bucks if you knock the next one in." I holed the next one. Then he says, "You got $100 if you hole the next one." In it went for three in a row. As he peeled off the bills he said, "Boy, I've never seen anyone so lucky in my life." And I shot back, "Well, the harder I practice, the luckier I get." That's where the quote originated.
>
> — Gary Player, *Golf Digest* (Oct 2002), in interview with Guy Yocom. Often misattributed to Arnold Palmer.

Having found suitable candidates, how can we best teach them military deception and train them to use it effectively? Here are some suggestions:

The Israeli Army and Government gaming experience (Case 85) holds a lesson for all of us. They have used it to refine both operational plans and cover plans, but it would seem a promising way for teaching and training in both deception and counterdeception. Moreover, this type of role-playing game need not cost a lot. At the bottom end the whole cost can be only the players' time (as little as a single day) plus some pencils and paper. At mid-range, as the Israelis did it, inter-team communication was by messenger-distributed xeroxed messages, teletype, or computer printer networks. In its most expensive and elaborate form, as the Israelis also sometimes preferred, it tied the teams to a Command Post Exercise (CPX) or even to a full-fledged Field Training Exercise (FIX).

Appendices

This section reprints in their entirety two major deception planning documents. The first is typical of German strategic level ones developed and used throughout WW2. The second, a British tactical level plan against the Japanese in Burma, was Col. Peter Fleming's most successful one. Both give us a close look over the shoulders of deception planners at work.

Appendix A: "Guidelines for Deception of the Enemy," 15 February 1941

Basic German Strategic Deception Plan for Operation BARBAROSSA (invasion of Russia)

[NOTE: This document was the basic German order governing deception for Operation BARBAROSSA, the planned invasion of the Soviet Union. It was generated at Hitler's military headquarters, the Oberkommando der Wehrmacht (OKW). Introduced in evidence at the Nürnberg trials but not published at that time. It was updated by the document #42 below in Appendix B.]

[SOURCE: A microfilm of the original document is in the National Archives, Washington, D.C., Microcopy Series T77, Roll 792. Also published in F. A. Krummacher and Helmut Lange, *Krieg und Frieden: Geschichte der deutsche-sowjetischen Beziehunger: Von Brest-Litovsk zum Unternehmen Barbarossa* (Munich: Bechtle. 1970). 554-557. The following translation was made c.1969 by Mrs. Rodica Saidman and myself.]

TOP MILITARY SECRET
[stamp]

The Führer's Headquarters
15 February 1941

High Command of the Armed Forces [OKW]
No.44 142/41 Top Military Secret/Senior Officers Only
WFSt/Abt.L (I Op.)

MATTER FOR CHIEFS! [stamp]   15 copies

THROUGH OFFICER ONLY! [stamp]   9th copy

Reference: OKW/WFSt/Abt.L No.22048/40
Top Military Secret/Senior Officers
Only of 3 February 1940

Guidelines for Deception of the Enemy

A) 1) The *aim* of the deception is *to conceal* the preparations of *Operation BARBAROSSA*. This essential goal is the guiding principle for all the measures aimed at keeping the enemy misinformed. It is a matter of maintaining uncertainty about our intentions during the first period, that is, until the middle of April. In the ensuing second period the misdirecting measures meant for BARBAROSSA itself must not be seen as any more than misdirection and *diversion for the invasion of England*.

   2) *Guidelines* applied to misleading intelligence and other measures are:

      a) *during the 1ˢᵗ period:*

Strengthening the existing impression of a coming *invasion* of England. Enclosed are instructions about new means of attack and transportation.

Exaggeration of the significance of the *secondary operation* (MARITA), SUNFLOWER, the Xᵗʰ Flying Corps, and the forces engaged therein. *Reason for the troop movements connected with* BARBAROSSA are to be presented as an exchange operation between the West, the [German] Homeland, and the East, as a concentration of reserve units for Operation MARITA, and in the final analysis as defensive rear cover against Russia.

      b) *during the 2ⁿᵈ period* the *troop movement* for BARBAROSSA *is to be seen as the greatest deception operation in the history of war*, intended as a cover-up for the final preparations for the invasion of England.

This measure is made possible by the fact that the first surprise attack against England would be carried out with relatively weak forces, thanks to the strongest concentration of the new [German] combat methods and in recognition of the superiority of the English fleet. As a consequence, the bulk of the German forces could be chiefly engaged in the deception undertakings. The deployment against England, however, will be initiated simultaneously with the surprise attack.

B) *Execution of the Deception:*

   I) *Intelligence Service* (under the guidance of the Chief of the Abwehr [Admiral Canaris]): Efficient use of the general policy of going only through the channels established by the Chief of the Abwehr.

The latter channels infiltrate false intelligence among the routine information of our own attachés in neutral countries and the neutral attachés in Berlin. The pattern will be a mosaic picture, determined by this general policy. In order to bring the actual measurers, especially the troop movements, of the High Commands into agreement with the intelligence service and to make full use of suggestions, the OKW/WFSt/Abt. L will hold a briefing on the general guidelines for the time periods depending on the situation. in coordination with the High Commands and the Abwehr. During the first briefing it will be established, among others:

a) how long the intended transport movements are to be interpreted as normal West-to Homeland-to East commutings,

b) which westbound transports could be used in counter-espionage for the deception "invasion" [of England] (for example, concentration of camouflaged new weapons).

c) if and how to disseminate the intelligence that the Navy and Luftwaffe were held back according to plan and because of bad weather conditions, in order to spare their forces for the main attack.

d) how to prepare the Codeword ALBION (see below) preliminary operations.

II) *Measures of the High Commands:*

1) In spite of the further relaxation of the preparation for SEA LION, everything should be done to maintain the impression that the landing in England is being prepared, although in a new form, although the troops stationed there would be withdrawn at a later date. Even the troops deployed in the East are to be kept as long as possible under the impression that this was simply conceived as a deception, that is, as defensive rear cover for the forthcoming blow against England.

2) The Army High Command is requested to check if measures connected with BARBAROSSA, such as introduction of the full capacity timetable, leave cancellation, etc., could be synchronized with the beginning of MARITA.

3) Particular significance for the deception is attached to intelligence about the airborne forces, pointing to their use against England (assignment of English interpreters, newly pringed English maps, and the like). The Luftwaffe High Command is requested to make the appropriate arrangements in cooperation with the Abwehr.

4) The stronger the troop concentration in the East, the harder the attempts to foster uncertainty about our plans. In addition the plan for the sudden "closing" of certain areas around the Channel and in Norway is to be prepared by the Army High Command in cooperation with the Abwehr. (Codeword for its initiation: ALBION.) In doing so it is less a question of carrying out this blockade in minute detail by engaging a great concentration of forces, but much more to create great effect through the appropriate measures. In this manner an impression should be created that surprises are in store for the British Isles, as well as by using other measurers, for example, the disposition of instruments that would look to the enemy like hitherto unknown "rocket batteries." The more the preparations for BARBAROSSA stand out, the more difficult it will be to maintain a successful deception. However the utmost must be done to keep to these guidelines to ensure the secrecy of the operation.

Suggestions and proposals of the participating service are desired.

Chief of the High Command of the Armed Forces

Keitel
Field-Marshal

[illegible signature]
Captain

Appendix B: Chronology of 67 Further German BARBAROSSA Deception Plans, 1941

These 67 implementing and elaborating documents cover the contributions of specific units of the German war machine. They are listed and separately summarized in Whaley, *Codeword BARBAROSSA* (Cambridge, Mass.: The MIT Press, 1973), 251-266.

Appendix C:
Plan CLOAK, 25 January 1945
British Tactical Deception Plan against Japanese in Burma, February 1945

[NOTE: This document gives the basic plan for Operation CLOAK, the key British deception for the crossing of the Irrawaddy River in Burma, by Gen. Slim's IV Corps which took place in mid-February 1945. It was prepared in Delhi, India, at the headquarters of "D" Division, the central deception planning group for Mountbatten's South East Asia Command. The original principle drafter was probably the chief of "D" Division, Col. Peter Fleming with, I presume, refinements by staff at IV Corps. Together with "Deception Scheme CONCLAVE" (see Appendix D-4, below) these are, so far, the only published deception plans for the China-Burma-India (CBI) Theatre.]

SOURCE: P. N. Khera & S. N. Prasad, *The Reconquest of Burma*, Vol.2 (Calcutta: Combined Inter-Services Historical Section—India & Pakistan, 1959), "Deception Scheme CLOAK", 499-502. [Also published in Major-General S. Woodburn Kirby, *The War Against Japan*, Vol.4 (London: Her Majesty's Stationery Office, 1965), 501-505. Kirby's text is identical to the above except that Kirby has inexplicable dropped the sign-off of BGS E. H. W. Cobb and for euphemizing the original racial slur of "JAPS" into "Japanese".]

Information

1. The presence of IV Corps in the GANGAW VALLEY is believed to be still undetected by the Japanese, but as soon as the corps begins to emerge into the open country east of PAUK they will realize that we are a strong force and that we intend to cross the IRRAWADDY.

Intention

2. To continue to conceal from the Japanese for as long as possible the presence of the corps in the GANGAW VALLEY.

3. Subsequently to mislead the Japanese about the corps' crossing place over the IRRAWADDY and about the corps' objective east of the IRRAWADDY, at the same time misrepresenting to them the composition of the corps.

Method in Outline

4. (a) To continue, as long as possible, the methods at present being employed to conceal the composition of IV Corps and the presence of a corps in the GANGAW VALLEY.

   (b) To make a feint crossing at CHAUK, three or four days before our actual crossing elsewhere.

   (c) To simulate preparations for crossing the IRRAWADDY at PAKOKKU shortly before our actual crossing elsewhere.

   (d) To 'sell' YENANGYAUNG to the Japanese as the objective of IV Corps east of the IRRAWADDY.

Method in Detail

Concealment of the Location and Composition of IV Corps

5. The present restrictions on the use of wireless will continue until relaxed by Corps H.Q.

6. 17th Division and 255th Tank Brigade will remain on wireless silence til deployed east of the IRRAWADDY.

7. No formation signs will be displayed on uniform, vehicles, notice-boards or elsewhere until permission to do so is given by Corps H.Q.—but see para.9(a) below for special instructions for one brigade of 7th Indian Division.

The Feint Crossing at Chauk

8. As soon as possible after securing PAUK area 7th Indian Division will despatch one brigade with some artillery in support (28th (E.A.) Brigade simulating 11th (E.A.) Division) down the YAW Chaung towards SEIKPYU. During this advance, the brigade will 'sell' to the Japanese the bogus fact that it is a brigade of 11th (E.A.) Division and that the whole of this division is advancing by the same route. One section 'D" (from 11th (E.A.) Division) and 57th Company 'D' Force will be under command this brigade to assist in the deception. C.S.O.IV Corps is issuing separately details of W/T deception methods to be employed as part of this 'selling' of 11th (E.A.) Division.

9. Methods to be employed by this brigade for simulating the presence of large numbers:

   (a) They will wear on their uniforms the sign of 11th (E.A.) Division. Corps H.Q. will arrange a supply of these.

(b) Movement wherever possible by day.

(c) Movement on a wide front, and widespread patrolling.

(d) Faked dust clouds, simulating the movement of large columns of transport or troops.

(e) Wherever contact is made with the enemy, the use of tactical deception devices to simulate considerable firepower and strength.

(f) The spreading of rumours that 20,000 E.A. troops are advancing down the YAW Chaung axis, and that airborne troops will be co-operating in advance of them in considerable strength.

10. On arrival at the IRRAWADDY, preparations will be made for a divisional crossing, as described in paras. 13 and 14 below.

11. At the appropriate moment this brigade will carry out a diversionary crossing over the IRRAWADDY. At least one company of infantry will be employed for this crossing. The deception units with the brigade will be able to assist in magnifying the strength of our force which lands on the far bank. This diversionary crossing will take place a few days before the real crossing by 7th Division elsewhere. To support the illusion that this diversionary crossing is the real thing, Corps H.Q. will arrange for dummy paratroops and other deception devices to be dropped from the air on the east side of the IRRAWADDY to assist this diversionary crossing.

12. Only negligible engineer assistance is likely to be available for this whole operation, since all available engineer resources will be required for the main crossing. Spurious Preparations for Crossing at Pakokku.

13. These preparations will be made by 7th Indian Division, who will send one brigade and engineers with river crossing stores into PAKOKKU itself. The activities of this brigade will conform as nearly as possible to those of a brigade which Is, in fact, going to cross the river and will include:

(a) Reconnaissances for crossing places by suitable reconnaissance parties. In addition to reconnoitering the near bank, some of these parties will reconnoiter the far bank at a number of different places during darkness, making sure that their presence becomes known to the locals.

(b) Visits to selected crossing places by an officer wearing a red hat and red tabs.

(c) Inquiries from local inhabitants concerning speed of current, sandbanks, nature of far bank, time required for crossing, exits from the river opposite PAKOKKU, enemy strengths and dispositions opposite PAKOKKU.

(d) The 'losing' on the far side of a marked map, showing a few sketchy details of projected reconnaissances and Japanese positions. This map will be prepared at Corps H.Q.

(e) The collection of country boats from local boatmen-demands to be sufficient for the crossing of a whole division.

(f) Work on the approaches to the river bank.

(g) The establishing of dummy camps and dumps in the crossing area.

(h) Unloading bridging equipment from M.T. in the PAKOKKU area. If this can be arranged so that the local boatmen become aware of the activity, or even so that the Japanese hear the work in progress, the effect will be improved.

14. Throughout these preparations, efforts will made to confuse and jitter the Japanese on the far bank by dropping deception devices from the air and floating them downstream on rafts and boats at night and by any other means by which these devices can be usefully used.

15. 51st Company 'D' Force will be under command 7th Indian Division to help carry out 'these various deception measures.

The 'Selling' of Yenangyaung as the IV Corp Objective

16. On arrival of 28th (E.A.) Brigade in the SEIKPYU area, a force of armoured cars and artillery will operate south from there along the west bank of the IRRAWADDY, to simulate a threat to YENANGYAUIVG. This force will:

    (a) Create a strong show of force wherever possible.

    (b) Shoot up any Japanese positions or movement seen on the east bank of the IRRAWADDY.

    (c) Publish amongst locals rumours of large forces due to arrive from the PAUK area to operate on west bank of the river.

    (d) Make inquiries concerning roads, water and enemy dispositions on both banks of the IRRAWADDY as far south as YENANGYAUNG.

    (e) Make inquiries regarding suitable landing areas for airborne forces in the same area.

17. The CHIN HILLS battalion moving on the general line TILIN-SAW-SIDOKTAYA PT 4886-NGAPE PT 7241, will also simulate a threat to YENANGYAUNG, by exaggerating their own strength and making similar inquiries about the area west of the IRRAWADDY as far south as MAGWE.

18. Corps H.Q. will arrange leaflet drops to indicate an interest in YENANGYAUNG.

19. An interest in YENANGYAUNG will also be 'sold' to the Japanese through certain reliable secret channel. Corps H.Q. is arranging this.

Wireless Deception

20. The question of wireless silence and of a bogus network representing 11th (E.A.) Division have already been dealt with (paras. 5, 6 and 8 above).

21. In addition Corps H.Q. will arrange for a few intentional mistakes to be made in our own wireless transmissions with the object of supporting the overall deception. Details will be worked out at Corps H.Q. and notified to those formations required to participate.

22. Wireless activity by 28th (E.A.) Brigade will show a considerable increase during the days immediately prior to the feint crossing at CHAUK. Details are being issued separately by C.S.O. IV Corps.

23. The armoured cars and artillery force will maintain a high level of wireless activity from the time of their arrival at SEIKPYU onwards.

Air Activity

24. Dropping of deception devices to jitter the Japanese will be carried out under arrangements to be made by Corps H.Q. and on request from 7th Division in support of bogus activity and the feint crossing.

25. Air reconnaissance, air photography and air attacks will be asked for by Corps H.Q. in areas away from our real crossing places and objectives, in order not to draw the Japanese attention to any particular area through undue air activity over it.

Date of Crossing the Irrawaddy

26. By other means arrangements are in hand to convey the impression to the Japanese that our crossing over the IRRAWADDY is going to occur one month later than we do, in fact, intend to cross.

Security

27. The deception plan to be known by the code work [sic, meaning code word] CLOAK.

28. As far as possible everyone taking part in these deceptive activities should believe them to be genuine. Where the personnel involved are bound to guess that their activities are not entirely genuine, they may be told

confidentially—in order to obtain their wholehearted co-operation—that they are taking part in a deception.

29. Signal instructions with wide distributions will not be issued in connection with this scheme.

30. Acknowledge.

Appendix D: Checklist of Other Deception Plans

D-1. Directive Establishing the LCS, 1942.

This brief directive was issued on 21 Jun 1942.

SOURCE: Michael Howard, *British Intelligence in the Second World War*, Vol.5 ("Strategic Deception") (New York: Cambridge University Press, 1990), 243.

LOC: BW.

D-2. BODYGUARD, 1944

This directive was issued 23 Jan 1944.

SOURCE: Michael Howard, *British Intelligence in the Second World War*, Vol.5 ("Strategic Deception") (New York: Cambridge University Press, 1990), 247-253.

LOC: BW.

D-3. FORTITUDE, D-Day 1944

The British official history of the D-Day 1944 deceptions. Written by Colonel Hesketh who was one of the main FORTITUDE planners.

SOURCE: Roger Hesketh, *Fortitude: The D-Day Deception Campaign*. London: St. Ermin's Press, 1999, xxii+513pp. Introduction by Nigel West.

LOC: BW.

D-4. CONCLAVE, Burma 1945

This was the deception plan for British IV Corps against the Japanese forces in Burma in 1945.

SOURCE: P.N. Khera & S. N. Prasad, *The Reconquest of Burma*, Vol.2 (Calcutta: Combined Inter-Services Historical Section—India & Pakistan, 1959), "Deception Scheme CONCLAVE", pp.515-517.

D-5. Plan NORTHWOODS, Cuba 1962

NORTHWOODS was a set of JCS recommendations for a series of deceptive psychological operations intended as "pretexts which would provide justification for US military intervention in Cuba." NORTHWOODS is interesting for showing the quality of deception and psyops thinking at the upper level of staff planners for the JCS, specifically BG Edward Lansdale and BG William H. Craig. Major portions of this plan were signed off by JSC Chairman L. L. Lemnitzer and all other members of the JCS.

I would judge this a highly amateurish example of deception and psyops planning. It took no account of any possible backfire and the potentially enormous consequences for the American government's reputation for credibility and respect for international law. That low echelon planners would put forward even outlandish options is acceptable, even commendable, in the intellectual effort to analyze all relevant hypotheses. But for these to be recommended to high echelon such as the JCS much less being approved by that exalted body is ridiculous—proving only an inept understanding of the limits of psyops and deception. In this case, it was probably just as well that this particular plan was never implemented, having been flatly turned down by the Secretary of Defense (McNamara) and the President (Kennedy). Indeed, the President was sufficiently disappointed that he fired the Chairman of the JCS.

SOURCE: *Memorandum for the Chief of Operations, Cuba Project, Subject: Tasks 33c and 33d* (Washington, DC: Office of the Secretary of Defense, 19 Feb 1962). Declassified from TOP SECRET - SPECIAL HANDLING.

LOC: Internet.

SOURCE: *Memorandum for the Secretary of Defense. Subject: Justification for US Military Intervention in Cuba (TS)* (Washington, DC: The Joint Chiefs of Staff, 13 Mar 1962). Declassified from TOP SECRET SPECIAL HANDLING - NOFORN.

LOC: Internet.

REF: *Wikipedia*, "Operation Northwoods" (accessed 20 Feb 2010).

D-6. KINGFISHER, An Israel War Game, 1979

KINGFISHER Game: Summary of Procedures and Analysis (Tel Aviv: July 1979, v+189pp). Declassified from "CONFIDENTIAL".

LOC: BW (Copy #129).

Bibliography

This bibliography is a preliminary effort to collect unclassified works by or about specific, identifiable military deception planners. Some other, more marginal, references are fully cited in the footnotes if they apply only to the details of a single case. Brief annotations are included as a guide to critics, serious readers, and any future researchers.

Barkas, Geoffrey (1896-1979)
> *The Camouflage Story*. London: Cassell and Company, 1952.
>> Light-hearted but perceptive memoirs of the first Director of Camouflage in North Africa during WW2. Lieut.-Col. Barkas had been, appropriately, a film producer. Particularly relevant to this paper because it shows the author's military deception learning curve.

Bittman, Ladislav (1931-)
> *The Deception Game: Czechoslovak Intelligence in Soviet Political Warfare*. Syracuse: Syracuse University Research Corporation, 1972.
>> Maj. Bittman was for three years, from February 1964 until December 1966, Deputy Director of the Czechoslovak Interior Ministry's Department for Active Measures. He fled to the West in 1968 at the time of the Soviet invasion of his country.

Brown, Anthony Cave (1929-2006)
> *Bodyguard of Lies*. New York: Harper & Row, 1975.
>> A pioneering study of Allied deception operations in the European theater of operations during WW2. However, should be used with considerable caution as the author's facts and conclusions are frequently wrong. Fortunately now superceded by Holt (2004).

Callwell, Colonel C. E. (1859-1928)
> *Small Wars: Their Principles and Practice*. 3rd ed., London: His Majesty's Stationery Office, 1906.
>> The first textbook of counter-guerrilla operations. For the role of tactical deception and related topics see particularly Chapters 4, 6, 7, 8, 11, and 15.

Callwell, Major-General Sir C. E.
:   *The Dardanelles*. London: Constable, 1919.

Cave Brown, Anthony
:   SEE: Brown, Anthony Cave

Churchill, Winston S. (1874-1965)
:   *The World Crisis, 1915*. London: Butterworth, 1923; New York: Scribners, 1923.

Churchill, Winston S.
:   *The World Crisis. 1911-1914*. New York: Scribners, 1924.

Clarke, Dudley (1899-1974)
:   [Official history of "A" Force]. Manuscript, 1945.

    Brigadier Clarke was the founder and director of "A" Force until VE-Day when he remained only long enough to liquidate his organization and write this official history.

Collins, Major-General R. J. (1880-)
:   *Lord Wavell (1883-1941): A Military Biography*. London: Hodder and Stoughton. 1948.

    Includes information on Wavell's learning and practice of deception.

Connell, Brian (1916-1999)
:   *Knight Errant: A Biography of Douglas Fairbanks. Jr.* Garden City, NY: Doubleday & Company, Inc., 1955.

    See chapter 13-14 (pp.143-173) for Fairbanks WW2 service in U.S. Navy deception. Unfortunately Fairbanks' own autobiography (1988) stops just short of his wartime service.

Connell, John [pseudonym of John Henry Robertson] (1909-1965)
:   *Wavell: Scholar and Soldier, To June 1941*. London: Collins, 1964.

    A biography of Field-Marshal Wavell that includes important details of his attitude toward and use of deception planning.

Connell, John
:   *Wavell: Supreme Commander, 1941-1943*. London: Collins, 1969,

    A continuation of the above work.

Daniel, Donald C. (1944-), and Katherine L. Herbig (1940-) (*editors*)
Strategic Military Deception. New York: Pergamon Press, 1982.

> A useful collection of 16 original papers generated by a CIA supported project at the Naval Postgraduate School at Monterey, California.

Dayan, Major-General Moshe (1915-1981)
Diary of the Sinai Campaign. Jerusalem: Steinmatzky's Agency, 1966.

> Includes several examples of Dayan's own contribution to the deception planning for this 1956 campaign.

Dayan, Moshe
Moshe Dayan: Story of My Life. New York: William Morrow and Company, 1976.

> Autobiography of the stratagemic Israeli soldier. Important to this paper because it shows Dayan's military deception learning curve.

De Guingand, *Major-General* Sir Francis (1900-1979)
Operation Victory. London: Hodder and Stoughton, 1947.

> WW2 memoir of a British intelligence officer under Wavell and Auchinleck who, later, as Monty's Chief of Staff contributed to the deception plan for the Battle of Alam Halfa in 1942 (Case 37).

Delmer, Sefton (1904-1979)
Black Boomerang: An Autobiography. London: Secker & Warburg, 1962.

> The author was a British journalist who headed the Black Propaganda division of the Political Warfare Executive in WW2. This, the second volume of his autobiography, covers his wartime years with PWE.

Delmer, Sefton
The Counterfeit Spy. New York: Harper & Row, 1971, 256pp.; London: Hutchinson, 1973.

> One of the earliest public accounts of British WW2 deception planning and operations (including the running of double agents). The author had good access to intelligence sources. His principal source for this book was the personal recollections of Col. Noël Wild and the then still secret documents provided by him, including a copy of Roger Fleetwood Hesketh's official top secret history of

FORTITUDE. The fact that Wild's disclosures were unauthorized led to the official suppression of Delmer's British first edition.

Despres, John (1942-), Lilita Dzirkals, and Barton Whaley (1928-)
"Timely Lessons of History: The Manchurian Model for Soviet Strategy". Santa Monica: The RAND Corporation, July 1976, 84pp. (RAND Report R-1825-NA)

Analyzes the Soviet surprise-through-deception planning of the invasion of Japanese-held Manchuria in August 1945.

Fisher, David (1946-)
The War Magician. New York: Coward-McCann, 1983.

A carelessly researched and quite unreliable biography of Jasper Maskelyne (1902-1973) based largely on Maskelyne's own 1949 memoir. The author is a former reporter and writer of popular non-fiction who even after researching this book evidently understands little of either military deception or conjuring.

Fleetwood Hesketh, Lieutenant-Colonel Roger (1902-1987)
FORTITUDE: A History of Strategic Deception in North Western Europe. April 1943 to May 1945. [1945].

The British official history of Operation FORTITUDE as written by a member of the Committee of Special Means, SHAEF. Although still unpublished, large parts were copied without authorization by Delmer (1971) and its author's "Conclusion" is reproduced in Daniel & Herbig (1982), 233-242.

Fleming, Colonel Peter (1907-1974)
[Official history of D Division.] Manuscript, 1945.

The author was head of this British deception planning unit in Delhi during WW2.

Foot, M. R. D. (1919-), and J. M. Langley (1916-1983)
M19: The British secret service that fostered escape and evasion 1939-1945 and its American counterpart. London: The Bodley Head, 1979.

Foot, M. R. D.
"Conditions Making for Success and Failure of Denial and Deception: Democratic Regimes," in Roy Godson & James J. Wirth (*editors*), *Strategic Denial and Deception* (New Brunswick: Transaction Publishers, 2002), 95-114.

A concise history of the British tradition in military deception. It substantially but independently covers much of the ground in Whaley (1969), Chapter II-A. Relevant to this paper for its tracing the history of the military deception tradition in the British Army from the mid-1800s through WW2.

Garfield, Brian (1939-)
The Meinertzhagen Mystery: The Life and Legend of a Colossal Fraud. Washington, DC: Potomac Books, 2007.

A scathing biography of Col. Richard Meinertzhagen (1878-1967) that exposes most of his autobiographical exaggerations and fabrications and raises dark questions about all his other claims. See also Whaley, Meinertzhagen's Haversack Exposed: The Consequences for Counterdeception Analysis (FDDC, 2007).

Harding, Major Edwin Forrest (1886-1970)
SEE: Lanham (1939).

Hart-Davis, Duff (1936-)
Peter Fleming: A Biography. London: Jonathan Cape, 1974.

Biography of noted traveler, writer, and WW2 deception planner Peter Fleming (1907- 971). the older and then much better known brother of Ian Fleming. Chapter 12 (pp.257-303) is specifically on Fleming's service as chief of deception in the China-Burma-India Theatre for Wavell and Mountbatten. Particularly relevant to this paper because it shows Col. Flemings deception learning curve.

Holt, Thaddeus (1929-)
The Deceivers: Allied Military Deception in the Second World War. New York: Scribner, 2004.

The most comprehensive, finely detailed, and best documented history.

Hoopes, Roy (1922-)
Ralph Ingersoll: A Biography. New York: Atheneum, 1985.

A detailed and psychologically probing biography of Ralph McAllister Ingersoll (1900-1985). For his brief but sparkling career as a U.S. Army deception planner in the European Theater, 1943-45, see Chapter 12 ("Lying to Hitler", pp.264-289) and Chapter 13 ("Invading Fortress Europe", pp.290-310). The author, an American journalist and biographer, is a bit too credulous of Ingersoll's often exaggerated claims about his personal contributions to deception.

Howard, Michael (1922-)
British Intelligence in the Second World War, Volume Five ("Strategic Deception"). New York: Cambridge University Press, 1990.

Hunt, Sir David (1913-1998)
A Don at War. London: Kimber, 1966.

> Superb, frank WW2 memoirs of an Oxford anthropology don who served as a Military Intelligence officer in the Greek, North African, and Italian campaigns. Disclosed some new information on British deceptions at Alam Halfa, El Alamein, and Sicily.

Irving, David (1938-)
The Trail of the Fox. New York: E. P. Dutton, 1977.

> The most psychologically revealing of the several biographies of Field-Marshall Rommel (1891-1944), as British historian. Fortunately this book is largely free of flawed judgments that have made Irving controversial.

Jackson. W. G. F. (1917-1999)
The Battle for Italy. New York: Harper & Row, 1967.

> This is the first published book to do systematically what every standard military history of a campaign should do. For each successive battle it gives the attacker's appreciation of the enemy, the battle plan. the deception plan, and the enemy's intelligence picture before proceeding to the battle itself.

> Major-General Jackson was a British regular officer who had served on Alexander's staff during the Italian campaign. For unexplained reasons—perhaps the Official Secrets Acts were belatedly invoked—Jackson abandoned his own exemplary format in his several later books.

Jones, R[eginald] V[ictor] (1911-1997)
"The Theory of Practical Joking-Its Relevance to Physics", *Bulletin of the Institute of Physics* (June 1957), 193-201; revised as "The Theory of Practical Joking—An Elaboration", *Bulletin of the Institute of Mathematics and Its Applications,* Vol.11, No. 1/2 (Jan/Feb 1975), 10-17.

> Dr. Jones is a leading military deception planner, experimental physicist, and practical joker—three activities that he links by theory in this landmark paper. For a biographical article on Jones

see Norman Moss, "The Theoretical Joker," *The Sunday Times Magazine* (18 February 1973), 44.

Jones, R. V.

Most Secret War. London: Hamish Hamilton, 1978; republished in the USA with slight changes as *The Wizard War: British Scientific Intelligence, 1939-1945.* New York Coward, McCann & Geoghegan, Inc., 1978.

A superb and amusing account. I cite from the U.S. edition.

[Lanham, Capt. C. T.] (1902-1978) (*editor*)]

★★ *Infantry in Battle.* 2nd edition, Washington, DC: The Infantry Journal, Inc., 1939, viii+422pp. Introduction by Col. George C. Marshall.

LOC: WorldCat.org; Internet.

Facsimile reprints 1993, 1996, 1997, 2006.

A leading US Army textbook, prepared for the Infantry School at Fort Benning. See particularly Chapter VIII ("Surprise," pp.107-121) for some rare case studies of US Army small-unit tactical surprise operations in WW1. Major Harding had begun writing the 1st edition (1934) as a textbook for the Army Infantry School at Fort Benning when George C. Marshall was, as Assistant Commandant, in charge of curriculum.

This book is a substantial rewrite by Capt. C. T. Lanham of the 1934 first edition, whose editor had been Major Edwin F. Harding.

Col. Charles T. "Buck" Lanham (West Point 1924) became a close friend of Hemingway in 1944 when they met in France. He was Hemingway's overly admired model for "Col. Richard Cantwell" in *Across the River and Into the Trees* (1950). The much-decorated Maj. Gen. Lanham retired in 1954 and began a second career in private industry, initially with Colt and then with Xerox until final retirement in 1970.

Lawrence, T. E. (1888-1935)

Seven Pillars of Wisdom: A Triumph. Garden City, NY: Doubleday, 1935.

Written in 1921 and privately published in 1926, Lieut.-Colonel Lawrence's controversial memoir of irregular warfare in Arabia in the Great War includes important case material on surprise and deception guerrilla operations conducted by him in the trans-Jordan in support of Allenby's campaign in Palestine. As a self-serving liar, all his assertions must be cross-checked with other sources.

Layton, Rear Admiral Edwin T. (1903-1984), and others
"And I Was There": *Pearl Harbor and Midway—Breaking the Secrets*. New York: William Morrow, 1985.

The principal author served throughout WW2 in the Pacific as a U.S. Navy combat intelligence officer.

Lewin, Ronald (1914-1984)
Ultra Goes to War: The First Account of World War II's Greatest Secret; Based on Official Documents. New York: McGraw-Hill Book Company, 1978.

The British author is a well-known military historian. During WW2 he served as a field-artillery officer with Eighth Army from the Battle of Alam Halfa until the end in Germany.

Lewin, Ronald
The Chief: Field Marshal Lord Wavell, Commander-in-Chief and Viceroy. 1939-1947. New York: Farrar, Straus and Giroux, 1980.

A sensitive, probing biography.

Liddell Hart, B. H. (1895-1970)
Great Captains Unveiled. Edinburgh: Blackwood, 1927.

Case studies of the strategic and tactical planning and operations of senior commanders.

Liddell Hart, B. H.
The Decisive Wars of History: A Study in Strategy. London: Bell, 1929.

A classic study of military surprise through deception.

Liddell Hart, B. H.
Strategy: The Indirect Approach. New York: Praeger, 1954.

The enlarged and rewritten version of the author's *The Decisive Wars of History* (1929) and *The Strategy of Indirect Approach* (1946).

MacArthur, General of the Army Douglas (1880-1964)
Reminiscences. New York: McGraw-Hill, 1964.

Valuable because it gives the author's highly colored view of himself. Must always be cross-checked with other sources. The

220,000-word handwritten manuscript was written over a period of six months in 1962-63.

Macintyre, Ben (1963-)
Operation Mincemeat. London: Bloomsbury, 2009.

Mao Tse-tung (1893-1976)
On the Protracted War. Peking: Foreign Languages Press, 1954.

Chairman Mao's theories of guerrilla warfare including the elements of surprise and deception, which he stressed. Originally published in 1938.

Maskelyne, Jasper (1902-1973)
Magic—Top Secret. London: Stanley Paul & Co., [1949].

Memoir of WW2 camouflage by a British professional stage magician-turned-camoufleur. Major Maskelyne headed the Camouflage Experimental Section of Brigadier Dudley Clarke's "A" Force deception-planning team in Egypt. His biography, a poor one, is Fisher (1983). Both Maskelyne's memoir and Fisher's biography are shabby pieces of publicity puffery, greatly exaggerating his role. A more sober and authoritative view is Mure (1980), 63, 95-96.

Masterman, [Sir] J[ohn] C[ecil] (1891-1977)
The Double-Cross System in the War of 1939 to 1945. New Haven: Yale University Press, 1972.

During WW2, Major Masterman, an Oxford history don, was an M.I.5 officer serving as Chairman of the Twenty Committee (so-called from twenty = XX = double cross) that coordinated the interdepartmental activities of the German double-agent deception system run from London. Written in less than 2½ months in 1945 as the Committee's official classified history. Published in slightly abridged form, the publisher accepting only about 12 of the 60 or so deletions requested by British officials. Otherwise the author took the occasion of publication for minor revisions in language to make his book more accessible to general readers. Gives rich details of the thinking behind deception planning in general, the reasoning out of specific plans, and the crucial element of feedback for their fine-tuning. Particularly important to this paper because it shows the deception learning curve of a tightly knit intelligence unit.

With 45,000 hardcover and 200,000 paperback sales, this esoteric work became an unexpected best-seller.

Masterman, J. C.
On the Chariot Wheel: An Autobiography. London: Oxford University Press, 1975.

Gives some new details of the author's role in LCS and as a writer of several distinguished mystery novels.

Meinertzhagen, Colonel R. (1878-1967)
Army Diary. 1899-1926. London: Oliver & Boyd, 1960.

A much rewritten "diary" with largely fabricated after-thoughts of the most creative British deceiver in East Africa and Palestine during WW 1. His elaborate lies are thoroughly untangled in Brian Garfield, *The Meinertzhagen Mystery: The Life and Legend of a Colossal Fraud* (Washington, DC: Potomac Books, 2007) and Barton Whaley, *Meinertzhagen's Haversack Exposed: The Consequences for Counterdeception Analysis* (FDDC, May 2007).

Montagu, Ewen (1901-1985)
The Man Who Never Was. Philadelphia: Lippincott, 1954.

A semi-official account of Operation MINCEMEAT, a minor but interesting British deception operation of 1943. Lieut.-Cmdr (RNVR) Montagu, as the Royal Navy representative on Twenty Committee, was the principal planner and case officer for this clever but risky ruse.

Montagu, Ewen
Beyond Top Secret U. London: Peter Davies, 1977; and in the USA as *Beyond Top Secret Ultra*, New York: Coward, McCann & Geoghegan, 1978.

Some important details on British WW2 deception planning and operations, particularly as related to MINCEMEAT, ULTRA, and the double-cross system. I cite from the American edition.

Mure, David (1912-1986)
Practise to Deceive. London: William Kimber, 1977.

A history-memoir of the British "A" Force deception team in Cairo of which Major Mure was a member from November 1942 to the end of WW2 as, successively, head of the double-cross agent committees in Baghdad (32 Committee) and Beirut (31

Committee). Republished in paperback in 1979 as *The Phantom Armies.*

Mure, David
Master of Deception: Tangled Webs in London and the Middle East. London: William Kimber, 1980.

Biography of Brigadier Dudley Clarke (1899-1974) who was the chief of "A" Force throughout WW2.

Official History of the 23rd Headquarters Special Troops.
[Pine Camp, NJ: September 19451, 37pp. plus appendices.

Written anonymously by Lt. Frederic E. Fox, a long-standing (87-points) member of the 23rd. Light on deception planning itself as this unit was the operational arm of the Special Plans Section (See Case 80).

Palmer, Dave Richard (1934-)
The Way of the Fox: American Strategy in the War for America. 1775-1783. Westport. CT: Greenwood Press, 1975.

A major reassessment of Lieutenant General George Washington's abilities as a strategic planner. Includes his deception operations, particularly during the march to Yorktown in 1781.

Prange, Gordon W. (1910-1980)
At Dawn We Slept: The Untold Story of Pearl Harbor. New York: McGraw-Hill, 1981.

Professor Prange gives us the most detailed insight into Admiral Yamamoto's planning style for the 1941 Pearl Harbor attack.

Price, Alfred (1936-)
Instruments of Darkness: The History of Electronic Warfare. London: William Kimber, 1967; revised edition, London: Macdonald and Jane's, 1977.

Excellent, detailed account of the electronic measures and countermeasures used by the RAF and Luftwaffe in WW2.

Rommel, Erwin (1891-1944)
Infantrie Greift An [The Infantry Attacks]. 1937; English translation as *Attacks*, Vienna, VA: Athena Press, 1979.

Rommel's famous study of infantry tactics that drew heavily upon his own battle experiences in WW1. Stresses his philosophy in always seizing the initiative at the earliest feasible moment in order to take the enemy by surprise.

[Rommel, Erwin]
The Rommel Papers. New York: Harcourt, Brace. 1953.

Collected papers of the "Desert Fox" giving much insight on how he viewed and solved problems. Particularly important to this paper because it illustrates Rommel's personal deception learning curve.

Saxe, Marshal de (1696-1750)
"My Reveries Upon the Art of War" in Major Thomas R. Phillips (*editor*), *Roots of Strategy: A Collection of Military Classics* (Harrisburg, Pa.: Military Service Publishing Company, 1940), 189-300.

The Maréchal de Saxe of France was not only the most consistently successful commander of the 1700s, he was the first modern military writer to stress the importance of maneuver and surprise and the many ruses, stratagems, and feints that can support these ways of diverting the enemy's reserves. He was strongly influenced on these points by Machiavelli. For surprise and ruses see pp.235, 239, 261-262, 263, 267-268, 271274, 285, 294.

Saxe also had a keen understanding of the psychological factors bearing on the discipline and behavior of soldiers, officers, and commanders—enemies as well as his own. Saxe took as his principal models the Roman Legions and the campaigns of Turenne.

His *Reveries sur l'art de la guerre* was written in 1732 and published posthumously in 1757. It enjoyed an immediate success, but one that was quickly superceded by the fames of Frederick the Great and Napoleon. His recent influence is largely limited to Col. T. E. Lawrence and Capt. B. H. Liddell Hart.

Smyth, Denis
Deathly Deception: The Real Story of Operation Mincemeat. Oxford: Oxford University Press, 2010.

Shtemenko, *General of the Army* S[ergei] M[atveevich] (1907-1976)
General'nvi shtab v godv voiny [The General Staff during the War Years]. Moscow: Voenizdat, 1968, 415pp.; English translation as *The Soviet General Staff at War. 1941-1945*. Moscow: Progress Publishers, 1970.

A uniquely revealing account of the Soviet General Staff throughout WW2 by a key member of that team. Each major operation is described in chronological sequence and the deception plan summarized for each. This exemplary format gives us our best single source for tracing the evolution of Soviet deception planning from the primitive plans of 1941 through the highly sophisticated one employed against the Japanese in 1945. The only comparable early Western study is Jackson (1967), which similarly traced the deception planning for each battle throughout Alexander's 1943-45 Italian campaign.

Swinton. Major-General Sir Ernest D. (1868-1951)
Over My Shoulder. Oxford: George Ronald, 1951.

Posthumously published and incomplete autobiography of an innovative British officer.

Verbatim Transcript of Stratagem Conference, Pentagon, 21 June 1971.
Syracuse: Syracuse University Research Corporation, 1971, 180pp.

Host and Chairman: Lt. Col. (USAF) Leonard E. Durham, Special Operations Officer for the JCS Joint Staff. Members of the SURC staff then involved in deception research: Howard K. Alberts (Col. USMC Ret.), Albert L. Jones (Col. USMC Ret), Leo N. Huddleston (SURC Project Coordinator), A. R. Spadaro (SURC physicist and analyst), Clement T. Tamraz (Lt. Col. USAF Ret.). Interviewees (all had been senior US deception planners for the European Theater in WW 11): William H. Baumer (Maj. Gen. US Army Ret.), Prof. H. Wentworth Eldredge, William A. Harris (Maj. Gen. US Army Ret.).

von Greiffenberg, General Hans (1893-1951)
"Deception and Cover Plans, Project #29", *Foreign Military Studies*, MS #P-044a, U.S. Army, Historical Division, MMR, NA.

A review of the Wehrmacht's WW2 experience with cover and deception. Written in 1950 by a German Army officer involved in these matters. His main points are summarized in Daniel & Herbig (1982). 16, 17-18, 20, 21.

Watts, Stephen (1916-)
"I Was Monty's Double Once Removed", in the author's *Moonlight on a Lake in Bond Street* (London: The Bodley Head, 1961), 158-173.

Memoir of the infamous "Monty's Double" ruse (Operation COPPERHEAD) by its M.I.5 case officer, Major Watts, who in peacetime was a professional journalist.

Wavell, General Sir Archibald (1883-1950)
Allenby: A Study in Greatness. 2 vols., London: George G. Harrap & Co., Ltd, Vol.I (1940); Vol.II (1944).

One deceptive commander's appreciation of another.

Wavell, General Sir Archibald
"Ruses and Stratagems of War", in the author's *Soldiers and Soldiering* (London: Macmillan, 1946), 80-83.

A paper originally published in pamphlet form in July 1942 marked "NOT FOR PUBLICATION" that Wavell used to indoctrinate his commanders in the India-Burma theater in the art of deception.

West, Nigel (pen name of Rupert Allason) (1951-)
MI5: British Security Service Operations 1909-1945. New York: Stein and Day, 1982.

A British journalist & politician who is extraordinarily well-informed on his country's security and intelligence services.

Whaley, Barton (1928-)
Stratagem: Deception and Surprise in War. Cambridge, MA: Center for International Studies, M.I.T., 1969, 965pp., multilithed.

A comprehensive study. Based on a data base of 158 military operations in the period 1914-1968. See also Whaley, DECEPTR.

Whaley, Barton
Codeword BARBAROSSA. Cambridge, MA: The MIT Press, 1973.

Detailed study of the German deception planning and operations that contributed to their surprise invasion of the USSR on 22 June 1941. The research itself is a case study in counterdeception—the detection of deception.

Whaley, Bart, *et al*
'Thoughts on the Cost-Effectiveness of Deception and Related Tactics in the Air War 1939 to 1945." Washington, DC: Mathtech and AMR/ORD/CIA, March 1979, 170pp.

A study of deception cost-benefits and the cycle of electronic counter-measures (ECM) and counter-countermeasures (ECCM) used by the British and German air forces in WW 2. The "et al" of authorship acknowledges Mary Walsh as the CIA sponsor and L. Daniel Maxim as the project director who appended a statistical analysis.

Whaley, Bart
DECEPTR.

A computerized data base of 230 military operations, as expanded from the original 158 in Whaley (1969). Copyright by the author, it resides in the CIA data base at Langley, Virginia, together with documentation prepared by MATHTECH, Inc.

Whaley, Bart
"Deception: Its Decline and Revival in International Conflict". In Harold D. Lasswell, Daniel Lerner, Hans Speier (*editors*), *Propaganda and Communication in World History*, Vol.II (Honolulu: University Press of Hawaii, 1980). 339-367.

Examines deception in international politics and war across four cultures and throughout their history. Provides a model (still the only one published) for analyzing the ups-and-downs of cultural acceptance or rejection of military and political deception.

Whaley, Barton
Covert German Rearmament, 1919-1939: Deception and Misperception. Frederick, Maryland: University Publications of America, Inc., 1984.

LOC: BW.

Whaley, Bart
"Toward a General Theory of Deception", *Journal of Strategic Studies* (London), Vol.V, No.1 (March 1982), 179-193; reprinted Epoptica, No.5 (January 1984), 170-177.

Proposes a general model of the categories of deception.

Whaley, Barton
The Maverick Detective: or, The Whole Art of Detection. Manuscript in progress 8 Jun 2009, 1,253pp.

Much relevant material on the psychology, thinking, and procedures of deceivers and their detectors. As of Dec 1988 the manuscript had only c.300 pages.

Wheatley, Dennis (1897-1977)
: *The Deception Planners.* London: Hutchinson, 1980.

    Memoirs of a member of Col. J. H. Bevan's London Controlling Section (LCS) in WW2.

Wingate, Sir Ronald (1889-1978)
: *Not in the Limelight.* London: Hutchinson, 1959.

    Memoirs of a senior British WW2 deception planner in London (as Bevan's deputy on LCS) and the CBI. As Wingate was an intelligent and perceptive man, it is unfortunate that the censorship of the time kept him from writing more than a few of the tantalizing snippets about deception that he presumably including in the following manuscript.

Wingate, Ronald
: [Official history of the London Controlling Section.] 1947, manuscript.

    Written in a six months period in 1946-47. Reportedly two copies were given the Americans, one to the Joint Chiefs of Staff, the other to Office of Naval Intelligence. See *Verbatim Transcript of Stratagem Conference* (Pentagon, 21 June 1971), 36-37, 170-171.

Winks, Robin W. (1970-2003)
: *Cloak & Gown: Scholars in the Secret War, 1939-1963.* New York: William Morrow, 1987.

    A superb biographical study of Yale University graduates and faculty recruited by the OSS and CIA. Most relevant is Chapter 5 (pp.247-321) on Norman Holmes Pearson (1909-1975) who served in WW2 with the OSS X-2 section in London as its liaison with the LCS. Winks was a Professor of History at Yale and, although never in the game itself, a most knowledgeable student of Intelligence.

Winterbotham, F. W. (1897-1990)
: *The Ultra Secret.* New York: Harper & Row, 1974.

    The first disclosure in substantial detail of the British ULTRA code-breaking and intelligence system. RAF Wing-Commander F. W. "Freddie" Winterbotham wrote as an insider, having initially handled ULTRA security and later coordinated its dissemination to the senior British and U.S. field commanders. Because it is a memoir, written without benefit of the essential documents and with little understanding of the technical side, many details are garbled and others missing. The most serious error of omission leaves the false impression that ULTRA was a near-seamless system. In fact it was usually incomplete and, when the Germans changed codes or routed key messages by hand (as during the Battle of the Bulge), occasionally blind. Should always be doublechecked against the several later ULTRA histories.

Wright, Peter (1916-1995), with Paul Greengrass (1955-)
Spycatcher: The Candid Autobiography of a Senior Intelligence Officer. New York: Viking, 1987.

> Must reading for its step-by-step recollections of how one trained scientist assigned to counter-espionage thought his way into his assignments. It is this man's account of his thinking and planning process in deception and counter-deception that is important. Do not be deterred from reading this merely because of the controversy surrounding the author's nasty motives (vindictiveness and money-grubbing) for publishing, much less that all its major revelations and speculations had been previously leaked in Chapman Pincher's Too Secret, Too Long (1984).

Yadin, Y[igael] (1917-1984)
"'For by Wise Counsel Thou Shalt Make Thy War': A Strategical Analysis of the Arab-Israeli War", in Liddell Hart (1954), 386-404.

> The author describes his role as a deception planner in Operation AYIN, 1947-48, when he was the Israeli Army's Chief of Operations. This article was originally published in Hebrew in September 1949.

List of Cases

Learning to Deceive

CASE 1:   *Maj.-Gen. Sir Garnet Wolseley, Night Advance on Tel el-Kebir, Egypt 1882*

CASE 2:   *Lieut.-Col. G.F.R. Henderson, the Relief of Kimberley, South Africa 1900*
The Commander's chief of Intelligence emulates Stonewall Jackson.

CASE 3:   *Major Ernest Swinton, The Boer War, South Africa 1900*
A Royal Engineer sets two ambushes.

CASE 4:   *Lieut.-Gen. Charles Monro, Suvla Bay and Anzac Beach, Gallipoli 1915*
Wherein the Commander throws away the rule books and succeeds.

CASE 5:   *Lieut.-Gen. Monro, Helles Point, Gallipoli 1916*
If the trick worked once, play it again.

CASE 6:   *Lt. Erwin Rommel, Italy 1917*
The future "Desert Fox" learns the value of surprise and practices his first deceptions.

CASE 7:   *Lt. Col. George C. Marshall, St.-Mihiel, France 1918*
The future US Army Chief-of-Staff learns to practice deception and creates a cadre of deceptive American commanders.

CASE 8:   *Maj. Heinz Guderian, The Swedish Connection 1929*
The future Panzer general learns the ways of deception.

CASE 9:   *Corps Commander Georgi K. Zhukov, Khalkhin-Gol, Mongolia 1939*
A future Marshal of the Soviet Union acts as his own deception planner.

CASE 10: *Gen. Wavell creates the world's first deception team, Cairo 1940*
The origin of "A Force."

Case 11: *Col. Dudley Clarke, Italian East Africa 1941*
A first lesson hard-learned.

CASE 12: *Lieut. Barkas, 1940-1942*
A film director becomes Director of Camouflage in North Africa.

CASE 13: *Brig. Shearer, North Africa 1941*
The Intelligence chief for British Middle-East Command devises a ruse.

CASE 14: *Capt. Thynne. North Africa 1942*
The "new boy" gets his first lesson from the "Master of Deception".

CASE 15: *Col. Peter Fleming, Operation ERROR, Burma 1942*

CASE 16: *Maj. Orde Wingate, Palestine 1938*
The modern Gideon rediscovers the night ambush and teaches Dayan and other future Israeli generals.

CASE 17: *Lt.-Col. Orde Wingate Improvises a Ruse, Ethiopia 1941*

CASE 18: *Maj. Ralph Ingersoll, OVERLORD and FORTITUDE 1943-44*
A devious journalist is ordered to found a deception planning team and learns the ruses of war.

CASE 19: *Dr. R. V. Jones, 1930s-40s*
A physicist evolves the Theory of Practical Joking and teaches the RAF the Theory of Spoof.

CASE 20: *Sun Tzu—The Chinese Tradition of Deception, c.350 BC - AD 2010*

CASE 21: *Mao's Theory of Asymmetry, 1965*

CASE 22: *The Warrenpoint Double-Ambush, Northern Ireland, 1979*

Planners in Specific Operations

CASE 23: *Gideon's Trumpet, Israel c.1249 BC*

CASE 24: *Maj.-Gen. James Wolfe, Quebec, Canada 1759*
The commander heeds timely intelligence, devises a battle-winning stratagem, loses his life, and gains immortal fame.

CASE 25: *Lt. Gen. Washington, Yorktown, Virginia 1781*
A commander proves his mastery of the strategic lie.

CASE 26: *Maj. Gen. Sherman, The March to Atlanta 1864*
The Commander plans a campaign of deception by alternating his left-right options.

CASE 27: *Maj. Gen. Sherman, The March to the Sea 1864*
The Commander plays his options of goals.

CASE 28: *Col. Frederick Funston, The Philippines 1901*
The future US Army Chief-of-Staff disguises his small column and effectively ends the Philippine Insurrection.

CASE 29: *Winston Churchill creates a dummy fleet, 1914*

CASE 30: *Churchill, The Ostend Demonstration, Holland 1914*
The First Lord of the Admiralty as his own deception planner.

CASE 31: *Gen. Freddy Mercer, Neuve Chapelle, France 1915*
The British 1st Army artillery chief recommends a tactical surprise.

CASE 32: *Commander Unwin and the Wooden Horse, Gallipoli 1915*
A Naval Officer Draws a Lesson from History.

CASE 33: *Lieut.-Gen. Allenby, Third Gaza, Palestine 1917*
The new Commander proposes a plan to end stalemate by a surprise attack.

CASE 34: *Maj. Meinertzhagen and the Haversack Legend, Palestine 1917*
One of Allenby's intelligence officers plagiarises a real plan and pretends to carry it out—thereby fabricating the celebrated legend of the "Meinertzhagen Haversack Ruse"

CASE 35: *Lieut.-Gen. Allenby, Megiddo, Palestine 1918*
The Commander keeps his own counsel.

CASE 36: *Major T. E. Lawrence, Arabia 1917-1918*
A case of deception and self-deception.

CASE 37: *Gen. Von Hutier, St.-Quentin, France 1918*
The German Chief of Artillery plans a tactical surprise.

CASE 38: *Marshal Mustapha Kemal, Dumlupinar, Turkey 1922*
The future Atatürk acts as his own deception planner and operator.

CASE 39: *Gen. Hans von Seeckt, Germany 1919*
The "disarmed" Commander deceives the arms controllers.

CASE 40: *Hitler, Europe 1935-38*
The Führer plans a bluff in grand strategy.

CASE 41: *Gen. Rojo, The Ebro, Spain 1938*
The Spanish Loyalist Chief of Staff devises a baited attack.

CASE 42: *Lt.-Gen. Rommel, Mersa el Brega, North Africa 1941 & 1942*
The "Desert Fox" twice preempts ULTRA.

CASE 43: *Lt.-Gen.Rommel, Gazala, North Africa 1942*

CASE 44: *Hitler, Russia 1941*
The Führer plans a strategic deception.

CASE 45: *Brig. De Guingand, Alam Halfa, Egypt 1942*
Monty's Chief of Staff devises a ruse.

CASE 46: *"A" Force, Plan BERTRAM, Alamein, Egypt 1942*

CASE 47: *"A" Force blows its camouflage, Alamein, Egypt 1942*

CASE 48: *Wing-Commander Winterbotham, ULTRA Security 1942*
A security officer plugs a breech of security with a ruse.

CASE 49: *Flight Lieutenant Cholmodeley, Sicily 1943*
The RAF Intelligence officer with Twenty Committee cooks up MINCEMEAT.

CASE 50: *Field-Marshal Alexander, Italy 1943-45*
The Commander encourages deception for an entire campaign.

CASE 51: *Lt. Cmdr. Douglas Fairbanks Jr, Operation ROSIE, Genoa, Italy 1944*
A movie star steps off the screen to found the Navy Seals and lead them in battle.

CASE 52: *Dr. R. V. Jones, channel deception for "Gee", 1942*
The RAF deception planner camouflages a navigational device.

CASE 53: *Dr. Jones versus the V-Bombs, England 1944*
The deception planner diverts Luftwaffe Intelligence.

CASE 54: *Maj. Ingersoll and the Battle of the Bulge, France 1944*
Wherein an American ex-publisher improvises the "Two Pattons Ruse".

CASE 55: *Lt. Col. Truly, Crossing the Rhine, Germany 1945*
An American deception liaison officer concocts a tactical cover plan.

CASE 56: *Col. Fleming's Operation CLOAK, Burma 1945*

CASE 57: *Brigadier Yadin, Palestine 1948*
The Director of Operations remembers Liddell Hart In the nick of time.

CASE 58: *Col. Haney, Guatemala 1954*
The CIA's field director invents "token insurgency".

CASE 59: *O/C Eamon Timoney, Northern Ireland*
The IRA'S O/C Derry plans a diabolical ambush.

CASE 60: *Maj.-Gen. Dayan and the Sinai Campaign, Egypt 1956*
The Israeli Chief of Staff plans a strategic surprise.

CASE 61: *Defense Minister Dayan and the Six-Day War, Israel 1967*
Dayan does it again at the level of grand strategy.

CASE 62: *President Anwar Sadat, Israel 1973*
A President plans a strategic surprise.

CASE 63: *Col. Robin Olds, Operation BOLO, Vietnam 1967*
The North Vietnamese thought their nimble MiG-21 interceptors were ambushing the usual bomb-laden F-105 Thunderchiefs. Instead they were counterambushed by Col. Robin Olds and his Wolfpack, flying the new F-4 Phantom IIs.

CASE 64: *Jody Powell and the Iranian Rescue Mission, 1980.*
An amateur reads The Bodyguard of Lies and meddles in an ops plan.

Selling the Commander

CASE 65: *Gen. Odysseus, Troy 1183 BC*
A wily warrior convinces his reluctant heros to use a ruse.

CASE 66: *Gen. Manstein, The Ardennes, France 1940*
Selling the Führer.

CASE 67: *Capt. (USN) Francis S. Low, The Tokyo Raid, 1942*
A submarine officer solves an aerial problem and sells his plan to the bosses.

CASE 68: *Adm. Nimitz, Midway Island, Pacific 1942*
The U.S. Pacific Fleet Commander sets a counter-trap.

CASE 69: *Col. Evans F. Carlson, Tinian Island, Pacific 1944*
A US Marine planning officer sells his deception to the CO.

CASE 70: *Lt. Col. Leonard Durham, The Pentagon 1970s*
Selling deception planning to US generals.

CASE 71: *General MacArthur, Inchon, Korea 1950*
Selling the idea to the JCS.

CASE 72: *Castro and His Invasion of Cuba, 1956*
Wherein Fidel wisely rejects the advice of both his teacher and his principle field commander.

CASE 73: *Richard Bissell and the Bay of Pigs, Cuba 1961*
A failure to communicate the CIA deception plan.

CASE 74: *Capt. Liddell Hart, 1927-1954*
The historian as teacher.

CASE 75: *Plan JAEL, London 1943*
Col. Clarke convinces the Supreme Command to drop the previously failed plan.

CASE 76: *Plans BODYGUARD & FORTITUDE, London 1943-44*

Institutional Deception Planning

CASE 77: *The Barcelona Defense Committee, Spain 1936*
A committee of Anarchists plans an ambush that wins the Battle of Barcelona.

CASE 78: *The German General Staff in WW2*

CASE 79: *The British "global deception" System in WW2*

CASE 80: *The U.S. Army creates its first deception units, 1943-45*

CASE 81: *Admiral Halsey's "Dirty Trick Department" in WW2*

CASE 82: *Admiral Yamamoto and His Staff in WW2*

CASE 83: *MacArthur's Deception Planners, 1942-51*

CASE 84: *The Soviet General Staff in WW2*

CASE 85: *The Israeli Deception Planners, 1948-1986*

CASE 86: *The KGB's Role in Political-Military Deception Planning, 1960s*

CASE 87: *Gen. Schwarzkopf's Deception Planners, Iraq 1991*
The American planning team for Desert Storm emulates the Russian Autumn Storm.

CASE 88: *Brigadier Clarke's Ideal Deception Planning System*

BARTON WHALEY received his bachelor of arts degree in Chinese studies from the University of California, Berkeley, before serving with the intelligence section of U.S. Army Psychological Warfare headquartered in Tokyo during the Korean War. Following the war he attended London University School of Oriental and African Studies before receiving his PhD at Massachusetts Institute of Technology. He was affiliated with the Department of Defense Analysis at the Naval Postgraduate School in Monterey, California, and worked for the director of National Security's Foreign Denial and Deception Committee of the Director of National Intelligence. He passed away in 2013.

The Naval Institute Press is the book-publishing arm of the U.S. Naval Institute, a private, nonprofit, membership society for sea service professionals and others who share an interest in naval and maritime affairs. Established in 1873 at the U.S. Naval Academy in Annapolis, Maryland, where its offices remain today, the Naval Institute has members worldwide.

Members of the Naval Institute support the education programs of the society and receive the influential monthly magazine *Proceedings* or the colorful bimonthly magazine *Naval History* and discounts on fine nautical prints and on ship and aircraft photos. They also have access to the transcripts of the Institute's Oral History Program and get discounted admission to any of the Institute-sponsored seminars offered around the country.

The Naval Institute's book-publishing program, begun in 1898 with basic guides to naval practices, has broadened its scope to include books of more general interest. Now the Naval Institute Press publishes about seventy titles each year, ranging from how-to books on boating and navigation to battle histories, biographies, ship and aircraft guides, and novels. Institute members receive significant discounts on the Press' more than eight hundred books in print.

Full-time students are eligible for special half-price membership rates. Life memberships are also available.

For a free catalog describing Naval Institute Press books currently available, and for further information about joining the U.S. Naval Institute, please write to:

>Member Services
>**U.S. Naval Institute**
>291 Wood Road
>Annapolis, MD 21402-5034
>Telephone: (800) 233-8764
>Fax: (410) 571-1703
>Web address: www.usni.org

www.ingramcontent.com/pod-product-compliance
Lightning Source LLC
Chambersburg PA
CBHW021056080526
44587CB00010B/261